Hiroshima Immigrants in Canada 1891-1941

Hiroshima Immigrants in Canada 1891-1941

MICHIKO MIDGE AYUKAWA

UBCPress · Vancouver · Toronto

16 15 14 13 12 11 10 09 08   5 4 3 2 1

Printed in Canada on acid free paper ∞

Library and Archives Canada Cataloguing in Publication

Ayukawa, Michiko Midge, 1930-
Hiroshima immigrants in Canada, 1891-1941 / Michiko Midge Ayukawa.

Includes bibliographical references and index.
ISBN 978-0-7748-1431-7 (bound); ISBN 978-0-7748-1432-4 (pbk.)

1. Japanese – Canada – History. 2. Hiroshima-shi (Japan) – Emigration and immigration – History. 3. Japanese Canadians – History. 4. Canada – Emigration and immigration – History. I. Title.

FC106.J3A98 2007   971′.004956   C2007-904259-7

Canadä

UBC Press gratefully acknowledges the financial support for our publishing program of the Government of Canada through the Book Publishing Industry Development Program (BPIDP), and of the Canada Council for the Arts, and the British Columbia Arts Council.

This book has been published with the help of a grant from the Canadian Federation for the Humanities and Social Sciences, through the Aid to Scholarly Publications Programme, using funds provided by the Social Sciences and Humanities Research Council of Canada.

UBC Press
The University of British Columbia
2029 West Mall
Vancouver, BC V6T 1Z2
604-822-5959 / Fax: 604-822-6083
www.ubcpress.ca

To my late parents:

Ishii Kenji (1895-1971)

Ishii Misayo (1900-2001)

Contents

Illustrations ix

Acknowledgments xi

Prologue xiii

1 The Hiroshima Homeland 3

2 The First Ones 12

3 Sojourning and Beyond 23

4 The Women Come 35

5 Farmers 58

6 The Divided Urban Community 79

7 Nisei, the Second Generation 98

Conclusion 119

Epilogue 125

A Note about the Sources 128

Notes 132

Bibliography 164

Index 175

Illustrations

Maps

1 Modern Japan, showing Hiroshima prefecture with former fiefs Aki and Bingo 2

2 Hiroshima prefecture with county divisions and the numbers of Canadian immigrants in 1920 7

3 Vancouver's Powell Street Japantown area 24

4 British Columbia coast, showing some major Japanese communities pre-1942 60

Photographs

1 Ishii Chōkichi and Kenji, [1917?]. *Author's collection* xvi

2 The results of the September 1907 riot on Powell Street. *UBC Rare Books and Special Collections* 37

3 Takata Misayo, [1920?]. *Author's collection* 38

4 Japanese brides aboard ship. *Japanese Canadian National Museum 97/200* 39

5 Ishii Kenji and Misayo in wedding photograph, Japan, 1921. *Author's collection* 40

6 Ishii Kenji and Misayo in Canada, 1922. *Author's collection* 40

7 Tree stump removal in British Columbia. *UBC Rare Books and Special Collections* 61

8 Ready to drive to the Hiroshima kenjinkai picnic. *Japanese Canadian National Museum 92/20.008* 89

9 The Japanese Women's Association in Ocean Falls, 1 July 1937. *Japanese Canadian National Museum 94/65.3.002* 96

10 Japanese-Canadian community entry in a parade celebrating Vancouver's silver jubilee in 1936. *Japanese Canadian National Museum 94/71.003* 99

11 Michiko Ishii and friend at *chigo* parade in celebration of the Buddhist Church completion, November 1934. *Author's collection* 100

12 Grade six class, Strathcona School, spring 1941. *Author's collection* 103

13 Japanese school play at the Alexander Street language school. *Author's collection* 106

14 Ishii family in 1940. *Author's collection* 123

Acknowledgments

The generous financial support of the Social Sciences and Humanities Research Council of Canada and the University of Victoria helped defray the costs of research trips across Canada and Japan during the writing of this book.

During those years, I received the assistance of many friends, colleagues, and relatives in Japan and Canada who encouraged me, gave me suggestions, and provided important information. Many welcomed me into their homes and shared their stories.

At both the University of British Columbia and the University of Victoria, office and library staff, fellow students, and professors gave me invaluable aid and support. I am indebted to Tim de Lange Boom for the maps that he painstakingly prepared and patiently altered several times over. His technical expertise was also required for the reproduction of my family photographs and other images. All this was a generous gift from a fellow "Tai Chi'er." The Japanese Canadian National Museum, in particular Reiko Tagami, gave me invaluable aid.

This research into the pre–Second World War Japanese-Canadian society, primarily on the west coast of British Columbia, would not have been carried out without the perspicacity and encouragement of Dr. E. Patricia Tsurumi, who believed that the vivid memories of my childhood and of this now lost community should be probed and analyzed. The writing of this book was stalled for a time, until a number of historians urged me to complete it and offered assistance. I am especially indebted to Dr. Patricia E. Roy for her kind patience and expertise at this stage.

During the research period, my mother, Ishii Misayo, encouraged me and shared with me her many memories. It is unfortunate that she passed away in her 101st year, before this book came to fruition. My five children, their spouses, and my grandchildren, who now total ten, unselfishly carried on without the full attention of the family "matriarch."

If I have in some small way been able to paint a picture of the early lives of pioneer immigrants from Hiroshima and the milieu in which they lived – covering both the positive and the negative aspects – I am sure my parents will be happy. I regret now that I had little understanding of their world prior to conducting my research.

Prologue

November 1983, Hisayamada, Onomichi city, Hiroshima prefecture. After a treacherous drive along a narrow, hilly road, we stopped in front of a small residence attached to a long, barrack-like building. My blonde friend, my maternal uncle Takata Tomoki, and I stepped out of the car and were immediately surrounded. My eyes fell in turn on four people: a beautiful woman in a pale-green kimono, an older woman, a toddler, and a young mother. They all smiled and bowed repeatedly as the young driver, my late cousin's son, Ishii Kazuhiko, gravely introduced us. I was tongue-tied, partly owing to my inability to voice appropriate Japanese phrases, but much more by the emotional impact of meeting kinfolk for the first time in my life.

I recovered sufficiently to introduce Helen, a friend since my youth. During our struggle through honours chemistry at McMaster University from 1948 to 1952 we had developed a strong bond, and she had eagerly accompanied me on this, my first trip to my parents' homeland. My relatives had rarely seen a *hakujin* (literally "white person") and had certainly never hosted one. Her red pantsuit, unusual on an adult in Japan, added to their bewilderment. They were shy but recovered their innate hospitality and ushered us into the *tatami* room (a formal parlour with rush mats), where a familiar photograph of Ishii Chōkichi, my paternal grandfather and Ishii Kazuhiko's great-grandfather, looked down upon us.

My hosts were descendants of my father's eldest brother, Ishii Seiichi, who had assumed the headship of the household when my grandfather left his humble terraced farm in 1906 to seek his fortune overseas. Seiichi, then a young man of twenty, had struggled to provide for his mother, his siblings, and later his own family of six children. Yet he had lived ninety-nine long years, twenty-three longer than my father, who had been nine years his junior.

It was obvious that my hosts had made careful preparations for my visit. Although my father's relatives were now professional people, they had had a humble past. Placed close to the cushions on which Helen and I kneeled uncomfortably were old photographs of their family and mine. I recognized many as similar to those I had often lingered over during my childhood in Vancouver. As we studied them together, I identified some people – in particular, the one in the kimono who now sat across from me. I asked what had happened to some of the others. Two male cousins had died, but three of the women were now living in Osaka. I resolved then that I would make efforts to meet my Osaka cousins, especially Nobuko, the one who was the same age I was. I wondered how my life might have gone had my father not immigrated to Canada.

During that visit, my hosts took me to the family grave, where I awkwardly stood by, uncomfortable with my ignorance of the customary ritual. To this day, I muse about what they thought of my unusual behaviour as they lit some incense and placed some greenery before the stone markers. I understood that their present home was not the ancestral family farm. In answer to my query about where my father's home had been, Kazuhiko pointed to a distant wooded area and told me, "Way over there."

That evening, my Takata uncle and his wife held a dinner party for me to meet my maternal relatives. Kazuhiko and his younger sister were also invited. Unlike my father's family, my mother's family had always been affluent and had an impressive lineage. My uncle, who was my mother's half-brother, lived in a renovated mansion, the ancestral home in which my mother had been reared. He also had rental houses nearby and a newly built guesthouse, as well as fig and mandarin groves. Perhaps because of the easy-going personality of this uncle, the Takata family was much more relaxed with us and welcomed us with light-hearted warmth. At the dinner was another uncle, Kōmoto Noriyoshi, and his married daughter Kiyomi. Noriyoshi had taken the surname of his wife when he married; that is, he had become a *yōshi* (adopted husband). He had fathered only one daughter, Kiyomi, who in turn had an adopted husband. As the sake flowed, Noriyoshi regaled me with stories of his youth and of the years he had spent in China with the Japanese army. It appeared that the passing of years had erased the harshness of those experiences. His stories reminded me sharply of the very different lives of my brothers, who had been designated as "enemy aliens" in Canada and had not been recruited into the military.

That night, Helen and I, although exhausted from the long and eventful day, talked for hours as we struggled with the soft mattress and mounds of heavy quilts over the Western-style bed in the guesthouse. Well into the wee hours of the morning my brain whirled from one scene to another and from one puzzle to the next.

This visit sent me forward on an odyssey, a search for my roots. I considered the emotional and practical difficulties my father and grandfather must have endured when they left their village and, with no knowledge of its language or customs, had sought their fortune in a strange land. And how did my parents, who had such different backgrounds, meet and marry? But now, at least, I understood why my parents used to dream of returning to Japan for an early retirement. They had never been able to achieve that goal. When at long last they were able to return for a visit after forty years of marriage, they realized that they had become Canadians and that the Japan they yearned for no longer existed. Both became happy with their life in Ontario, and neither wished to return even for another visit.

I began to take some Japanese history courses at the University of Victoria. I also went to visit my elderly mother in her seniors' apartment in Hamilton. For two weeks we quietly talked in a way we never had before. She answered my many questions quite willingly when I explained that they were for a course assignment. She had always made great personal sacrifices for my education in my youth, and she still supported my academic endeavours.

I emerged with a sketchy picture of the lives of my pioneer grandfather and my parents. My grandfather, Ishii Chōkichi, had set sail in the early 1900s with several other men from his district. They had been enticed with promises that they would be able to solve all their financial problems by going to Hawaii for a few years. Stories about the men and women from the Hiroshima city area who worked in Hawaii's sugar cane fields and sent money home had reached as far as the eastern outskirts of Hiroshima prefecture, where the Ishii family tilled their modest rice plot. My grandfather and his neighbours were eager to try their luck.

They had passports for Hawaii, but the recruiters persuaded them to travel even farther, to North America. Since this extension was illegal, there are no immigration records.[1] I surmise that they were among the many who landed in Victoria, the Canadian port of entry, in 1906-07.[2] This sudden influx of Japanese immigrants aroused anti-Asian feelings, and in September 1907 a parade and Asiatic Exclusion League rally at Vancouver City Hall culminated in an ugly riot in Chinatown and

1 This photo of Ishii Chōkichi and Kenji was taken in Vancouver before Chōkichi returned to Japan, probably 1917.

Japantown. In its aftermath, Canada and Japan negotiated the Lemieux-Hayashi Gentlemen's Agreement, which was intended to limit Japanese male immigration. In fact, it led inadvertently to the arrival of wives and the beginnings of settlement.

Chōkichi worked here and there in coastal British Columbia and then urged his seventeen-year-old son, my father, to join him in 1912. Father and son laboured on the same work gangs for about five years. Then Chōkichi became ill and returned to Japan, where he died soon after. A few years later, my father's marriage was arranged, and in 1921 he returned to Japan to marry my mother, a pampered, adventurous young woman from a neighbouring village. He had promised her that they would return to Japan in five years, so she left her trousseau of quilts and furniture behind.

I thought about my parents' lives, both in Japan and in Canada, and reflected on my own childhood. My life had been devoid of cousins, aunts, uncles, and grandparents. My family had been "nuclear" before the term had been coined. Yet there had been "aunts" and "uncles" – surrogate relatives, who had always been around us to provide a support system. Most of these people had been born in Hiroshima. I wondered what Canada's society had been like for the Issei (literally, the first generation, the immigrants). How had it compared with the world they left behind? How difficult had it been for my parents to leave home to pursue their dreams – even if (so they believed) only for five years? It appeared inconceivable that my mother had actually believed that five years was a realistic period, or that my father had sincerely thought that it was possible.

Eager to learn more about my ancestors' past and the alien environment in which they had staked their dreams, I soon became a full-time student of Canadian and Japanese history. I also resumed my Japanese language studies, which had been interrupted in December 1941 after Japan bombed Pearl Harbor. Gradually, a picture emerged of the racist society that the Japanese pioneers had encountered in British Columbia. Xenophobia and notions of white supremacy had prevailed in British Columbia since the mid-nineteenth century, and lawmakers had imposed restrictions on Asian immigrants. Yet for the Japanese in Canada, persecution and racism did not plague every aspect of daily life. When I was a child in the 1930s, there had been a vibrant Japanese-Canadian community full of confident men and women, both young and old. My memory is not of people who were downtrodden or intimidated by the world around them. I felt the urge to probe and investigate the society of those people.

Ten years after that first trip to Japan in 1983, I made a much longer visit on my own, travelling from Tokyo as far as Nagasaki, partly as a tourist but primarily as a researcher. I met and talked at length with friends, relatives, and academics. At first I was overwhelmed by the complexities of the society and the language, and at times I was so discouraged that I was tempted to give up. But eventually I learned how to travel with ease on the trains and buses and even to roam around the streets of Hiroshima city and other areas of historic significance. In Hiroshima city, Nishimoto Masami, a reporter for *Chūgoku shinbun* who had interviewed me a few years earlier in Victoria, was of invaluable help. I had met him when he was on assignment to research the lives of Hiroshima immigrants in Canada. Through him and another contact I met some relatives of immigrants in Canada; I was also able to consult the authors of a series of books on the history of Hiroshima prefecture.

On returning to Victoria, I read the Japanese-language articles and books I had acquired. I also travelled across Canada to interview surviving early immigrants as part of an in-depth study of the people who had immigrated to Canada from Hiroshima prefecture. There was an urgency to this project, since the pioneers were now all elderly; even the Nisei (the second-generation Japanese Canadians) were now senior citizens.

I had planned to investigate the early history of Japanese immigrants: the reasons why they immigrated, their social backgrounds, their regions of origin in Japan, and their lives in Canada. It soon became clear that this history comprised a number of separate though intertwining stories of emigration from a number of different parts of Japan. Much like the stories of other ethnic groups who had immigrated to Canada, the story of the Japanese would have to involve a series of "micro studies that constitute the economic, social, and cultural conditions of the sending areas."[3]

Although Japan is a small country of only 142,707 square miles, variations in climate, proximity to the ocean, fertility of the soil, and other factors have generated regional differences.[4] Beyond these physical variations are social ones. For more than two-and-a-half centuries, the Tokugawa regime (1600-1868) had held on to power through strict measures, some of which precluded free movement. As a result of policies that forced peasants to remain on the land in their villages, rural communities became insulated and developed different customs and dialects. The demands of their lords and regional calamities also affected the lives of the villagers.[5] Although the Meiji government opened the doors to emigration in 1885 as a possible solution to rural poverty, actual emigration policies were determined by the prefectural governments. Some prefectures encouraged it; others discouraged it.[6] The zeal of the central government's recruiters, local economic conditions, village officials' predilections, and later, the activities of emigration companies, which went from village to village in some areas, also had a strong influence. How the immigrants lived in Canada, which jobs they took, and whether they settled permanently or saved their earnings with the goal of returning home also varied according to their roots.

Even during my period of investigation – the late Meiji, Taisho (1912-26), and early Showa (1926-89) – people from Hiroshima were seen as having different characteristics from, for example, those from Shiga prefecture, which also sent substantial numbers of emigrants to Canada. Shiga was noted for its entrepreneurs. *Ōmi-shōnin,* salesmen from that area, used to travel throughout Japan selling goods; later, in Canada, many people from Shiga became business proprietors. This is well illustrated by Audrey Kobayashi's study of the village of Kaideima, on the eastern shore of Lake Biwa in Shiga prefecture.[7] Kaideima was prone to flooding, and particularly severe floods in 1896 precipitated emigration from there, especially to British Columbia. The money these people earned in Canada, mainly by labouring in sawmills and by operating shops around Vancouver's Powell Street, did much more than keep their relatives alive. Almost 70 percent of the Shiga immigrants whom Kobayashi studied returned to their villages, bought land, built majestic homes, and donated money to the local Buddhist temple. Of the 135 Shiga households (535 immigrants), only 30 remained in Canada after the Second World War.[8] As we shall see, Hiroshima immigrants tended to settle and remain in Canada.

Emigration also varied according to region. For instance, in the Tōhoku region in northern Honshu (see Map 1), where poverty was often widespread and severe, villagers typically lacked even the minimum economic resources that would enable them to book passage to Canada. Yet some individuals were able to encourage and arrange emigration for their fellow villagers. Oikawa Jinsaburō made Herculean efforts to urge people from Miyagi prefecture in Tōhoku to emigrate.[9] Oikawa first went to Canada in 1896. On his return to his home village in 1899, he tried to recruit both men and women to work in his dog salmon (chum) and salmon roe salteries in Canada. Wherever he went in Miyagi prefecture, he heard heart-rending stories of the previous year's famine, which had caused many to die of starvation. But passage to Canada cost sixty yen – an impossible amount for any of the local villagers to accrue, so only nine people followed him. Seven years later, in 1906, he returned to the area with a daring venture. He was able to recruit eighty-two people, including three women, who sailed in September on the *Suianmaru,* which he had hired to transport them illegally to Canada. They landed at Becher Bay near Victoria and were caught, but were allowed to stay. These immigrants were eventually able to remit money to their home villages to keep their families from starving. This sort of desperate poverty was not a principal theme in the stories of the Hiroshima immigrant families.

Another man, Kuno Gihei, rescued Miomura, a fishing village in Wakayama prefecture broadly known as Amerika-mura (America village), from obliteration. Kuno's poverty-stricken village depended entirely on fishing. Once the fishers began venturing farther and farther out and returning with more and more meagre catches, Kuno urged them to go to Canada to fish for salmon. For a number of years those fishers who followed his advice returned to Miomura from Canada in the off-season; later, though, they immigrated with their families. The vast majority of these Wakayama fishers settled in Steveston at the mouth of the Fraser River. A fair number eventually returned to Japan to live comfortably on the fruits of their labour and on the monies remitted to them by sons left behind in Canada; many, though, realized that Miomura could not provide any permanent sustenance and chose to remain in Canada.[10] Like the Hiroshima emigrants, they stayed; unlike the Hiroshima immigrants, they fished.

In Hiroshima too, there were villages, especially in Asa, Aki, and Saeki counties, from which large numbers emigrated.[11] (See Map 2 of Hiroshima prefecture with the county divisions.) A table in a history of Hiroshima tells us that by 1910 there were twenty-six villages from which more than 270 people had emigrated. From as few as 3.1 percent to as many as 25.6 percent of these villagers had done so.[12] And these numbers do not include those who had moved to the colonies of Taiwan, Sakhalin, or Korea. So it is clear that emigration overseas was fairly common among villagers in some parts of Hiroshima. In fact, Hiroshima people often led the way to foreign lands, and their apparent success created many "emigrant villages" in the prefecture. The first to leave went to Hawaii as contract labourers in January 1885; 222 of this group of 945 were from Hiroshima.[13] In Canada as well, the first contract Japanese immigrants were all from Hiroshima. They arrived in 1891 to work in the mines at Cumberland, Vancouver Island.

Hiroshima was the third-largest source of Japanese immigrants to Canada, trailed by Shiga and Wakayama prefectures.[14] According to a study conducted in British Columbia in 1934, of the 574 Japanese immigrants surveyed, 8 percent were from Hiroshima. Of these, almost half lived in Vancouver, almost one-quarter on farms, and just over one-quarter in company towns. None of them were fishers.[15]

By focusing on Hiroshima immigrants to Canada, I hoped to show how regional identities influence personal behaviour and community networking. My family's own roots offered me special advantages as well as personal qualifications for this study. Having been born to Hiroshima immigrants and having lived within the rather narrow confines of Vancouver's Japanese-Canadian society in the 1930s, I had acquired useful tools for understanding these people and their history from their earliest days in BC. Every day, after primary school, I attended the

Alexander Street Japanese Language School in Japantown; then on Sundays I would go to the Buddhist Sunday School at the corner of Princess and Cordova Streets. I had probably been enculturated to Hiroshima customs and traditions and also to the regional dialect. Also, my 1983 visit to Japan had pointed me toward "insider" research into the history of the Hiroshima immigrants in Canada.

After first studying Canadian and Japanese history and improving my Japanese-language skills (which I sorely needed to do), I embarked on my study of Japanese-Canadian history. My BA essay and MA thesis both involved translating the memoirs of Mrs. Imada Ito, a pioneer woman who had arrived in Canada in 1911. Luckily for me, she had come from Saeki county, from a village that is now part of the city of Hiroshima. I gathered a vivid picture of village life from her descriptions of her childhood on a farm, her stay in her in-laws' home before she joined her husband, and her temporary return to the village with three children in 1918.[16] She was a product of her village, and the way she conducted herself in Canada must have partly reflected her background as a Hiroshima woman. She had written her memoirs in a unique blend of Meiji Japanese, fractured English, and a Hiroshima dialect, combining *hiragana* (cursive script), *katakana* (phonetic script, used for foreign words), and *kanji* (Chinese ideograms). Her language had been confusing to scholars from Japan, but it was very familiar to me. When I had some question regarding an idiomatic expression, a phone call to my elderly mother would answer it. In her memoirs, Mrs. Imada mentioned many people who appeared in my later research.

As I carried out my study, a picture emerged of both the homogeneity and the individuality of the immigrants. They had sought fortune in Canada for a variety of reasons. Some came alone; a number had been recruited by emigration companies; many others had been hired by a previous immigrant who had returned to his home village to gather a work crew for a specific venture. Some were wildly successful in Canada: Kaminishi Kannosuke and Sasaki Shūichi ended up owning lumber camps, sawmills, and forest tracts. Other immigrants became prosperous farmers, struggling farmers, mill workers, or small businessmen. Some were caring and family-oriented men; others were lazy and selfish; still others spent every penny they earned on gambling and liquor. Some community leaders sacrificed their own families in order to help others. There were adventurers and daredevils, and some who beat their wives, but most of them were like my father – just steady workers who sacrificed for their families.[17]

Some women had chosen to immigrate to "Amerika"; others had merely acquiesced to their parents' suggestions that they marry overseas men. These women found their lives in Canada extremely difficult: they had no extended family to help them, and they worked both inside and outside the home. Those who were burdened with irresponsible husbands became breadwinners; or they just gave up and abandoned their families, or committed suicide.

The pioneers waged an ongoing battle against racism; in this, they were supported and defended by the Japanese government through the consul in Vancouver. When the provincial legislature passed discriminatory laws against the Japanese immigrants, the Japanese government appealed to Britain on their behalf, citing the Anglo-Japanese Alliance, which was in force between 1902 and 1921. The Canadian government disallowed some of BC's laws; even so, the racism institutionalized by the ones that remained demoted the Japanese Canadians to an inferior status in the province. At the same time, BC's business community victimized Japanese labourers, paying them badly in order to maximize profits. And within the Japanese community, predatory contractors, "the bosses," actively participated in this process. They negotiated with the hiring companies, offering work crews at lower wages, and the Japanese labourers felt obligated and grateful to them. As the years went by, the economic gap between the labourers and their "benefactors" widened; and all the while, the *dekasegi* (literally, "going out to work" – that is, temporary migrant workers) evolved into permanent settlers as they married and raised families. Those who belonged to this immigrant community had a wide range of goals. The Nisei were exposed to mainstream culture at public schools and through the media, but most parents tried to raise them to be proud of their Japanese heritage and to be fluent in Japanese.[18] The province's social and economic climate made this necessary. Many Nisei struggled to make a living at hard labour and menial jobs, much like their immigrant parents; but some became successful businessmen and professionals.

The history of the Hiroshima people is a vital part of the history of British Columbia. It was in BC that these immigrants struggled against anti-Asian racism, discriminatory labour practices, and anti-Japanese legislation in the hope of achieving their dreams. Over the years, the Hiroshima immigrants largely succeeded in controlling and directing their own destinies – at least, until the bombing of Pearl Harbor by their ancestral country destroyed the Japanese-Canadian community.

Hiroshima Immigrants in Canada 1891-1941

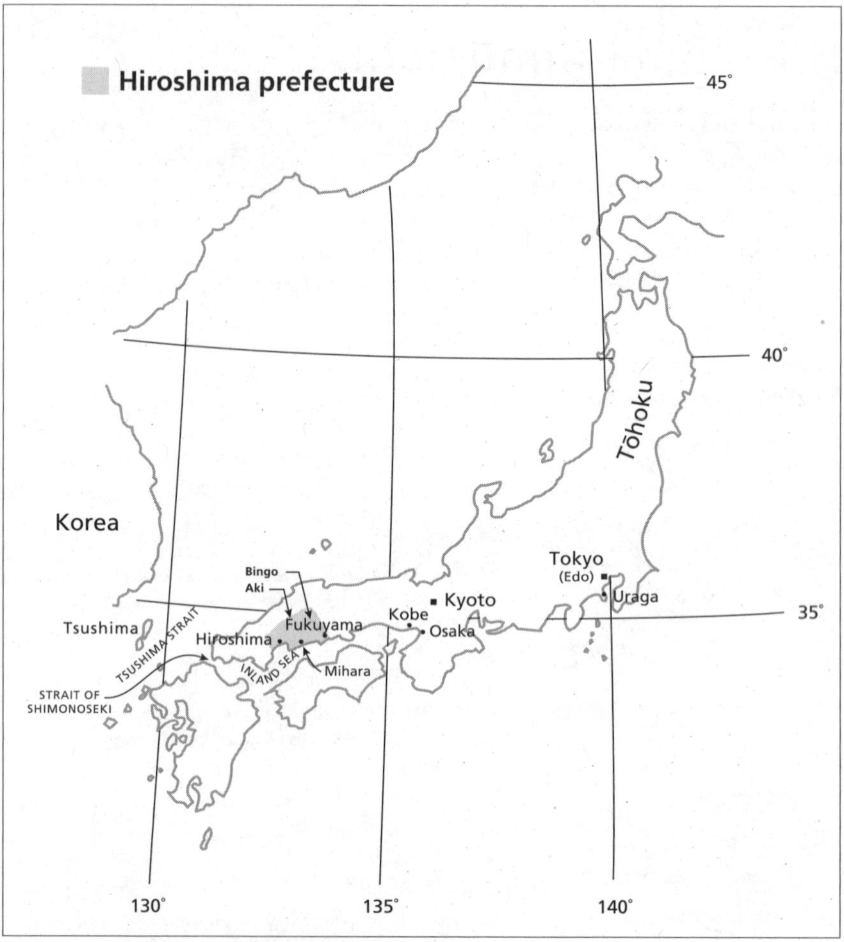

Map 1 Modern Japan, showing Hiroshima prefecture with former fiefs Aki and Bingo

Chapter One
The Hiroshima Homeland

One of the first questions that arose in my mind was why the people of my grandfather's prefecture had a greater propensity than many others in Japan to seek their fortunes abroad. Besides geographical, climatic, and economic variations among the four main islands of Japan, there were basic and long-standing differences in cultural and psychological attitudes that affected the acceptance of new ideas and that drove some people, but not others, to seek adventures. Undoubtedly, the proximity of the Setonaikai (Inland Sea) was a major factor; Hiroshima prefecture lies along its north coast. For many centuries, ships had been sailing to and from the continent of Asia through the Tsushima Strait (see Map 1).[1] From Korea, China, and other lands had come cultural ideas such as Buddhism and Confucianism, as well as the technical skills of indigo dyeing and ceramics making. Thus the sea did not frighten the people who lived near it; instead, they saw it as a passageway to a world of wonders. Thoughts of far-off lands evoked in many a yearning for adventure, a sense of awe, and an eagerness to explore.

During the Era of the Warring States (1336-1590), the samurai fought battles back and forth over the paddy fields. They constantly ravaged the farms; the peasants suffered, rebuilt, and carried on. Except when the samurai were fighting on their land, the peasants lived peacefully, though at subsistence levels, in hamlets surrounded by rice paddies and communal woodlands.

From 1590, Toyotomi Hideyoshi managed to maintain relative calm but the samurai conflicts ended only in 1600 when Tokugawa Ieyasu (1542-1616), having won the Battle of Sekigahara, completed the unification begun by Oda Nobunaga (1534-82) and Toyotomi Hideyoshi (1536-98). In Tokugawa's semi-unified state, slightly fewer than three hundred feudal lords – called *daimyō* – acknowledged him and his descendants as overlords. Ieyasu organized the *daimyō* into three categories: *shimpan,* relatives of the Tokugawa clan; *fudai,* those who had followed the Tokugawa family before the Battle of Sekigahara; and *tōzama* (the "outside lords"). Ieyasu, distrustful of the *tōzama,* situated their domains far from the capital of Edo (present-day Tokyo), between two *fudai* lords' domains.

To tighten its grip over the country, the Tokugawa regime maintained a rigid society, an adaptation of the Confucian four-class system in which the samurai or soldier-officials were at the top of the social hierarchy. Below them, "the peasants were to remain on the land, and the artisans and merchants were to keep their places and behave in a manner expected of humble people."[2] In each domain, the warriors, merchants, and artisans lived in the *daimyō*'s castle towns.[3] The entire population of Tokugawa Japan depended on the production of the peasants, who were about four-fifths of the population. Cadastral surveys by Ieyasu's predecessor had recorded the financial worth of each village in terms of its estimated rice yield, or *kokudaka*. The Tokugawa rulers continued to order these surveys and to use the resulting statistics. The status of the *daimyō* was determined by the *kokudaka* value of the entire domain.

At that time, what is now known as Hiroshima prefecture comprised two domains. Aki, in the west, stretched east as far as Mihara (see Map 1); Bingo was to the east. Aki was a *tōzama* domain held by the Asano clan; Bingo had since 1710 been ruled by a *fudai* lord, Abe.[4] Aki, whose castle was located in what today is Hiroshima city, boasted a *kokudaka* value of 426,000. Bingo, with its castle at Fukuyama, had a *kokudaka* value of 110,000 in 1867.[5] Like domain lords throughout the land, the *daimyō* of Aki and Bingo were responsible for their samurai vassals and paid them rice stipends. By the mid-1800s, rising living standards, the increased consumption of "luxury" goods and services, and demands made by the governing Tokugawa shogun had impoverished the country's *daimyō* and the rest of the samurai class. So, too, had the *sankin-kōtai,* which required all *daimyō* to alternate their residences between their Hiroshima and Fukuyama castles and Edo, while their families remained in Edo under the watchful eye of the shogunate.

Like the other lords, the Aki and Bingo *daimyō* looked for ways to supplement their domain incomes. Within their domains they encouraged cottage industries specializing in local materials and crops. Local entrepreneurs, who organized these ventures, hired peasants to work in their own homes or at nearby workshops. Villages were gradually converted from subsistence farming to production for the market; typically, they focused on cash crops of local products, including ones that could be used in cottage industries. The mild winters and the long growing season made it possible to use rice paddy fields for crops of winter barley, as well as mat rush and cotton for use in cottage industries.[6] The peasants grew whatever the market and the climate favoured. What they needed, they could now purchase. The percentage of cash crops varied from region to region. By the Meiji era (1868-1912) the national percentage was between 10.2 and 26.8 percent; around Aki and Bingo it was 13.7 percent in 1877.[7]

Since earliest times in Aki and Bingo, the peasants had farmed cooperatively, often organizing themselves by lineage. But as cash crops became more important, the trend grew toward individual farming, with families buying what they required – fertilizer, labour, thatch for roofing, lumber, food, clothing – instead of working cooperatively. As a result, they came to depend on the market. Not all succeeded. Some lost their land through foreclosure and survived as tenant farmers, by hiring themselves out as agricultural labourers, or by turning to other occupations. Women worked in village handicraft industries that were owned and controlled by the wealthier landlords. By the last decades of Tokugawa rule, the distance between the rural wealthy and the mass of peasants had grown wide.[8]

Landless peasants and those who owned plots so small that they could not survive on farming alone often left home to find work to supplement their incomes.[9] In Aki and Bingo, and elsewhere, some women left home to work in nearby villages or towns as maids and seasonal labourers. Most, however, stayed home and engaged in agricultural activities, which included growing, processing, and weaving cotton and silk.[10]

The Intrusion of the West

In the early seventeenth century the Bakufu (the central administration of the Tokugawa regime) was sharply restricting the country's contact with the outside world, especially the non–East Asian world. It forbade the building of ships large enough for ocean voyages, and it refused reentry to those who, carried by the winds, had landed on foreign shores. It also restricted trade to a handful of foreigners. This seclusionist policy was not seriously challenged until America's commodore Matthew Perry arrived with four warships in Edo Bay in 1853. In 1854, Perry forced the Bakufu to sign the Treaty of Kanagawa, and soon a number of European powers secured similar treaties. These unequal treaties imposed by the Western imperialists generated turbulence throughout the country, and by 1868 a new regime with the young emperor Meiji as a symbolic head had replaced the Bakufu. Rather optimistically, it declared itself the representative of a unified country.

At the time of Perry's intrusion, Abe Masahiro (1819-57), the *fudai daimyō* of Bingo from 1837 to 1857, as well as *rōju* (senior councillor) from 1843 until his death, wielded considerable influence in the Bakufu. As the chief elder of the Bakufu from 1843 to 1855, he undertook military and institutional reforms and handled the Perry negotiations.[11] The Asano rulers of Aki, on the other hand, presided over a *tōzama* domain. During the turmoil of the 1860s the Asano did not unequivocally support the challengers that eventually defeated the Tokugawa rulers. So they were unable to leverage Aki's historical distance from the Bakufu in order to receive favours from the new state that ultimately emerged from the struggles.[12] The vacillation of the Asano, and Abe's *fudai* connections with the defeated Tokugawa, meant that neither Aki nor Bingo could hope for much power in the Meiji government.

The new government faced enormous problems. In order to win back Japan's autonomy by eliminating the unequal treaties that gave the Western powers extraterritorial and other rights, the Meiji rulers needed to launch drastic economic and social changes. They converted domains into prefectures, and they pensioned off the former *daimyō* and samurai. Hundreds of young men and five girls of "impressionable ages" were sent overseas to study, while thousands of Western "experts" were brought in to train others.[13] The government imported modern machinery, erected huge factories, developed mines and railways, introduced compulsory education – with the costs borne by the local areas – and conscripted males from all classes. This last practice caused great hardship, especially in the rural areas, since it deprived the fields of the labour of young men in their prime. The new government financed these expensive ventures through a revised land tax levied on the peasantry, who still constituted around 80 percent of Japanese.[14]

In the early Meiji era in Hiroshima prefecture, the degree of stratification among peasants varied from area to area. In southern Bingo, about 70 percent of farmers owned less than three *tan* (1 *tan* equals 0.245 acres) and had to rent more land to survive. Farmers in other areas had slightly more land, but about half the farmers still owned less than three *tan*. In Bingo there were far fewer families of middle status – that is, who owned and worked five to ten *tan*. In both areas there were landowners who had amassed large tracts of land. One man in what is now Hiroshima city had by 1872 acquired more than 44 *chō* 9 *tan* (1 *chō* equals 10 *tan*, so approximately 110 acres); three others, near what today is Fukuyama city, had acquired even more property.[15] These land acquisitions preceded the Meiji tax law of 1873; clearly, then, by late Tokugawa times, land was an important investment for the wealthy, who rented it out to tenants or hired agricultural labourers.

Because the 1873 tax law required the holders of title deeds to pay taxes in cash at 3 percent of the assessed value of the land, the vagaries of the market caused much hardship for peasants. A reduction of the tax in 1876 to 2.5 percent did little to alleviate the problem. Moreover, by 1879, inflation had further accelerated land losses among non-tenant farmers. This was caused in part by the issuance of bank notes against bonds deposited by the *kazoku* (peers) and *shizoku* (one-time higher-class samurai) that had been paid to them by the government.[16] The situation grew worse when Matsukata Masayoshi, the finance minister in 1881, introduced deflationary fiscal policies that led to a sharp fall in the price of rice. This meant that the peasants had to pay twice as much in taxes.[17] Meanwhile, the central government was forcing local governments to levy additional taxes.[18] Peasants began to lose their land at alarming

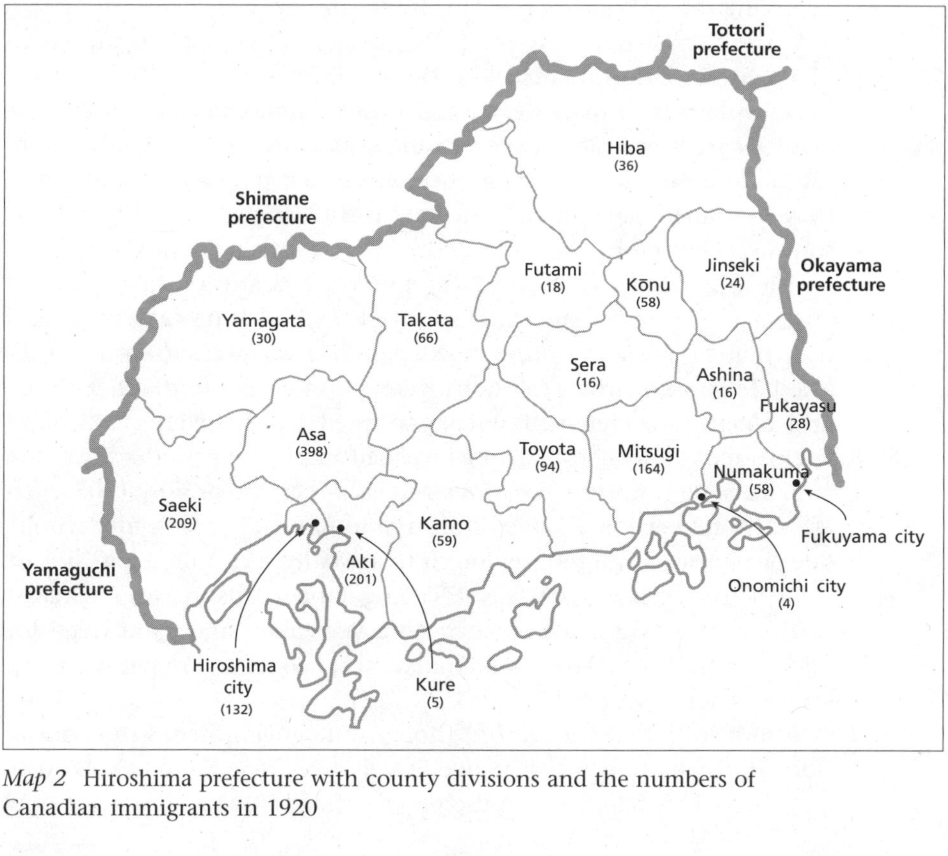

Map 2 Hiroshima prefecture with county divisions and the numbers of Canadian immigrants in 1920

rates. In Hiroshima between 1884 and 1886, 18.9 percent of the land in the prefecture changed hands; between 1884 and 1887, tenancy increased by 4 percent across the prefecture.[19] By 1889, the tenancy rates ranged from as high as 58.4 percent in Fukayasu county to 25.4 percent in Mitsugi county (see Map 2).

In 1884 and 1885 in the area around the Inland Sea, economic hard times were extreme. Prices were falling, as were interest rates; money-lenders were going bankrupt, unemployment was rising, and many farmers were becoming destitute. Matters went from bad to worse. By 1887 there had been a sharp decline in the market for cash crops such as cotton, indigo, sugar cane, tobacco, reed, and flax.[20] Cotton was especially important. It had been grown ever since Tokugawa times and by 1877 had come to represent 11.1 percent of the value of agricultural commodities. Rural households had supplemented their incomes by spinning and weaving cotton. Now, though, large-scale spinning mills built in 1882 and 1883 in the Hiroshima city area with *shizoku* and government funding, and using cheap imported cotton thread, were depriving the villagers of their livelihood.[21]

Another small-scale enterprise that had provided supplementary employment for Hiroshima blacksmiths and farmers was the manufacture of *yasuri* (files or rasps). After a long, arduous apprenticeship of seven or eight years, men learned how to make rasps from iron sand. Before mechanization, they could produce only about ten each day. By 1911, however, Japan had a modern steel industry,[22] so that by 1917, one person was able to turn out two hundred files in one working day.

As a consequence of industrialization, the peasants of the Inland Sea area, who since Edo times had survived by marketing cash crops and developing cottage industries, needed to find new ways to earn a livelihood. In some districts, solutions were found. In the former fief, Bingo area, enterprising merchants quickly adjusted to the marketplace. Around Fukuyama, wholesalers had long provided employment for local women who wove *Bingo-gasuri* on narrow thirty-six-inch looms.[23] By 1907, even after the conversion to large industrial looms, sixty to seventy wholesale dealers were still renting looms to agricultural families, and at least some *Bingo-gasuri* weaving was still being done.[24] This area also switched easily from growing cotton to raising vegetables and *igusa* (reed for *tatami*). The production of *tatami* mats and woven cotton products also absorbed surplus labour.[25]

In most other parts of Japan, though, the government's modernization efforts shattered people's livelihoods and drove them to seek work elsewhere. This happened to the people of Nihōjima near what is now the southern end of Hiroshima city. At nearby Ujina, over protests from the local peasantry and despite setbacks caused by storms, high tides, and funding shortfalls, the government built a deep-sea port, which was finally completed on 30 November 1889. The residents of Nihōjima were forced to abandon their oyster beds and to stop harvesting seaweed; the dredging of the seabed and the raising of the piers had destroyed both.[26] During the Meiji era, Sakamachi, on the Inland Sea just east of Hiroshima city, had had a population density of 861 per square kilometre – more than four times the average for Japan. Indiscriminate felling of trees eventually resulted in a severe flood there in 1907. Arable land was scarce and no side work was available. When the Ujina harbour was being constructed, men would pay five *rin* for a boat journey to work for five *sen* a day.[27] Few in Nihōjima went to school beyond the age of fourteen. As a consequence of all this, many in this region had no alternative except to go overseas to work.[28]

In the early 1880s, migration was chiefly within Japan. Many villagers moved to Osaka and other large cities, continuing the tradition of *dekasegi*. At the government's urging, some moved to Hokkaido. Between 1882 and 1884, Aki county was one of the main sources of settlers for Hokkaido.[29] In 1885, emigration to Hawaii began, and people from Aki county began going there instead, because the wages were higher and the transportation was free.

Until then, Japan had been reluctant to send its workers abroad. However, R.W. Irwin, the consul general for Hawaii, was a personal friend of Inoue Kaoru, the foreign minister, and the two of them signed an emigration agreement in September 1884.[30] The Japanese Foreign Office decided that if the Americans guaranteed the safety of the immigrants to Hawaii, it would permit temporary immigration.[31] Here, the government was remembering a fiasco dating back to the last days of the Bakufu, when around 150 men and women from Tokyo and Yokohama were "sneaked into" Hawaii to work in the sugar cane fields. Many were unable to cope with the hard labour, and the Meiji government had to transport some of them back to Japan. The government hoped that work overseas would provide employment, and that the income these sojourners remitted would ameliorate the hard times in Japan.

Among the first three groups of workers who embarked for Hawaii – on January 1885, June 1885, and January 1886 – the largest number were from Hiroshima prefecture: 963 out of 2,859 (33 percent). The Foreign Affairs Ministry's own statistics indicate that between 1899 and 1937, 96,181 people from Hiroshima went overseas. By 1940, Hiroshima prefecture led all of Japan in numbers of emigrants, with a total of 72,486.

(Presumably, about 23,700 returned to Japan.) In other words, by that time, 3.88 percent of the people of Hiroshima prefecture had gone to live overseas. Only Okinawa prefecture (9.97 percent) and Kumamoto prefecture (4.78 percent) exceeded Hiroshima in this regard. The average percentage for all of Japan was 1.03 percent.[32] These statistics include children who were born overseas but were registered in the family records in Japan.

Emigration was also driven by disasters such as the heavy summer rains and plagues of vermin that in 1889 destroyed crops in Hesaka, an area near Hiroshima city. Another important factor was the amount of money that could be earned in Hawaii.[33] There, a worker could earn the equivalent of 17.65 yen per month; in Hiroshima, carpenters made 4.68 yen and labourers 3.38 yen per month.[34] Three years' hard work in a foreign land could solve a person's economic problems. Many of the early emigrants from Hiroshima were household heads or first sons who were "saving" their families through *dekasegi*.[35] The amount of money sent back to Japan by Hiroshima emigrants between 1926 and 1938 represented 22.4 percent (in raw numbers, more than five million yen) of the total amounts sent back by all the emigrants overseas.[36] Remittances by Wakayama prefecture emigrants came second, amounting to 12.9 percent of all funds remitted to Japan.

Why were so many emigrants from Hiroshima prefecture? Although the Tokugawa regime had discouraged movement around the country, going elsewhere to work was a well-established custom even in the Tokugawa period.[37] Hiroshima farmers for centuries had gone to other parts of the country by way of the Inland Sea, and bold fishermen had sailed as far as Korea. Was Hawaii the next logical step? The inhabitants of the Hiroshima area were certainly more willing to go overseas than were people in the far more destitute Tōhoku region (see Map 1). In Tōhoku, desperate peasants were practising infanticide and selling their daughters to brothels, yet they were extremely reluctant to go abroad. In places such as Nagano in the Japanese Alps, young daughters were being sent to work in the spinning mills of Suwa, where they were forced to work under atrocious conditions.[38] The men and women of Hiroshima chose *dekasegi* instead, as far as Hawaii.

There was a push-pull effect in emigration. In Hiroshima, as soon as money from overseas began to arrive in the villages, others were drawn to the idea of going abroad, and emigration accelerated. After all, families of emigrants were buying property and household goods and repaying their debts.[39] The amount of money remitted in 1891 was equivalent to 54.3 percent of the annual budget of Hiroshima's prefectural government that year.[40]

Figures for Hawaii compiled by Japan's Ministry of Foreign Affairs for the years 1885 to 1894, and similar data gathered on the Hiroshima *dekasegi* between 1885 and 1893, reveal that emigrants from Hiroshima tended to stay overseas rather than return to Japan.[41] How did the Hiroshima immigrants who followed the first "wave" find their way overseas? And what did they do in their new environment?

After 1894, it was private companies that organized emigration; before then, the government had sponsored it. In order to control emigration, which so far had been unregulated, the Japanese government drew up the Emigrant Protection Ordinance in 1894; this was followed by the Emigrant Protection Law of 1896. Prefectural authorities gradually took over the paperwork for emigration, and some local authorities, especially in certain prefectures, encouraged overseas work and helped popularize it. Private businesses shipped labourers to Southeast Asia, Hawaii, and North and South America. In December 1891, even before emigration companies were officially sanctioned, the Kobe Emigration Company (later known as the Meiji Emigration Company) began operations, sending one hundred labourers from Hiroshima prefecture to the Union Colliery in Cumberland, Vancouver Island. According to Sasaki Toshiji, at the time these men were sent to the Union Colliery, there were only two hundred Japanese in all of Canada. How many of those two hundred were from Hiroshima we do not know.[42]

Chapter Two The First Ones

One of the most fascinating parts of my study was the search for information on the first arrivals from Hiroshima. It was also one of the most frustrating parts, because there was so little primary material. Diary keeping is quite popular among the Japanese, and a number kept up the practice in Canada. Many of my interviewees, children of the pioneers, told me that their parents (usually the father) had done so. However, either these books had been destroyed or they had been stored in a locked room or attic at the time the Japanese were forced from their homes on the coast during the Second World War. When the British Columbia Security Commission sold these homes, the diaries disappeared along with other stored materials. I was able to locate a few diaries, but families were extremely reluctant to release them: they were unable to read the contents themselves and were afraid that sensitive private matters might become public. One set of diaries was briefly in my possession. The section chronicling the early years was missing, and family members told me that it had been left behind in their farmhouse. Before I had the chance to examine them, another member of the family claimed them, alarmed that I had been given the set by her sibling.

According to Sugimura Fukashi, the Japanese consul in Vancouver, there were approximately two hundred Japanese in Canada in 1891.[1] However, he did not say how many were from Hiroshima prefecture. Canada did not keep records on Japanese immigration before 1900.[2] It is difficult to determine with certainty who the first immigrant from Hiroshima prefecture was. Ueda Minoru, who arrived in 1886 from Narahara village in Kamo county, may have been the "*senpai* [senior] from Hiroshima prefecture."[3] Ueda worked at Vancouver's Hastings Mill for six months. He was not the first Japanese worker there; evidence indicates that the mill hired its first Japanese worker in 1883.[4] Japanese immigrants referred to the Hastings Mill as *otasuke gaisha* (saviour company) because it provided employment for many men when little other work was available.[5] This sawmill, which started operations in 1867, was at the foot of Dunlevy Street on Burrard Inlet (see Map 3). It employed "Indians, Kanaka and Scandinavian deserters from the sailing ships and 'busted' refugees from the gold mines," and still later, Chinese and Japanese.[6] It was one of the first large-scale steam-powered sawmills on the west coast. The workers lived nearby on scows and in shacks.[7]

One block south of the mill was Powell Street, "with the Tivoli and Cisne Saloons, Fook's Columbia Hall." The footloose, the unemployed, and the labourers at Hastings Mill headed to Powell to relax, to drink, and to be entertained.[8] Soon it became the centre of the Japanese community. By the turn of the century, Powell Street between Main and Princess was completely lined by Japanese shops and boarding houses, which provided the Japanese immigrants with many of the amenities of their homeland.[9] Japanese labourers usually left the Powell Street area as soon as they found jobs elsewhere. Ueda followed this pattern of moving on to other occupations from Hastings Mill. He did heavy physical labour in Seattle and Portland and then worked under a labour contractor ("boss") at the English Cannery in Steveston.[10] Soon afterwards, he himself became a boss at the Skeena Balmoral Cannery, where he was in charge of sixty Japanese fishers. Packing companies dealt with white fishermen as individuals, but Japanese fishers were generally under contract to a labour contractor, probably because of the language barrier.[11] The special status of labour contractors like Ueda will be discussed in more detail in the next chapter.

Ueda later became a "top-level Hiroshima person" who helped his fellow Japanese through his activities with the Steveston Fisherman's Association. In 1903 he launched a magazine, *Shokumin no tomo* (The Settler's Friend). According to his biography, he discontinued the magazine once "the period was over" – which leads one to surmise that the magazine published advice, instructions, and information for new immigrants. Ueda opened the Umegaya Restaurant on Main Street near Powell and as a sideline provided supplies for fishers.[12]

Another early arrival from Hiroshima prefecture was Matoba Toyokichi. In the 1909 list of Canada's Japanese residents published by *Tairiku nippō* newspaper (henceforth *Tairiku, 1909*), he is recorded as a labourer, married with two children and living at 223 Cordova Street in Vancouver. We know almost nothing else about him, even from his descendants. According to his granddaughter, Raye Shin, Matoba came from the town of Onomichi.[13] His wife, Nishimura Chiyoko, from Hikone city in Shiga prefecture, was one of the first Japanese women in Canada. There is no record of her arrival; we do know that her sons were born in British Columbia in 1896 and 1898. One contact told me that Matoba's son was the first Japanese born in Cumberland; however, no Matoba is listed among the contract immigrants brought to Cumberland in 1891 and 1893.[14] The Matoba family's second son, Tom Niichi, was born in Vancouver. It is possible that Mrs. Matoba found her life in Canada unbearable, for she took the drastic step of leaving her husband and sons in Canada and returning alone to Japan. Matoba remained, and died in 1918 in a sawmill accident. I was told that his eldest son died of unknown causes three years later but there is a discrepancy, since, according to BC death records, he died in 1915 of tuberculosis.[15]

The earliest Japanese immigration to Canada seems to have been by individuals or small groups. Then a group of contract miners arrived in Cumberland on Vancouver Island. Knowledge about them was scanty until Sasaki Toshiji of Ritsumeikan University in Kyoto investigated the activities of the Kobe Emigration Company (later Meiji Emigration Company), which brought labourers under three-year contracts to the Union Colliery in Cumberland (see Map 4).[16] Sasaki published three articles in a Japanese journal in 1987 and 1988.[17] All of the first group of one hundred, who arrived in December 1891, were from Hiroshima prefecture; a high percentage of those who arrived through the same company in 1893 were also from Hiroshima. The list Sasaki offers is incomplete and not totally reliable, but his articles certainly fill a gap in our knowledge about the Hiroshima immigrants.

The Union Coal Company, registered in 1872, was founded by seven Vancouver Island coal miners and was associated with the Union Pacific Railroad in the United States.[18] It owned many coal deposits on Vancouver Island, including the Comox coal seam. In 1881, Robert Dunsmuir and the Southern Pacific Railroad bought out the company.[19] Dunsmuir, elected to the British Columbia legislature in 1882, was probably BC's wealthiest and most powerful entrepreneur. Through astute negotiations with the Canadian government when he was constructing the Esquimalt and Nanaimo Railway, he had acquired a land grant of 200,000 acres, which included "all substances whatsoever thereupon, therein, and thereunder."[20] Dunsmuir died in 1889. His son James took over his financial empire and tried to overcome the problems of using Chinese miners by importing Japanese labourers.

To reduce labour costs, the Vancouver Coal Mining and Land Company had been employing Chinese miners as early as 1867. Chinese workers could be hired at half the wages of white workers. "Boys and Indians were paid $1.50 per day; white mine workers received between $2.00 and

$3.50 while the Chinese earned between $1.00 and $1.25. Contract miners, the elite workers in the mine who were paid by the ton, averaged between $3.00 and $4.00 per day."[21] At first, white miners tried to protect their interests by claiming that the employment of the Chinese was a safety issue: their inability to understand English, they argued, had led to accidents. Investigations failed to show any grounds for these accusations; even so, in February 1888 the mining companies in the Nanaimo area agreed to exclude Chinese from employment below ground. Yet by late 1888, Dunsmuir was employing Chinese in his new operation, the Union Colliery in Cumberland, maintaining that the February 1888 agreement applied only to the Nanaimo area. Then, in 1890, the BC legislature passed the British Columbia Coal Mines Regulations Act, which prohibited the employment of Chinese underground. But this law had no "teeth," in that it did not prescribe any penalties for the unlawful employment of Chinese, and the Dunsmuir group continued to use Chinese miners while lobbying for the repeal of the act. To hedge his bets, Dunsmuir imported Japanese miners to work on contract in the Union mines.[22]

Dunsmuir's representative, Frank Casper Davidge of Victoria, contacted Frank Upton of the Upton Steamship Company of Portland, Oregon, to make the required arrangements. Upton's company advertised for "round trips to Yokohama, Kobe and Hongkong [*sic*] ... including stop-over privileges ... sailing monthly from Victoria," with F.C. Davidge and Company of 131 Government Street, Victoria, as agent. Upton, an Englishman living in Kobe, drew up an agreement on 3 March 1890 with the director of Union Pacific to carry wheat between Portland and Kobe. Before all his ships were ready, realizing he would be facing direct competition from the Canadian Pacific Steamship Line, he decided to look into transporting labourers from Japan to the United States. He formed a partnership with two *shizoku* (ex-samurai) from Yamaguchi and Kagoshima prefectures, who by then had formed the Kobe Emigration Company.

On 10 September 1891, Davidge, as representative for Dunsmuir of the Union Colliery, the Upton Steamship Company, and the Kobe Emigration Company, drew up a three-year contract for the miners.[23] The overriding concern in the agreement was to maximize the profits for the Kobe Emigration Company. The miners were to be paid $1.25 for an eight-hour day; "outside the mine" (i.e., above ground), they would be paid $1.00 a day for ten hours' labour. The wages were the same as for the Chinese – that is, half what the whites were paid.[24] In other words, the Japanese would provide the same cheap labour as the Chinese, and the company would not have to prepay the fifty-dollar Chinese head tax.[25] The Kobe Emigration Company recruited one hundred Japanese, who paid fifty yen each in return for the company's promise that it would find them work and be responsible for them until they had worked at least five months.[26] However, the company did not keep these promises. The Japanese government had a special department for emigrants by 1891 (within the Ministry of Foreign Affairs' Bureau of Trade and Commerce), but it did not pass the Emigrant Protection Ordinance until 1894, and the Emigrant Protection Law until 1896.[27] These laws required companies dispatching Japanese citizens abroad to secure official permission, to make security deposits, and to assume financial responsibility for shipping back the ill and those unable to return on their own.[28] In this circumstance, the miners were offered little protection by their own government.

It was during this time of flux that the first Hiroshima immigrants sailed to Canada. They left Yokohama on 11 November 1891, two months before the Kobe company received official approval for the enterprise. This made the immigrants' situation especially difficult. The company had promised "better than average" accommodation in Western-style bunkhouses that slept twenty men and cost only fifty cents per month. It also claimed that other living expenses would be approximately ten dollars per month – that is, seven dollars for food and three dollars for personal expenses and sundries. In calculating the monthly expenditure for food, it quoted prices of five to six dollars for one hundred pounds of rice, noting that the average worker would be eating less than fifty pounds, or two-and-a-half to three dollars worth. Beef and pork were available at fifteen cents per pound; so, after various vegetables were added, the cost for food would be three dollars per month per person. On this basis, the company claimed that each person would have a surplus of twelve to thirteen dollars per month, out of which he would be able to send back three to five dollars to his family.[29] Sasaki, however, has calculated that since the Kobe Emigration Company claimed thirty-seven cents from each dollar earned, the surplus was actually less than three dollars per month rather than the twelve to thirteen dollars it was suggesting. The company was obviously painting a rosy picture to gain the confidence of the Japanese government.

Moreover, the local newspapers railed against the arrival of the Japanese. A long article in the *Nanaimo Free Press* of 19 December 1891 argued: "There is no question that the bringing in of the Japanese free of duty, while the ordinary so-called Chinaman has to pay $50.00, is a nice distinction without a difference ... If we want the Dominion of Canada to progress we have to provide a certain degree of protection to Anglo-Saxon labor against the Asiatic competitor, who will revel in luxury at wages that a white man would barely escape starvation."[30] Less than a month later, on 9 January, the same paper complained that the Japanese had replaced white men and "Chinamen" in jobs both above and below ground. Ominously, the *Free Press* warned: "If the Japanese are allowed to get a foothold in the Union Colliery, they will soon permeate every industry in the land."[31] In a report datelined Victoria, 12 January 1892, the *San Francisco Examiner* made the same complaint, adding that the expected arrival of two hundred more Japanese would be the beginning of the influx of another group of labourers who "will get into every other industry and prove as dangerous to white labourers as the Chinese."[32] These fear-mongering reports were grossly exaggerated, as the actual experiences of the Hiroshima labourers would soon demonstrate.

The Japanese consul in Vancouver advised his ministry in Tokyo that only five or six of the miners who journeyed to Cumberland had worked underground before and that, because the others could not understand English, training them was difficult. Thus, the majority worked above ground. Once that work fell off in April, more than fifty fled, and only thirty were still employed at a dollar a day. Dunsmuir criticized them for deserting, but he also promised the immigrants other jobs at the mine or nearby lumber camps until experienced miners from Japan could train them for underground work. Some men took up his offer. By the end of May, sixty-five Japanese were employed at the Union Colliery.[33] Dunsmuir, however, operated his mines only when he could sell coal, and on 21 June 1892, when the San Francisco market slumped, he closed the mine.[34]

Without jobs, neither the immigrants nor their families in Japan could survive. Representatives of these stranded and unemployed men travelled to Vancouver, where, like peasants appealing to their lords, they "looked to the state for benevolence."[35] The consul offered some aid, but much more was required. Compounding the problem was the impending arrival of seventy-three experienced miners from Fukuoka prefecture. As soon as he learned that the mine had closed, Davidge sent telegrams telling them not to come and the consul sent a similar message to the Ministry of Foreign Affairs. But Davidge's messages went unheeded and the consul's report did not arrive at the ministry until mid-July, several days after the Fukuoka men had sailed.

The arrival of the experienced miners made a serious situation worse for the Cumberland labourers. The Kobe Emigration Company representative had disappeared in Yokohama before the ship sailed for Canada without having issued the promised blankets and clothing.[36] The Japanese consulate in Vancouver found it necessary to become more and more involved in providing money and aid. On 1 October 1892, representatives of the troubled immigrants again approached the consulate asking that they be returned to Japan. This request was refused, given the prohibitive costs. Whenever he obtained small sums from the Kobe company, Davidge took his percentage, leaving very little for the Japanese. This was extremely greedy and insensitive, but since he was acting for the Dunsmuirs, who had provided the passage money, his heartless actions were legal.[37]

When autumn arrived, the demand for coal rose again and the mine gradually reopened. The Japanese started back to work – at sixty cents a day. By 21 December, all the men who had remained in the area were working. However, they often protested with strikes and petitions to the Japanese consul about unwarranted pay deductions for equipment, and about poor working conditions and the lack of Japanese bathhouses. Many deserted. By February 1893 there were 2,309 white miners, 483 Chinese (17 percent), and 70 Japanese (2.5 percent) at the Union Colliery.[38] More than half the first hundred immigrants from Hiroshima and the seventy-three from Fukuoka had left the mine.

There is no doubt that the first group of contract labourers from Hiroshima brought over by the Kobe Emigration Company realized immediately that they had been conned by both the emigration company and the Union Colliery. Many broke contract and ventured onto the mainland, to the Cariboo, the fishing villages, and the embryonic Japanese community along Powell Street in Vancouver. Others hired themselves on with Vancouver Island sawmills and paper mills. A few of them formed the Royston Lumber Company. The first arrivals attracted others, which undoubtedly explains the disproportionate number of Hiroshima immigrants in Canada. As for Cumberland itself, only thirteen of the original group settled there. In later years, these veterans, "as seniors, gave guidance to the newcomers" who arrived either directly from Japan or from other parts of the province.[39]

Because there was no profit in recruiting and carrying contract labourers, the Kobe Emigration Company – now renamed the Meiji Emigration Company – decided in 1893 to focus on recruiting independent immigrants.[40] It brought a total of 458 labourers to the United States and Canada (see Table 1).

From the first half of 1893, the Meiji Emigration Company began carrying fewer Hiroshima immigrants and more from other prefectures. This tells us, perhaps, that Hiroshima people had become aware of the unreliability of this particular company. Also, fewer Japanese were immigrating to the United States, probably because American authorities were more carefully enforcing an 1885 law forbidding contract labour.

Table 1

Japanese emigrants to Canada and the United States in 1893

	Canada from		United States from		Both countries from	
Sailing date	Hiroshima	Japan	Hiroshima	Japan	Hiroshima	Japan
January 7	2	2	2	2	4	4
February 23	36	36	27	27	63	63
March 25	14	34	61	61	75	95
April 12	19	25	2	2	21	27
May 13	44	75	1	4	45	79
June 4	24	41			24	41
June 24	6	61			6	61
July 29	13	88			13	88
Total	158	362	93	96	251	458

Source: Sasaki Toshiji, "Meiji imingaisha ni yoru jiyūtōkōsha no okuridashi," *Han* 8 (April 1988): 162-64.

That law prohibited the signing of contracts beforehand with, or the payment of a passage in advance by, someone other than the immigrant.[41] On 20 August 1893, the US immigration authorities refused to admit fifty-five Japanese men carried on a Meiji ship. As a consequence, they were "forwarded" to Victoria a few days later.

Meiji had protected itself by demanding from each immigrant a guarantor, who had to either pay at least a five-yen tax or make a deposit of one hundred yen in a secured bank in Kobe to ensure passage home in case of an emergency. In addition, the immigrant was to carry at least twenty yen for Western-style clothes. Recruiters claimed that jobs were plentiful. They offered, for a commission of three yen, to find jobs for the men at wages of at least $1.50 to $1.60 per day – a considerably inflated sum, since there was a depression at the time and unemployment was high. Wages were more likely to have been seventy-five cents a day at the most. Sasaki writes that greed, misrepresentation, corruption, and failure to keep its promises sealed the fate of the Meiji Emigration Company. After four years' operations, it closed in 1893.[42]

The Vancouver consulate, in a report to Tokyo dated 12 October 1893, deplored the arrival of Japanese immigrants at a time when the BC economy was depressed and unemployment was rampant. It noted that the new arrivals were being hired at the lowest wages for the most unskilled jobs and were being called *guriun Jappu* ("Green Japs").[43] The consul referred to this name-calling as a national shame. Consular reports like these undoubtedly sealed the fate of the Kobe/Meiji company. The Ministry of Foreign Affairs soon took steps to control emigration in order to preserve Japan's pride and honour. In 1894 and 1896 it finally passed legislation to regulate the activities of private emigration companies.

Thanks to Sasaki's study, Canadian immigration and statistical records, and interviews with descendants, we now know the names of some of the men who were sent to Cumberland, as well as some biographical details (see Map 2 for location of counties).

Doi Umatarō (1870-194?) is listed as a member of the first Hiroshima group. He renegotiated his contract and remained in Cumberland after 1892.[44] He was the eldest in a family of seven sons and one daughter that farmed in Kaitaichi in Aki county, about four miles east of Hiroshima city.[45] Doi had spent three years in Hawaii. He then returned to Japan, only to leave almost immediately for Canada with the first group of labourers for the Union Colliery. At that time he was twenty-one years old. He lived in Cumberland for around forty years. There is no record of his wife Tomiyo's (1875-?) arrival in Canada, but Chiyono, a daughter, was born in 1900, and a son, Kenichi, in 1902. According to his grandson George, there was another daughter, who died when she was three. At any rate, Tomiyo returned to Japan for a short while with Chiyono and Kenichi. While there she gave birth to a daughter, Shimayo, whom she left behind when she returned in 1908 with the two Canadian-born children.[46] Shimayo joined her family in 1917.

The economic status of the Doi household in Japan is difficult to assess, but undoubtedly the sons needed to seek independent livelihoods. An adventurous streak in the family drove many of their sons overseas; the eldest Umatarō (1870-194?) and the youngest Denjirō (1896-?) both came to Canada.[47] Immigration records reveal that Umatarō's youngest brother, Denjirō, then twenty-one years old, arrived in Cumberland in 1917 to work in the mines. Denjirō's son Manabu said that his father's life was difficult in Kaitaichi and that he felt he had no choice but to emigrate. On his first attempt, the Japanese authorities rejected him because of an eye infection, so he stowed away. Ten minutes after the boat left Kobe, he was discovered and sent back.[48] Denjirō's wife, Fusayo, arrived in 1926.

Iwaasa Matsutarō (1868-1957) was from Higashishiwa village in Kamo county, just east of Hiroshima city. There is some uncertainty about the date of his arrival, but he was certainly one of the early contract labourers.[49] He assumed leadership in the group, negotiated with the mining company, and approached the Japanese consulate in Vancouver for monetary assistance and for help dealing with the Kobe Emigration Company. After working for a time at the Hotel Vancouver, probably in a menial job, he returned to Cumberland and opened a boarding house and grocery store. Matsutarō's relative Kōjun (1882-1968) came to Canada when he was fourteen to help in Iwaasa's businesses. In 1907 he moved to southern Alberta to farm and became a leader in the Japanese community that formed there.

Nakanishi Kanekichi was in the first group of contract labourers from Hiroshima and is listed as one of the forty men who left the mines.[50] His home village was Kawauchi in Asa county, just north of Hiroshima city.[51] Apparently, Nakanishi went to the Cariboo for three years. Later, he lived in Vancouver, where he ran a real estate business as well as a lumber business, besides operating as a labour contractor.[52]

The Union Colliery experience was a disastrous episode for the earliest immigrants from Hiroshima. Even so, thirteen of them stayed in that area, and their presence attracted many friends and relatives, who worked in the local mines and in the nearby lumber camps. For example, Iwaasa Matsutarō's fellow villager, Okuda Kasaku (1879-1969), arrived in Canada in 1900 and within a few years had gone to Cumberland to work at the Iwaasa store there.[53] In 1911 he began to produce *miso* (fermented bean paste) and *kōji* (a type of yeast made from rice used to make *miso,* soy sauce, and sake) and sold ice cream. He also worked in the mines.[54] Kasaku's wife, Haruka (1892-1975), joined him in 1914, and they had two sons and a daughter.

Another immigrant, from Kamimizu village in Saeki county, west of Hiroshima city, was Hirose Tokuji. He was the fourth son of a prominent family. Yet, seeking adventure, he immigrated to Portland, Oregon, at the age of eighteen. The following year, in October 1898, he settled in Cumberland, where he worked in the mines. By 1900 he had become the Japanese labour boss and the liaison between management and the miners of Number Five Mine.[55] He also arranged jobs and work schedules.

Two Japanese communities developed beside the Union Colliery in Cumberland. They were referred to as Number One Jap Town and Number Five Jap Town. Comox Valley local historians D.E. Isenor, E.G. Stephens, and D.E. Watson contend that the term "Jap town" was "more a shorthand rather than derogatory term or indication of racial tension." However, the Nisei who grew up there were sensitive to the term and asked an interviewer to refer instead to Number One Village and Number Five Village.[56] The Japanese were not the only segregated group in the Cumberland area. Black residents lived at "Coontown," whereas the Chinese resided in "Chinatown."[57]

Because mining was marked by seasonal unemployment, the Canadian-born sons of the Hiroshima miners found work in the lumber camps, though they and their families continued to live in the two Japanese "towns" near Cumberland until their wartime removal in 1942. At least ten Hiroshima men became farmers in the Courtenay area in the early 1920s.[58] Their immigration dates to Canada range from 1892 to 1907. All had spent some time mining in Cumberland, some continuously; some had also fished out of Steveston. A number began farming by leasing land from white farmers; doing so, however, required an investment in farming implements. Others, by saving carefully and shifting regularly to the most lucrative jobs, were able to buy considerable acreage outright. Some grew potatoes and turnips, others wheat and hay; still others kept poultry and dairy cattle.

Kishimoto Yūkichi, from Kinomura village in Saeki county, was one of the most successful of these Comox farmers.[59] By 1921 he had thirteen or fourteen hired farmhands of various backgrounds, as well as 130 head of cattle, and he was providing milk for the two Cumberland Japanese towns and a variety of hotels, restaurants, and homes, as well as the Courtenay Condensed Milk Company. He kept more than twenty horses for his deliveries.

Another farmer, Kobayakawa Giichi, from Zōka village in Kamo county, came to Vancouver Island in 1892 as one of the first contract miners. There is a detailed record of his early experiences that leaves little doubt he was among the earliest arrivals. He claimed to have arrived in Victoria in October 1892, but it was more likely to have been December 1891, with the very first group, for he noted that he and his fellow "miners," distressed with only part-time work and an idle life, made representations to the Japanese consul, who helped them to the tune of twenty cents a day.[60] Kobayakawa left Cumberland and went on to other jobs in lumbering and fishing. Eventually he returned to Cumberland, where he resumed mining, made and sold tofu (bean curd), and started a Japanese-style bathhouse with the help of his wife. In 1908 he purchased 160 acres in the Comox Valley for six thousand dollars. That was a great deal of money at the time; clearly, saving it would have entailed much hard work and diligence. He acquired twenty-eight head of cattle and five horses and also grew grain. In 1912 he bought more land and a house.

Some Hiroshima people remained in the Cumberland-Courtenay area, where they farmed or worked in lumbering; others, like Nakanishi, moved to Vancouver. Some fished out of Steveston, but many more gravitated toward the Powell Street district, where they worked at Hastings Mill and became part of Vancouver's rapidly growing Japanese community.

Chapter Three Sojourning and Beyond

Vancouver's Japanese community developed around Powell Street because Powell Street was near Hastings Mill, the *otasuke gaisha,* where many Japanese worked. Parallel to Powell Street one block inland was Cordova Street, which until the early 1890s was Vancouver's choice residential street. The adjacent streets offered hotels, boarding houses, saloons, shops, and entertainment houses. Then, during the depression of the 1890s, the small merchants along Cordova and Powell went bankrupt, the buildings emptied, and the Japanese slowly moved in, establishing their own community.[1] After 1908, with an increase in female immigration from Japan, Powell became more settled. In April 1911, a writer for *British Columbia Magazine* described Powell Street, noting that it hardly appeared to be a Japanese neighbourhood:

> For half a mile of its length the men of cold bosom [?] have printed their pleasant-sounding names on the shop windows of Powell Street, in English, and in their own symbols, but they have not printed the marks of their individuality upon it, as the Chinese have on Pender Street – they have not cared to. They are not here to do that sort of thing. There is no money in it, and they are here to make money, as much as they can. Money is at the back of every Japanese motive. At first glance only the window signs and the dried devil fish [squid] and straw sandals and sake bottles in the window themselves tell you that you are in the Japanese quarter ... Look for something picturesque and having Oriental character on Powell Street ... and you will look in vain. You will see no Japanese wearing a single rag of the costume of his country ... Powell Street is a monochrome, there is no colour. There is not a suggestion of the Japanese architecture in any of the buildings. The shop windows have little in them that's interesting or curious. Little

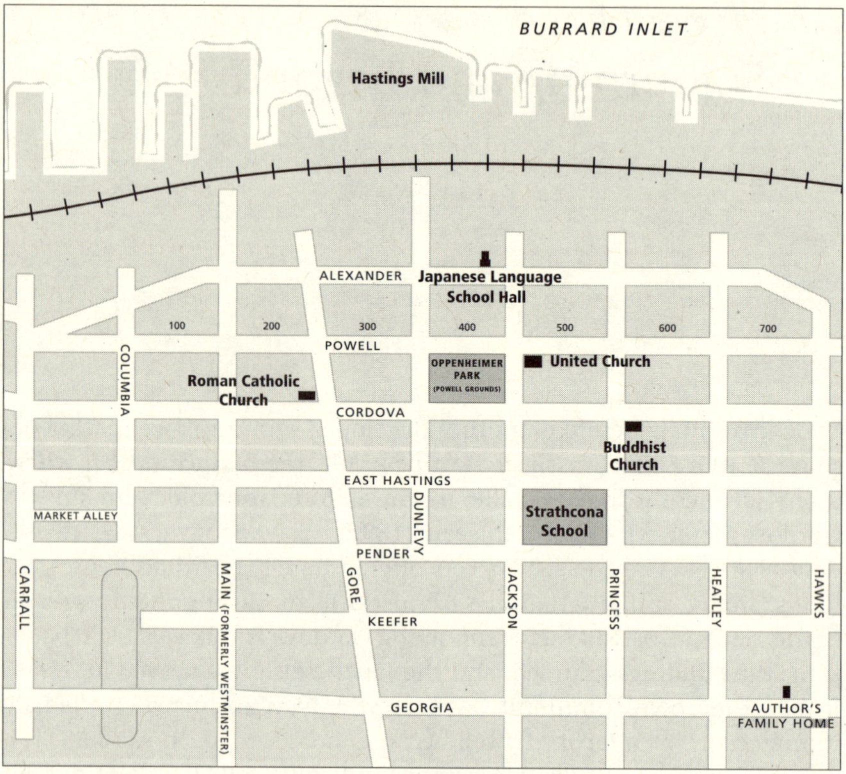

Map 3 Vancouver's Powell Street Japantown area

of the stuff is Japanese ... There are plenty of Japanese real estate offices on Powell Street and they do a good business.[2]

Early Japanese society in Vancouver was predominantly a sojourner society – something not unique to the Japanese immigrants. Vancouver at that time was a city of migrants; in 1911 its sex ratio was 3:2 male to female, and its population fluctuated with the seasons. Once winter shut down the province's resource industries, men flocked to Vancouver, where they could live for a time free of the "isolation, wetness, and arduous toil of coastal logging camps [and get] good and drunk."[3] Powell Street provided cheap rooms for both white and Japanese transients. In the late 1930s, rooms were still available for a dollar a night.

The new immigrants had no knowledge of English and were mystified by the local mores and working and living conditions. To find and learn jobs, they needed the help of a compatriot or "boss" who spoke English. This circumstance, of course, was not unique to Vancouver. It also existed among Japanese immigrants to the United States, who relied on labour contractors to find work in agriculture, mining, lumbering, and fishing.[4]

The "boss" phenomenon developed early on at Hastings Mill, even though that business was eager to employ Japanese. Richard H. Alexander, the long-time manager, bluntly explained to the Royal Commission on Chinese and Japanese Immigration in 1902 that

> The Japanese supplies the want of the proportion of cheap labour that is necessary to compete in the markets of the world. I submit that there is great necessity that they should be here to supply that proportion of cheap labour in order that we may employ a larger number of whites. The point is this: We have always had a certain proportion of cheap labour, and in order to operate successfully we must have it yet, and having that cheap labour we are enabled to employ white men in the higher branches of industry.[5]

The "proportion of cheap labour" that the mill always hired included first, local Indians; later, Chinese; and still later, Japanese. Alexander stated that the Japanese workers at the mill were "all in inferior positions, with the exception of the lath mill, at which there are six or seven of them at the cut-off saws and trimmers." They were generally used "in and about the mill trucking lumber and piling it."[6] At the time, the Indians were paid seventy-five cents a day plus board, equal to a dollar a day. The Royal Commission of 1902 reported that in sawmills,

> The Japanese are paid from 90 cents to 1.00 a day and board themselves; in a few instances they are paid as high as $1.50 to $2 and for semi-skilled from $2 to $2.50, and skilled labour from $2.50 to $3.50, and in a few instances $4.50 to $5, the fact being that nearly all of the strictly common labour in and about the mills and yards is performed by the Japanese and Chinese.[7]

The Japanese called Hastings Mill the "saviour company" because it provided work for new arrivals, whether they were sponsored by a friend or relative or "on the run" like the Union Colliery absconders. Yet at the same time, the mill itself was "saved" by the Japanese, who provided not only a good supply of cheap and docile labour but also their own "bosses," who acted as brokers. When Yamada Suteya became "boss" in 1899, he was placed in charge of more than two hundred workers. Japanese was the mill's working language, and Yamada kept his employee records in Japanese.[8]

Only through a boss (the Japanese pronounced it "*bosu*") could jobs be obtained at the mill – or, for that matter, in most BC industries that employed Japanese. Uyeno Ritsuichi (1889-1994), a pioneer from Hiroshima, wrote in 1981 that when he arrived in Canada in 1907, it was difficult to get a job in a sawmill unless one was from Shiga prefecture.[9] Since bosses tended to hire men who shared their prefectural origins, this suggests that in 1907 the Japanese sawmill bosses were mainly from Shiga.

The immigrant workers were highly mobile, both occupationally and geographically. When they were dissatisfied, "they just moved along" and spent "years without definite occupations, shifting from job to job, place to place." Then, in the summer of 1908, the United States began strictly enforcing a "right" of the Gentlemen's Agreement: "the right to deny admission to any laborer whose passport was issued for any destination other than the United States."[10] Until then, many Hiroshima emigrants had been moving back and forth across the Canadian-American border. Between 1897 and 1901, 15,280 Japanese had arrived in Canadian ports, and about 10,000 had gone on to the United States.[11] Over the next few years an even greater influx of people, these with passports for Hawaii, took advantage of this easy movement.

Occupational mobility applied to entrepreneurs as well. Miyake Ryūkichi (1879-1953) came from Kabe village in Asa county, now a suburb of Hiroshima city. His father had opened a *terakoya* (temple school) to teach basic reading and writing to the neighbourhood children.[12] After coming to Canada in 1900, he learned English by working in white homes and in a hotel. He then started a "servants' registry" for Japanese seeking work in white establishments and homes. In 1910, after a real estate venture with Nakanishi Kanekichi went bankrupt,[13] Miyake became a foreman at a camp near Stave Falls that produced cedar shingle bolts.[14] He returned to Japan in 1921, married, and brought his wife back to Stave Falls. When his eldest child was born a few years later, he returned to Vancouver, where he worked as the secretary of the Canadian Japanese Association and became highly active in the Japanese community.[15]

Wherever they went, the Japanese turned to people from the same prefecture for aid and friendship. To increase business, entrepreneurs from prefectures from which relatively few Japanese immigrated advertised their services to people from prefectures adjacent to their own. For men without family ties, prefectural networks were an important substitute. Immigrants quickly established friendships with men from the same prefecture, who shared a dialect and tastes in food, thereby softening the hardships of the New World. Japanese-operated hotels and boarding houses served as important points of contact and also as employment agencies.[16] The bachelors who lived in primitive shacks and bunkhouses in logging and fishing camps, and in boxcars when working on the railways, all straggled back to Powell Street once their contracts were over. There they moved into boarding houses, where they could find beds and hot baths, get their laundry done, and perhaps find other jobs. By providing "homes" for Hiroshima natives and sources of potential jobs, boarding house proprietors offered a lifeline, especially for newcomers, that was grasped eagerly both in Canada and along the Pacific coast.

The most enterprising of the early arrivals saw good business in providing food and lodging for their fellow countrymen. These men then brought wives over from Japan to help run their boarding houses. Hiroshima immigrants preferred establishments run by Hiroshima owners, because they provided familiar foods (different regions of Japan had their own special dishes) as well as opportunities to meet and make friends. Moreover, they could speak the Hiroshima dialect: a Hiroshima immigrant could barely understand the speech of people from Wakayama or Kagoshima prefectures.[17] Tight bonds developed among the Hiroshima people in Canada.[18] At least four Vancouver boarding houses were owned by Hiroshima natives.

To a Japanese bachelor immigrant, the boarding house was a home – it provided regular meals, a bed, companionship, and recreation. Four men often occupied one room, and whatever the frictions, close friendships often resulted. The proprietor's wife looked after the laundry, cleaned the rooms, and served as a surrogate mother. Kazuta Kiyoso recalled that when he arrived in Vancouver in 1917 he stayed at a Hiroshima boarding house, where he paid about sixteen dollars a month for room and board and ten cents for a bath at a local Japanese-style bathhouse. He did not feel as if he was in a foreign country.[19] He remembered, too, that the people who worked in the logging and sawmill camps, and in fishing, returned to Powell Street in the off-season to "cure their solitude," and that "many were destroyed by sake and gambling."[20] Kazuta became an active member of the Japanese community and especially of the young men's branch of the Hiroshima kenjinkai (Hiroshima Prefectural Association), the Kōryō seinenkai.[21]

Kurita Shōjirō (or Sōjirō) (1877-?), who ran another boarding house, arrived in 1897.[22] At one point he was a contractor for the fishing industry in the Skeena area. In 1917 he bought the Maple Rooms at 391 Powell Street; the following year, in partnership with another person, he bought the Imperial Hotel at 403 Powell Street.[23]

Fukui Yajū and his wife, Chika, opened a popular boarding house and grocery store at 433 Alexander Street in 1911. Fukui was from Mikawa village in Asa county, from which a number of immigrants came. This may well explain the popularity of his establishment. Before opening the boarding house, he had followed a pattern quite common among Japanese immigrants. He arrived in Victoria in 1900, went to Vancouver, and found work in a sawmill, probably Hastings Mill.[24] He then worked in a sawmill in Seattle for a few years, returned to Japan, and served in the Japanese army during the Russo-Japanese War. That may have been a patriotic gesture, since Japanese men living abroad enjoyed deferments from military duty but lost it "if they returned for more than thirty days."[25] After the war he returned to Seattle, where he worked in a store operated by a Caucasian. When his wife was refused entry to the United States due to an eye disease, they went to Vancouver.

The Fukui boarding house charged one dollar for one night's stay and three meals.[26] When the Fukui opened their business, the average pay of a Japanese labourer was about two dollars a day. Given that a hundred-pound sack of potatoes then cost two dollars, this was not a large sum.[27] Two decades earlier, a hundred pounds of rice cost around five dollars, but it is difficult to determine what its price would have been in 1911.[28] The meals would have been simple – rice and *miso* soup for breakfast; rice, vegetables, and some fresh or dried fish for supper. Red meat was rarely part of the diet.

The Hiroshimaya boarding house was operated by Satō Mohei (1869-1934). Satō arrived in 1899 from Hikino village in Fukayasu county, now within Fukuyama city on the eastern border of Hiroshima prefecture. He was the eldest son of an "average" peasant family; that is, they owned sufficient land to grow enough for their survival.[29] He married in 1897. Dreaming of making his fortune abroad, he gave the land and home he was to inherit as eldest son to his married sister and emigrated, leaving his wife and baby daughter behind temporarily. He must have saved his money conscientiously, since by 1901 he had opened the Hiroshimaya on Market Alley, west of Main Street, between Hastings and Pender. Because that was a few blocks from the centre of the Japanese area, he later moved his business to 230 Alexander Street. His wife and daughter joined him in 1904. A photograph of his establishment taken in 1912 shows a sign saying "Grocer," so it seems he also sold groceries.[30]

Another early arrival who opened a boarding house was Taniguchi Kumatarō from Yahata village in Saeki county. He came to America in 1893, worked in a sawmill near Seattle for several years, fished on the

Fraser River, and laboured in a sawmill in Chemainus, where he also owned a food and sundries store. He established himself on Powell Street in 1900.[31] A 1907 photograph shows a building called the Taniguchi Inn; barely legible lettering on the storefront reads "Takahashi Labor Agent." This tells us that Taniguchi worked as a labour contractor (possibly in partnership with a Takahashi) while his wife ran the boarding house. Through him it was possible for sojourning bachelors to find work in lumber camps.

When Imada Ito (1891-1987) arrived in Vancouver in November 1911 to join her husband Imada Kaichi (1884-1947), they stayed at the Taniguchi Inn. She wrote that people said Taniguchi "was the most successful of all the Hiroshima Prefecture immigrants at that time."[32] Within days of arriving, she secured housework in a house belonging to white people. Frightened after the mile-and-a-half walk back to her lodgings through dense fog, she began working in Taniguchi's boarding house.[33] She later wrote that this too was an unpleasant experience:

> The female boss [presumably Mrs. Taniguchi] and I made the beds, cleaned and cooked. It was unsanitary. I was shocked at the many lice in the beds where the white men stayed. I encountered these only after I came to this country ... We had to use cold water for our cleaning. The people who stayed there went to the bath-house and did their laundry there ... I worked at this rooming-house for two months, from December to January but I did not get paid. My husband and I just received free room and board.[34]

The boarding house owner was more than just a supplier of food and lodging. Yoshida Ryūichi observed: "If the owner knew you, if you seemed to be an honest person, they would advance the room and board until you had a job."[35] Immigrants usually obtained jobs through a boss, as in the case of Hastings Mill. Typically, a boss operated out of an office on Powell Street and acted as a liaison between the mill, camp, or cannery and the Japanese workers employed there. Some bosses worked on the same site as the men under them. The chief criteria for being a boss were experience in the workplace and facility with English. A 1920 *Nikka Times* publication, *Kanada zairyū dōhō sōran* (General Survey of Compatriots Resident in Canada) listed thirteen Hiroshima men as labour contractors. The sectors in which these men specialized – lumbering, railways, fishing, canneries – were also listed.

Labour contractors also established themselves in the Chinese community. In this case, whether they were Caucasian or Chinese, they imported and exploited Chinese labourers and underbid white labourers. The Chinese contractors were often immigrants themselves who, "after a period of time in Canada became petit bourgeois merchants, traders, shopkeepers, and labour contractors."[36] In the white community as well, employment agencies were common. In Vancouver between 1898 and 1915, there were "anywhere from thirty to sixty of them [male employment agencies] operating at peak seasons ... They were small, marginal, delicate businesses which operated in an intensely competitive environment only during periods of labour shortages, and whose operators emerged from and often returned to the same background as their working clients." Such businesses "attracted those hoping to escape wage labour."[37] Unlike the white operators, the Japanese labour contractors usually rose socially and economically above their clients.

In her memoir, Imada Ito wrote about Katō Tōsaku, her first boss.[38] Katō was referred to as a "commission boss" because he took a commission of twenty-five cents from every cord of shingle bolts a worker cut. Apparently, this was extremely high. A Japanese contractor for shingle bolts told the Royal Commission in 1902 that

> I contract to get out bolts, $2.05 per cord delivered on the scows. I pay $2 per cord and get 5 cents and what I make on supplies. The men do not have to buy in my store; they can buy in any other place. I take out about three thousand cords a year. We employ all Japanese, 36 men in the camp ... I buy groceries at the wholesale store. I keep store and buy $2,000 a month; $360 a month goes into camp. I supply them with overalls and working clothes. I buy some from white men and some from Chinese.[39]

The Royal Commission summary stated: "The Japanese contractors pay the Japanese the contract price within a few cents and make their profits on their supplies."[40]

Katō thus appears to have deserved his title. At first he hired Imada Ito to cook and do the laundry for forty men at a shingle bolt camp two hours by rowboat beyond Indian River on the north shore of Burrard Inlet. Later Katō asked her to go as cook to a camp at Seymour Creek. There, with difficulty, she cooked for twenty-seven men, rising at 4:40 a.m. to prepare fifty pounds of rice for their breakfasts and to pack lunches.

Stories abound of fast-talking contractors offering work in lumber camps where (so they said) the facilities were good, the food plentiful and nutritious, and the pay better than average. The reality many times fell far short. Some camps purchased small quantities of poor-quality food and skimmed a profit that way.[41] Imada Ito recalled how the men paid a great deal of money for their food but got a diet consisting mainly of rice and dried foods:

> The only fresh vegetables were potatoes, carrots, onions and cabbages. The rest was all dried. Everything was almost always cooked with *iriko* [small parched sardines]. In the five months period, meat came only once and after only two or three meals it was consumed. It could not be kept long at any rate, because it was in April or May. The dried foodstuffs were burdock, lotus root, long white radish, gourd, kelp, dried bean curd and devil's tongue that I made myself. Canned fish, each can contained about six to seven pounds, came just once in a while, so everyone bought such things as eggs and ham and every morning they fried their own and ate it. Thus, the cost of food was low: for each day it cost only six or seven dollars to feed all these men.[42]

Others profited from the extensive gambling that went on in the camps. Possibly, as in the Alaska salmon canneries, contractors and foremen promoted gambling. The labourers gambled on credit so that by the end of the season some *owed* money to the contractor.[43] One pioneer recalled: "Camps were always full of fights – fights and gambling. Men played cards, especially Black Jack. Fights would start over gambling ... Some people in those camps gambled from supper until it was time to go to bed."[44] Some contractors may not have supported gambling but were completely unscrupulous and victimized their clients. When Maehara Takuji, from Yoshino village in Kōnu county in east-central Hiroshima, came to Canada in 1907 after two years in Hawaii, the Canadian Nippon Supply Company (Nikka yōtatsu kabushiki kaisha), which had an exclusive contract with the Canadian Pacific Railway (CPR), sent him and others to Maple Creek, Saskatchewan. When they arrived, they discovered that there were no jobs. No one gave them any assistance for returning to the coast. Maehara had no alternative but to walk back to British Columbia. It took him forty-two days to reach the Okanagan Valley. He settled there and eventually became a successful apple grower.[45]

The labour contractors who ran agencies in cities such as Vancouver had underlings who handled their affairs in the isolated areas. There were also many small-time operators who hired a few men and worked alongside them. Imada Ito mentioned a number of the latter type of bosses, including at times her husband, as well as her brother-in-law,

Imada Heiichi, from Hatsukaichi in Saeki county, who had come to Canada at eighteen. After learning English, he contracted small labouring operations here and there.[46]

Several other Hiroshima immigrants became contractors. Sunada Naotarō (1879-1962), from Suzuhara village in Asa county, immigrated to the United States in 1899 when he was twenty. After a few years, he moved to Canada and became an independent logging contractor in places such as Minstrel Island, Lasqueti Island, and Bowen Island. Unfortunately for him, the 1902 legislation that prohibited the employment of Japanese on Crown land was vigorously applied in December 1924, and by 1927 he was unable to continue in this line of work.[47]

Nakanishi Kanekichi was one of the earliest Hiroshima labourers at the Union Colliery. He broke his contract there but later returned and became the mine workers' boss. In 1909 he was a contractor residing at 421 Powell Street and had one employee. Nakanishi even went to Japan to recruit workers, so presumably the employee looked after the business while he was away.[48] As noted earlier, for a brief time Nakanishi also conducted a real estate business with Miyake Ryūkichi. There were several real estate offices on Powell Street; however, of the Hiroshima immigrants, only Saeki Tadaichi seems to have been involved in real estate for any length of time. Saeki had come to Canada in 1894, from Kameyama village in Asa county, and became a real estate broker in 1905. By 1911 he had white partners. Some real estate offices on Powell Street probably sold farmland, for by 1911 some Japanese were beginning to farm in the Okanagan, Comox, and Fraser Valleys. Saeki was heavily involved in the gradual settlement of Japanese on the high-quality farmland in the vicinity of Vancouver.[49]

We should not assume that all new arrivals required help, although many would have needed some at first. Uyeno Ritsuichi (1889-1994), the second son of a family of six children, was an independent adventurer. He was from Misono village in Kamo county, the present site of Hiroshima University in what is now Higashi Hiroshima city. After eight years of elementary school and higher elementary school, he apprenticed as a carpenter for four years before going to Hawaii in 1906 and then on to Canada in 1907. He moved about the Lower Mainland and other areas in British Columbia, as receipts from paid poll and road taxes in Vancouver, Burnaby, and Delta and provincial taxes in Comox and Golden attest.[50] Uyeno probably resorted to the services of labour contractors in the early years, when he was working for sawmills and fish canneries and for the CPR in Golden. We know that in 1913 he went to Skagway, Alaska. He crossed Atlin Lake by dogsled to the Atlin

Gold Mine, where he worked as a flume carpenter for two years. At Atlin, Uyeno built a wooden channel to carry river water to the sluices into which the gravel was shovelled. The sluices would "disintegrate the gravel and free the gold."[51] These sluices were made of rough timber and were probably built by Uyeno. He told his son that the company trusted him and did not worry that he would steal any gold nuggets that might appear when the sand was washed down the flume.[52] Uyeno became a Canadian citizen in 1914. Many Japanese had become citizens, but it was usually so that they could fish. Uyeno had no intention of fishing, so taking citizenship was obviously a sign that he expected to make Canada his home. Back in Vancouver in 1917, he married Matsumiya Kuye (1896-1989), the daughter of an immigrant from Shiga prefecture.[53]

Not all immigrants maintained close ties with the Japanese community. Hoita Rikuzo (1890-1948), from Hiura village in Asa county, arrived in Canada in 1909. He did not seek the companionship of fellow Japanese. Instead he went to Cranbrook, where he attended school while working as a houseboy. Then he worked in a white man's store for four years, before serving in the Canadian army (which decorated him). He later attended the University of British Columbia, presumably taking advantage of his educational right as a veteran. Through the Soldier Settlement Board, he bought twenty acres of land.[54]

Men such as Uyeno and Hoita may have come to Canada as sojourners, but in the end they made it their home. Others, however, clung to their dreams of returning to Japan. My paternal grandfather, Ishii Chōkichi (1862-1918), came to Canada in 1907 from Hisayamada in Mitsugi county, near Onomichi, via Hawaii. In 1912 he persuaded my father Kenji (1895-1971) to join him. My father was seventeen at the time and had completed his apprenticeship as a carpenter. They worked together in various jobs until my grandfather became ill and returned to Japan. The year of his return is uncertain, but he died in 1918, according to the family records kept at the municipal office in Onomichi. According to family lore, when my grandfather returned to Japan, his wife was furious and refused to receive him since he had not sent her any money during his stay in Canada. My grandfather's large family struggled to survive on their little terraced rice paddy in a mountainous area north of Onomichi.

On my most recent trip to Japan, an elderly cousin, the daughter of the eldest son of Chōkichi, and therefore living in the home to which my grandfather should have returned, recalled that as a young girl she had often visited our grandfather at the home of her uncle in Onomichi. She believed that our grandfather lived there because it was closer to medical help and not because his wife had refused to care for him. Whatever the truth, my grandfather had not been able to help his family the way he had dreamed of doing. Undoubtedly there are many stories like his.

If returning to Japan after a sojourn in Canada was a sign of success, then the story of Nakashima Kumakichi (1868-?) is exemplary. Nakashima, from Hatsukaichi in Saeki county, arrived in the United States in 1889. From there, he boarded a coal ship and travelled to Nanaimo. He fished out of Steveston during the summer months and worked in a sawmill in Chemainus during the winter months. He was soon in charge of more than two hundred Japanese at a lumber camp on Saltspring Island. In 1899 he returned to Hiroshima prefecture, bringing back ten people the following year.[55] His success suggests that he was a hard worker, strongly driven, and a compelling leader. As a boss on Saltspring Island he would have taken a percentage of the wages of the others; that would easily have financed his trip to Japan to bring back the ten men. His son Giichi came to Canada in 1906 to help him; Giichi's sixteen-year-old wife came in 1907. According to *Tairiku, 1909,* by 1909 Kumakichi had a wife and four children and was running a general store in Chemainus with two employees. Nakashima Kumakichi apparently returned to Japan with his wife and four of his children in 1914. One cannot be certain exactly how many children he had or whether they were born in Canada, since in Japan adults are adopted into the family readily.[56] At any rate, by the time Nakashima Kumakichi returned to Japan in 1914, his son Giichi was able to take over the store, a boarding house, and an eighty-acre farm – all in Chemainus.[57]

Upon returning to Japan, Nakashima went to Itsukaichi, now a suburb of Hiroshima city. He leased some waterfront land, reclaimed more land, and operated a beach playground with boats, a waterfall (created with a steam engine), and grand buildings. This became an extremely popular spot in summer.[58] Nakashima's triumphant return to Japan was, however, a rare case. For most immigrants, sojourning led to permanent settlement. Only a few were able to return to Japan, buy land, and rebuild their lives. Before 1909, 22.8 percent of Japanese labourers in Canada recorded two domiciles.[59] That is, they lived alone in Canada and sent money back to Japan to support their families. They soon realized the impracticality of this arrangement and had their families join them in Canada. Many bachelors, unable to achieve their dreams of a "glorious" return, asked their families to find wives for them. These wives became the picture brides, the harbingers of the settlement period.

Chapter Four
The Women Come

In 1893 in Canada, Japanese men outnumbered Japanese women thirty to one; by 1910 the ratio was five to one, and by 1920 it was two to one.[1] These ratios indicate the transition through the three stages of Japanese immigration that Audrey Kobayashi discussed in "For the Sake of the Children."[2] During the first sojourner stage, up until 1908, the Japanese population in Canada was predominantly male, and the few Japanese women present had been brought over to help their husbands with their enterprises. In the second stage (1908-24), the subject of this chapter, women began arriving and in doing so launched the settlement stage in the history of the Japanese in Canada.

The Canadian government did not keep any statistics on Japanese immigration before 1900. Furthermore, separate records for women were not kept until 1907, and even then not in every year (see Table 2).

The total number of male immigrants far exceeds the two-to-one ratio of men to women mentioned by Kobayashi for 1920. This apparent discrepancy, however, exists because men are included who arrived in Canada but then moved on to the United States or returned to Japan. The table also shows the pattern of immigration. The great increase in the number of Japanese immigrants between 1905 and 1908 has been "attributed to the desire of Canadian corporations for cheap contract labour" and to US regulations that made it impossible for Japanese immigrants in Hawaii to continue on to the American mainland.[3] As a consequence, many came to Canada from Hawaii as well as directly from Japan. Higher wages lured many to move from Hawaii to North America. Also, emigration companies placed their own profits above the well-being of the Japanese sojourners and enticed those bound for Hawaii to travel farther at an additional passage cost. Then, on 14 March 1907, President Theodore Roosevelt issued an executive order prohibiting aliens with passports issued for other than the United States from

Table 2

Immigration of Japanese women, 1900-34

Year	Number of female immigrants[a]	Total number of immigrants[b]
1900		6
1901		–
1902		–
1903		–
1904		354
1905		1,922
1906		2,042
1907	242	7,601
1908	566	858
1909	153	244
1910	134	420
1911	217	727
1912	362	675
1913	424	886
1914	447	681
1915	338	380
1916	233	553
1917	310	887
1918	370	1,036
1919	530	892
1920	389	525
1921	338	481
1922	300	395
1923	197	404
1924	233	510
1925	269	424
1926	214	443
1927	36	511
1928	57	535
1929	11	179
1930	29	217
1931	65	174
1932	48	119
1933	40	106
1934	25	125
Total	6,577	25,312

a Figures from Sumida Rigenda, "The Japanese in British Columbia" (MA thesis, University of British Columbia, 1935), 40. Data for years 1927-30 calculated from Japanese consulate data.

b Figures from Ken Adachi, *The Enemy That Never Was: A History of the Japanese Canadians* (Toronto: McClelland and Stewart, 1976), 412.

entering his country; as a result, many were unable to cross the border to the United States.[4]

As more Japanese arrived on Canadian soil, white labour groups became more and more vociferous in denouncing this "invasion," which was also attracting the attention of politicians at all levels. The Asiatic Exclusion League, patterned after similar leagues in the United States – but a "purely Canadian organization" (i.e., it was not a branch of an American group, although some Americans were involved) – met in August 1907 to agitate for "a white man's country."[5] A demonstration held by the league on 7 September at the Cambie Street grounds included a parade to City Hall that turned ugly. The angry mob surged into Chinatown, causing havoc, and then went on to the Powell Street district, where it was repelled, though not before many shop windows were broken.[6]

Negotiations between the Japanese and Canadian governments led to the 1908 Lemieux-Hayashi Gentlemen's Agreement. The terms of this agreement are unclear, because they were never set down in writing.[7] However, there seems to have been a general agreement that Japan would restrict the number of passports issued to male labourers and domestic

2 The results of the September 1907 riot on Powell Street. The mob broke practically all the storefront windows.

3 Takata Misayo, [1920?]. This is quite probably the photograph that she sent to Ishii Kenji, on receipt of which he decided to marry her.

servants to an annual maximum of four hundred. This number did not include "returning residents and their wives, children or parents."[8] However, the key restriction was that "labourers under specifically worded contracts (giving terms of contract, type of work, names and standing of employers) [had to be] approved by the Canadian government."[9] This condition halted the immigration of contract labourers. Thus, the numbers of male immigrants plummeted in 1908, as the table shows.[10]

Restrictions on the numbers of male immigrants, as well as the age of most of the men who were already in Canada, led to an influx of women, which changed the ratio of men to women. Years of hard labour, low wages, and miserable living conditions had frustrated many of the Japanese men in Canada, who then squandered their earnings on sake, prostitutes, and gambling. Both the bachelors and the men with families in Japan felt that wives would make their sojourners' lives more comfortable and help counter their wastrel ways. As well, the earnings of two might help them achieve the dream of returning. Moreover, men who had immigrated in their late teens and early twenties were of a highly marriageable age.

Some bachelors returned to Japan to marry, but not all could afford to take the necessary time off work, or to pay for the passage and finance a formal wedding. Furthermore, men who returned to Japan might be inducted into the military – a possibility that had induced many to emigrate in the first place. Men who were temporarily out of the country were entitled to a deferment, which, however, they would lose if they returned for more than thirty days.[11] So, in most cases, families in Japan selected the brides. Each of the families involved, with the help of a go-between, screened the other's wealth and genealogy, as well as the education and health of the future bride or groom. These two also exchanged photographs and, often, letters. Bride and groom sometimes already knew each other, however briefly, before the wedding ceremony.

In Japanese rural society it was not unusual for the family to wait until their daughter-in-law was pregnant or otherwise acceptable before entering her name in the family register. But in the case of picture brides,

4 Unlike English "bride ships," the Japanese ships carried women who were, following Japanese government rules, already legally married to the men. Most, however, were picture brides.

5 Ishii Kenji and Misayo. Wedding photograph taken after the ceremony in 1921. Note the formal kimono with the family crest on the sleeve.

6 Ishii Kenji and Misayo, after they arrived in Canada together, 1922.

Japanese regulations stipulated that the bride had to be entered in the register of the groom's family at least six months before her passport application.[12] Where there was no fear of induction into the military – as in my father's case (he had been diagnosed with a heart condition, which he admitted to many years later to my mother!) – some men who had saved enough money returned for longer periods. My parents lived in Onomichi for a year, where my mother learned how to use a Singer sewing machine. It later turned out to be a wise investment.

An adventurous woman who wanted to travel to "Amerika" could fulfill that dream only through marriage. Nakamura Tami (1896-1986), who immigrated to Canada in 1916, explained: "I didn't care what my husband would be like. I didn't even have marriage in mind. As long as I could go, that was all I wanted. I just wanted to go to a foreign country, because I wouldn't have to wear a pompadour."[13] Nakamura Tami had wavy hair that would have been impossible to arrange in the proper married woman's pompadour style (see photo 5). Other picture brides mentioned this perceived flaw of curly or wavy hair. Of the thinking in Japan at the turn of the century, Jūkichi Inouye wrote: "Women esteem glossy-black, straight hair. Curly hair is held in such horror that it is said to spoil any face however comely in other respects."[14] The *marumage* (pompadour, or "round chignon") of married women required an abundance of straight hair and was usually dressed "with a large tuft of false hair ... and formed by spreading out the hair."[15]

There were other apparently superficial reasons why some women wanted to become picture brides. Ishikawa Yasu (1896-?) came from Aburagi village in Jinseki county, about eighty kilometres directly inland from Fukuyama city. She was the fifth of twelve children. The family had a yard goods shop to which she contributed her labour by sewing, although she was never allowed to serve the customers. She dreamed of becoming a medical doctor, but her weak academic record prevented her from pursuing that goal, so she followed the footsteps of her elder sister and, after eight years of higher elementary and one year of supplementary education, attended midwifery school in Osaka for two years.[16] On graduating, she practised in her village.

Until the age of twenty – which was old by the standards of the day – Ishikawa Yasu, whose siblings teased her about her homeliness, had not had any marriage proposals. She made up her mind to go overseas to practise midwifery, to earn a lot of money, and to prove her worth. However, like Nakamura Tami, she learned that she could go only as a bride. A villager heard of Yasu's wishes and made all the arrangements, although Yasu's parents objected strenuously. They argued that they did not know the family of the prospective husband, but Yasu was adamant and they finally relented. She recalled: "I had no idea what kind of person I had married, and what kind of life he was leading. Anyway, I had my heart set on coming here, and that was all I could think of. That was my dream, and I thought things would turn out all right. I was just a child, you see."[17]

Yasu came to Canada in the summer of 1919 when she was twenty-two. She later marvelled that she had even brought her *biwa* (Japanese lute). What had her expectations been? On disembarking from the *Kagoshima-maru* in Victoria, she was shocked when she met her husband. He was handsome, just as in the photograph, but he was clearly feeble-minded. She had no alternative but to stay with him for a year. Then she left him, but only a year and a half later was she able to get a divorce.[18] Her almost daily letters to her parents bemoaning her situation did not draw any sympathy, only a reprimand – she had made the decision on her own, so she was not to write about it again. She never returned to Japan to see her parents. Her fellow Japanese in Vancouver criticized her separation from her husband. Undeterred, she survived by working as a midwife. Eventually she married another immigrant, from Tottori prefecture, and led a happy life, continuing her midwifery.

It is likely that many picture brides decided to marry strangers in the belief that they were "marrying Amerika"; whatever the case, they were immigrating as wives of men they had never met. Yasu was not the only one to be disappointed with the spouse she met on arrival in BC. Glowing letters from prospective husbands (at times written by more educated friends), photos of them in homburgs and dark suits with white "high collars," and snapshots of them posed in front of a mansion or even the Hotel Vancouver certainly contributed to women's unrealistic expectations.

Some of them came to Canada to help a relative. Some immigrated to replace a relative who had died in Canada and left young children. Kuwabara Shigeno had a sweetheart, so she was reluctant to comply with her father's request that she go to Canada as the second wife of a widowed cousin, Kuwabara Bunpei (1889-1939), whose first wife, Masano, had died in 1913 at the age of twenty-nine, leaving two young children. Shigeno finally agreed and arrived in 1918 to take over the care of the children from Bunpei's sister. The latter woman had herself come as a picture bride; but on discovering that her husband was much older than she had been led to believe, she refused to remain with him. She later married a veteran of the First World War, Hoita Rikuzō (1890-1948).[19] Shigeno not only lovingly raised the two stepchildren but had six more of her own with her husband. Bunpei had many jobs but eventually worked for thirty-seven years as a part-time interpreter for the Canadian Department of Immigration. Almost every Japanese immigrant's recollection of his or her first days in Canada mentioned Kuwabara and the Immigration Building at the corner of Ontario Street and Dallas Road in the James Bay district of Victoria.[20] Bunpei's eldest son, Masao, recalled that his father's income from the interpreter's job was far from adequate to support his growing family.[21]

Stories like that of Ishikawa Yasu – who decided to marry a man completely unknown to her and her family – are rather rare. Even so, many women accepted at times unreliable information about prospective partners from people they trusted. Families often made decisions, but women could make choices within the parameters set by those decisions. Generally, spinsterhood was socially unacceptable in Japanese culture except in circumstances involving the natal family's needs.[22] So, some women who felt that their opportunities for marriage were scarce accepted marriage to an overseas man.

Kudō Hatsue (1895-?) was teaching school and was considered past the ideal age for marriage. Like a number of picture brides, she had spent so many years earning an education that she was past the "ideal" age for marriage. She was the eldest in a *shizoku* (ex-samurai) family of ten daughters and one son. Her father, a county clerk in the Hiroshima prefecture public service, who was often transferred to different postings, had a good education. He supplemented his children's studies by teaching them the Chinese classics at home. Hatsue graduated from the Onomichi girls' higher school; later, when her father was transferred to Hiroshima city, she attended normal school (teachers' training school) there. After graduating, she taught at Honkawa elementary school in Hiroshima city.

Hatsue was twenty-four years old, twelve years younger than her husband, when she arrived in Canada in 1919. When she married Kudō Minoru (1883-1957), she was aware that he had already settled permanently in Canada. He had come to Canada from Ariho village in Takata county in 1906, and he had worked in Vancouver for *Tairiku nippō,* the Japanese-language newspaper, while studying English. The stress of work and study broke his health, and in 1911 he purchased seven acres of land at Mission in the Fraser Valley and settled into a quiet life as a farmer. Hatsue joined him on the farm. When the Japanese schoolteacher who had been brought to Mission from Japan in 1926 returned to Japan after two years, she and her husband were asked to take over.[23] They moved with their children from the farm to the Japanese school building in town, where the two of them taught until the school was closed after Pearl Harbor.[24]

Divorcees also became picture brides. In the samurai class, prejudice against divorce had carried into the Meiji era; for peasants, in contrast, divorce was often a relatively simple matter and not necessarily a disgrace: "Even wealthy peasant daughters married repeatedly; in fact, some peasants practised what might be called serial marriage."[25] A few of the women whose lives I investigated had been divorced. Some, like Yoshida Hina from Kōi in west Hiroshima city, had been married but later returned to their natal home. Twenty-eight-year-old Yoshida Hina was making a good living sewing kimonos for geishas and actors; even so, when she was asked to "rescue" a widower with five children on Vancouver Island, she agreed to help. Yoshida Tomekichi (1881-1970) was from Ōsuga in north Hiroshima city. Tomekichi had immigrated in 1911, followed two years later by his first wife, Okie, who died in 1927, leaving behind five children. At first, Hina lived in Genoa Bay on Vancouver Island, where Tomekichi worked in the sawmill. Hina gave birth to a son in 1931. Later she mused that though she had endured hardships, she had had no choice – she could not return to Japan.[26]

So strong was the pressure against women remaining single in Japan that a number of *shizoku* (ex-samurai) women who had been married, divorced, and sent back to their natal homes were later urged to marry peasants who had emigrated. Becoming the picture bride of a peasant could be more tolerable than remaining single. Iwaasa Ito (1893-1983) had divorced her husband and with her two children returned to her natal home.[27] She had received an exceptional education. Not only was she a graduate of a secondary school for women (*joshi kōtōgakkō*), but she also sang, played the *koto* and the *shamisen*, wrote poetry, and did calligraphy. She was urged to marry a peasant, a relative, Iwaasa Kōjun (1882-1968), whom she knew only slightly and who was farming in southern Alberta. In April 1915, Ito and the wife and daughter of Kōjun's neighbour, a Mr. Tamaki, sailed from Kobe. When they arrived in Victoria, they waited anxiously for a few days for Iwaasa Kōjun and Tamaki; but when Iwaasa finally came, he was alone. To save money, the men had decided that only one would fetch the womenfolk. Iwaasa had even had to borrow a suit for the trip.

Accroding to Iwaasa's grandson David:

> Mrs. Tamaki was incensed that her husband had not missed her enough to come in person to meet her at the boat after a separation of four years. Mrs. Iwaasa was incensed because he had been late to meet his new bride by some two days. On the train to Raymond, Mrs. Tamaki and Mrs. Iwaasa sat on one bench, while Mr. Iwaasa sat alone another two or three seats back.[28]

Iwaasa Ito recalled years later that

> Her first home consisted of an old granary with a curtain in the middle to separate the kitchen from the bedroom. In order to provide more room during the day, the bed had to be rolled up and put away. During the winter the cold would penetrate the single-walled building freezing the water in the stove reservoir and making the walls white with frost. During the day, while her husband was away in the fields, she used to climb to the top of a nearby hill just to be able to see the smoke from the chimney of a neighbour some two miles away.[29]

But Iwaasa Ito adjusted to her new life, and with her husband raised nine children as active members of a vibrant Japanese-Canadian community in southern Alberta.

The family of Takata Misayo (1900-2001) had been headmen in Sanba, a village near Onomichi, and in the Tokugawa days had been the most prominent family of the area, the collectors of the rice tax for the *daimyō*.[30] Misayo had married the eldest son of a family of similar status, but her father brought her home owing to the profligate ways of her husband. Eager to make a new start and to have some adventure, she married a man of lower status who would take her to "Amerika." Her parents provided her with a substantial trousseau, but she left it behind because her new husband had assured her that they would be returning to their homeland in five years. This was never to be, and she often mused about what had happened to her trousseau. She was my mother.

Although picture brides included older women and divorcees, many were daughters of well-situated families, highly educated, and too independent to agree to enter the families of the eldest sons who would have been "suitable" matches for them. A life of subservience to a mother-in-law and possibly sisters-in-law was anathema for these spirited, adventurous, strong-willed women:

> The women who had the most difficult time in farm families ... were young wives married to eldest sons, since they had to live with at least three, sometimes four, generations of the husbands' families. A young wife was treated as an outsider and as the lowliest member of the family until her mother-in-law got too old to run the household. She was referred to as the *yome* [bride] and was expected to lead a life of total subservience.[31]

The women who consciously avoided such situations insisted that they had "married Amerika, not the man."

A surprising number of women had graduated from girls' higher school (*kōtō jogakkō*), even though such graduates were relatively rare in the 1910s. In 1900 there were only fifty-two higher schools for girls in the entire country, enrolling a total of twelve thousand students.[32] Although these institutions were called "high schools," the academic standards were said to be even lower than those of middle schools for males.[33] The girls' schools emphasized "development of national morality and the cultivation of womanly virtues."[34] Entrance examinations, tuition fees, and distances from homes made it impossible for many to attend the girls' higher schools.[35] Other options for higher education for women, apart from normal schools (teachers' training schools), were few.[36] Thus, by the time most picture brides were growing up – that is, by the 1910s – post-elementary education was within the reach of very few young women. It is easy to surmise that for many spirited women, emigration was an attractive choice.

They may have embarked on the adventure eagerly, but they could not have anticipated what awaited them. The usual experience of a picture bride was as follows. After waiting about a year while the necessary papers were processed, a picture bride received the fare from her groom, endured an arduous voyage of many days across the Pacific, and arrived at the port of Victoria. Even before she faced her "stranger" husband and her new life, she found herself bombarded by startling situations. Imada Ito recalled: "When I arrived at the Immigration Building, I thought it most peculiar that green grass was growing all around it. I had only seen long grass in Japan. I wondered why grass only one inch long was growing here. Inside the Immigration Building, everything I saw was completely strange and puzzling."[37] Imada described her encounter with the "white person who was as big as a giant" who taught her and another picture bride how to use the window blinds and the toilet, which had an overhead water tank. The two young women, puzzled and curious, tested everything and then spent anxious moments as the window blind rolled up completely and the water in the toilet appeared to run continuously. Fortunately, the food in the dining room was reassuring: rice and fresh fish. Imada's first meeting with her husband was full of anguish: "How embarrassing and awkward it was. There was no one to even introduce the new husband and wife to each other."

Embarrassment turned out to be the least of the troubles for these brides. Many were taken directly to remote lumber camps, sawmill towns, fishing villages, and untamed farms in the Fraser Valley, the Okanagan, and southern Alberta. Isolation and hard work was their common experience. They faced harsher lives than they had ever imagined in Japan – for example, the back-breaking labour of caring for the daily needs of as many as forty workers in lumber or fishing camps. This involved not only hauling water, washing and cooking many pots of rice, and preparing side dishes from dried fish and root vegetables, but also using washboards to launder work clothes covered with pine pitch or fish offal. Those living in urban areas managed or otherwise worked in boarding houses with tasks that included cooking, changing the linen, and doing all the laundry by hand. Some, while they struggled with the language barrier, did housework for white families.

Even harder than the strenuous labour was the isolation. Away from their friends and family, the women lacked the support systems they would have had in their native environment. The birth of children added to their already heavy burdens. If they were lucky, they were attended by midwives; more often, though, husbands assisted during the childbirth, which often took place in a lonely wilderness shack. Imada Ito wrote about the birth of her first child in a sawmill camp in the Fraser Valley:

> It was a difficult experience and I suffered for twelve hours. In this area there wasn't a single woman and the doctor was said to be ten miles away. I felt helpless and lonely, but somehow, thanks to the gods, I gave birth and was very happy. With no female beside me, in the woods without a doctor nearby me, I gave birth like a cat or a dog ... I felt desolate.[38]

This childbirth experience stood in stark contrast to the customary practice in Japan, where a new mother often returned to her natal home to be cared for by her mother. How different it was, to experience the pains of labour in an isolated cabin. Iwaasa Ito's "husband told her to bang a steel tub that hung outside the door with a wooden spoon when she thought that the baby was about to be delivered. This way he could hear it in the field and come to take her to the midwife."[39]

In Japan, convalescence was for at least three weeks; in Canada, women usually resumed their daily labour within a week of the birth.[40] Farmers' wives went out to work in their berry farms, strapping their babies on their backs or leaving them alone indoors in their wicker basket-cots. Traditionally, grandmothers or grandfathers might take care of the young while the parents laboured in the rice paddies or elsewhere. More affluent families hired wet nurses and maids. My mother, Ishii Misayo, who would have had a support system in Japan, lived in an isolated sawmill camp in Abbotsford. Her first-born cried constantly. Extremely concerned, she and my father consulted a doctor, who diagnosed the cause as hunger. Inexperience, stress, and anxiety had hindered my mother's ability to produce sufficient breast milk.[41]

Children, their care, and, later, their need for an education added further complications to immigrants' lives. The immigrants had been inculcated with the Meiji ideology, which stressed the importance of education. Also, provincial regulations required all children between seven and fifteen to attend school regularly, and the Japanese were law-abiding people.[42] At first children were sent to Japan for their education and later Japanese schools were established in BC. Most people, however, sent their children to regular schools in their area. Some mothers were the more determined of the two parents with regard to establishing a permanent home so that their children could attend school. Imada Ito was driven to labour alongside her husband, leaving her two young sons alone in the cabin, in order to earn the money for a down payment on land in Maple Ridge so that her eldest son, who was of school age, could attend school there.[43]

But even after Imada Ito acquired farmland in 1921 so that the family had a permanent home, her labour continued. The farmers' wives worked night and day:

> The distinctive feature of labour on the Japanese berry farm is the women's share in it. The picture bride worked with pick and shovel with her husband when they cleared the bush land to plant strawberries. Then hoeing and cultivating the berry patches besides her house chores. She would get up very early in the morning and go to bed at eleven at night. Upon arising in the morning, she fed the chickens and horses, then prepared breakfast; washed the dishes; after which she followed the family to the field where she may drive a horse with her husband, behind a plow or cultivator. She would come in shortly before dinner, prepare supper, and clean up then return to the field. During the berry picking season, she picked the berries or packed them, from dawn to dusk, taking very little time for the household chores. After the berry season was over some of them would work in the fruit cannery or hired [*sic*] out as a domestic worker.[44]

Nakashima Tsutayo recalled her busiest months:

> In four months, May to September, all kinds of strawberries come out, one after the other. Those months, it's war. My work was cooking and supervising the meals for the pickers. I'd get up at four in the morning, cook rice and *miso* soup, and feed everybody. It was food for 40 people at least, so we had a cook, but it was a lot of work just to manage the house. Anyway, I was busy, busy every day and I had no spare time at all ... For meals we had Japanese food, rice and *miso* soup. Sometimes for lunch I would broil salmon that the local Indians used to come selling in secret, and for the rest, I would cook vegetables from the fields. Once a week we could buy food, such as dried lotus root and burdock root, *hijiki* seaweed, tofu, and *kamaboko* [boiled fish paste] from a peddler from Vancouver. As long as you had money you could buy

> anything. My job was cooking more than anything else; day after day I would cook from morning on, all year long without stopping.[45]

Although the never-ending labour for the farmers' wives was difficult, the wives of non-agricultural labourers also had many fears and concerns. Most of the male Japanese immigrants were engaged in hazardous unskilled work in forestry or mining or on the railways. Their wives had to live with the constant worry that their husbands might be injured or killed. Mrs. Ishihara Kikuno (1894-1969), from Tosaka village in Aki county, had a difficult life owing to her husband's misfortunes. He and a partner had run a business that provided gravel, but the partner gambled away the company's funds. He then worked in a sawmill but lost his fingers in an accident there. Although he received some workman's compensation, his family of nine children had great difficulty surviving. The contributions some women like Mrs. Ishihara made are unheralded except in the recollections of the children. The Ishiharas lived with other Japanese families in a *nagaya* (longhouse), a cooperative shared by many families in Vancouver East, an area known as "Heaps." In order to support her family, Ishihara Kikuno took in laundry and ironing.[46] The *nagaya* was an adaptation of the cheap housing in the poorer districts of urban Japan.

> Cheap houses are built in long blocks; ... they are of one story, or if of two stories, the second has a very low ceiling ... The smallest of these houses is only twelve feet by nine. A block may be made up of a dozen such houses, six on either side with a wall running through the middle from end to end.[47]

The *nagaya* could provide some of the support that would have been available from a family and a village in Japan – support that was sadly lacking in the lives of many Japanese immigrants. Kyōshi Shimizu, who lived in such *nagaya* in the Heaps district, remembered:

> For the many families who lived in the *nagaya* it provided the kind of support to young families that housing co-ops try to generate for their members. I remember the nine years from 1924 to 1933 when I was four to thirteen years old as relatively stable years as we had five other mothers keeping an eye on us when our own mother had to be somewhere else. My sister and I were the oldest among the children, and we passed many happy and productive weekends and summers, playing "school" and organizing games, while minding the younger ones.

> Those years were difficult for our parents as our father had his left leg crushed in a logging accident shortly after we moved to the *nagaya*. He was in and out of hospital for the next nine years. Without the support of the other mothers, our mother would not have been able to survive.
>
> On the ground floor where our family lived there was a central corridor with four large rooms on the west side and a more open space at the back where a sink, two toilets, and a space with a kitchen stove and counter, were located ... On the east side were five rooms. Each room had a door into the corridor, and some of the rooms had interior doors connecting the rooms. The two families living on this floor rented three rooms each, using one room as a kitchen/dining area, and in the case of our family, one room as a bedsitting room with a simplified Murphy bed for our parents, and the third room with an adjoining door, as a bedroom for the three children. Three rooms at the back were occupied by single men who cooked on hot plates in their own room, except for the man occupying the rear room. He was able to use the stove in the alcove at the back. The facilities were pretty basic. We carried water from the sink to our kitchen, and heated water for dishwashing on the stove, using the kitchen table to do that chore. We took turns cleaning the toilet, sink area, and corridor. A telephone was installed in the front unit, and all the residents in the *nagaya* shared the cost. A *furo* [Japanese bath] was available in the basement and was maintained cooperatively. Water from the *furo* was used the following day for laundry by some of the families, but I can recall that our mother did her washing in the kitchen with water heated on top of the stove.
>
> In our *nagaya* there was a fairly stable population of six families during the nine years we were there. When a vacancy occurred, another family moved in soon after. Two of the single rooms were occupied by the same men. In the third single room, students from Japan seemed to come and go.[48]

The influence of a strong and determined woman was clearly evident in the family of Dr. Henry Ryusuke Shibata, a renowned cancer surgeon and specialist. Henry's father, Shibata Hatsuzō (1895-?), from Koami district in Hiroshima city, was the second son of a family that had been in the entertainment business and that at one time owned a great deal of property before losing much of it through bad management. Because there was little left that Hatsuzō could inherit, he immigrated to Canada in 1919 at the age of twenty-four. In BC he worked mainly as a cook, but he was restless. His wife, Tomoko (1906-62), whom he married in 1929, supplemented his earnings by working evenings as an entertainer. She played the *shamisen* (Japanese banjo) at Fukusuke, a restaurant in the Powell Street district. Their eldest son, Henry, born in 1930, said that while his parents were working, he looked after his younger siblings, even though he himself was a child.[49]

Especially unfortunate were widows. Imada Ito noted that when she returned to Japan temporarily in 1918, many of her shipmates were widows with one or two children. Their husbands had died in the influenza epidemic. All of them were poor.[50] For many widows, returning to Japan was not an option because their impoverished families there would not have been able to support them.

The situation in Japan was evident in the story Imada Ito told about her return to her native country in 1918 with three little children after she had been in Canada for seven years. Her husband had told her to return to Japan with the children:

> He said that the following year the eldest child would have to go to school. Besides, with a big family it would be hard to move around often. Also, if he alone worked and I loafed, we could not save any money. He said he would send me money. When I thought of the misery of going here and there like a migratory bird with the three children, and how hard I had worked, I was sure that if I worked that hard when I returned to Japan, I would be able to bring up the children.[51]

She stayed with her sister and her family, and soon realized that it would be extremely difficult to live in Japan alone with her three children. So, when her husband urged her to return to Canada after she had been in Japan for six months, she did, leaving her eldest, a daughter, behind with her sister.

Some women in special situations were able to survive in Japan. In 1910, Niiya Tsuruyo (1886-?) joined her husband, Kōtarō (1873-?), in Canada. Kōtarō was the *yōshi* (adopted husband) of Tsuruyo.[52] They were from Saka village in Aki county, one of the areas that had been devastated by deforestation and landslides. Kōtarō's three elder brothers had immigrated to the United States, so he wished to do so as well. He went to Hawaii first and then on to Canada, where he worked in a lumber camp in North Vancouver. Tsuruyo joined her husband and worked as a cook and washerwoman at the camp. She gave birth to three sons in three years; however, the first son died. When she was pregnant with her fourth child she returned to Japan, believing that if she worked in Japan as hard as she had in Canada, she would be able to survive. She was one of the fortunate ones, in that she could work with her father in the prosperous family business of growing wheat and barley and making noodles.[53]

In Canada, Japanese women without husbands had very few options. They struggled to survive in a world that assumed that all women were or should be financially supported by men. Nakata Ume became a widow when her husband, Kenichi, a fisher from Kanon village in Saeki county, was run over by a train. Ume already had an infant daughter, born in 1904, and was carrying another child. She somehow survived, doing housework and working in a fish cannery. Later, until the expulsion of all Japanese Canadians from the west coast, she lived with her daughter's family in the Fairview district of Vancouver, though she went to the Skeena during the fishing season to cook for the fishers and work in the cannery.[54]

Remarriage did not necessarily ease these women's lives. Miyamoto Sute (1887-1983) joined her husband, Naosuke (1883-1918), in 1910. Naosuke, from Miiri village in Asa county, had immigrated in 1900 and worked in the Cumberland mines. Sute operated a boarding house while bearing and caring for three sons and a daughter. In 1918, when the youngest was less than a year old, the Spanish flu claimed Naosuke. Sute later married Kaga, an immigrant from Okayama prefecture, who gave her children his name, and she had four more sons by him. Yet one sorrow after another besieged her. Her two eldest sons died in logging accidents in 1932 and 1939, and Kaga in 1936. In an interview, her son Tom, Kaga's son, related that his mother had not received any formal education; however, she had memorized Buddhist sutras, and every day she visited the Cumberland cemetery, where her sons and husbands were buried, to offer prayers. She also taught herself to write *kana* (simple Japanese characters) in order to correspond with her sons when they were away at work.[55]

Some widows remarried, such as Sute, whose children by Miyamoto all took the stepfather's name Kaga. Then there is the painful story of Enomoto Mume (1880-1970). Her husband, Enomoto Tsunetarō (1869-1921), immigrated in 1899 at the age of thirty from Matsukawa in Hiroshima city. Mume followed in 1907 at the age of twenty-seven, leaving their seven-year-old daughter behind with her parents in Chigiya district in Hiroshima city. A son, Steve Shūichi, was born in 1909, and a daughter, Suzue, in 1911. When Suzue was not quite ten years old, her father, Enomoto Tsunetarō, died in an accident at the sawmill at Fraser Mills, near New Westminster.[56] He had been an only son, so when his widow Mume went to Japan with his ashes ten years after his death and asked his family for permission to remarry, the request was granted.

However, they refused to allow her new husband to adopt the children and insisted that Steve carry the family name and responsibilities.

It was not just widows who struggled in a world that favoured men. Two well-educated sisters showed amazing independence. It is difficult to surmise why their father arranged for them to marry emigrants, though it may have been their local reputation for non-conformity. It is also possible that the family resources had been so diminished that the family welcomed the opportunity to avoid "the heavy outlays of marriage required by Japanese social custom."[57] Marrying and going overseas circumvented the need for a large trousseau, albeit in rural areas these requirements were less elaborate than they were for brides from well-to-do Tokyo families. Such a bride was expected to bring to her marriage "chests of drawers and several boxes containing her dresses, bedding, toilet articles, various utensils needed for tea-making and flower arrangements, a *koto* (Japanese harp), and work-boxes, and sometimes even kitchen utensils."[58] Much depended on the status of the families of the bride and groom as well as the customs of the area; even so, a trousseau would have been required. The Yokota of Kamo county had been well-to-do, and elaborate weddings would have been expected.

The two sisters, born in 1902 and 1906, grew up in a privileged family in a part of Kamo county that is now Toyota county. According to the younger sister, Kotoma (1906-2007), her family owned substantial land and hired people to work it. Their father, who had seven children, had been widowed and remarried. The two sisters were the offspring of the second wife. Her death from stomach cancer when Haruko (1902-89) was thirteen ended an idyllic childhood in a home surrounded by persimmon trees, lovely multipetalled cherry blossom trees, and chestnut trees under which pine mushrooms grew. Soon after her mother's death, Haruko left the village to attend the higher school for girls in Hiroshima city. Her father hired an older woman, "Baayan" (this seems to be a local dialect word for "granny"), to look after the family. Whenever Haruko returned home from school, Baayan and the neighbours told her about her difficult younger sister, Kotoma, who constantly defied the housekeeper.

In her memoirs, Haruko described her natal family, but it is difficult to be sure which of the seven children were born to which wife.[59] The eldest brother was a superintendent of schools for the county and was so stern that Kotoma was even afraid to call him to supper! The second brother was an agricultural engineer. Kotoma referred to the next brother as a *dōraku* (prodigal son) and blamed him for her family's financial ruin.

When I interviewed Kotoma, I had not yet read her sister Haruko's memoirs. However, Kotoma said that when she was sixteen, her "prodigal" brother persuaded her father to sell everything and move to Korea. Japan had annexed Korea in 1910 and had imposed military rule. The Japanese government was confiscating farmland from the Koreans and selling it cheaply to Japanese land development companies and immigrants; it was also undermining Korean industries by importing Japanese goods to Korea. It was into this milieu that the Yokota family moved. Kotoma was not clear about what subsequently happened except to say that she attended girls' higher school in Seoul and that her family eventually lost everything.

Haruko did not mention Korea in her memoirs, so it is likely that the family moved there after her marriage to Masao Kobayakawa, the Canadian-born son of Kobayakawa Giichi of Courtenay. Masao had gone to Japan to marry her. Haruko told her sister that she was startled when Masao rose from their nuptial bed and asked in English, "What time is it?" When she arrived at her in-laws' farm in the Comox Valley, Haruko learned that she would be expected to live with them and labour on the farm. Her husband worked elsewhere as a mechanic but turned all his earnings over to his parents.[60]

In 1982, Haruko told an interviewer about the loneliness she felt during her first few years in Canada, when the sound of the train whistle stirred her emotions. Her responsibilities on her in-laws' dairy farm were heavy. The men used mechanical seeders for planting the corn, turnips, and hay; in contrast, all of her tasks required hand labour. She rose at 6:00 a.m. to milk one hundred cows by hand. After that she washed the milk cans, drove the cows out to pasture, rounded them up again at 4:00 p.m. with the dogs, and milked them again. Most of the milk was hauled to the Cumberland Dairy; with some of it she made butter. Then she warmed buttermilk and skim milk to feed to the calves. Besides all this, she cooked for six or seven people and grew vegetables for home consumption. Order takers came around from Japanese stores in Vancouver, and from them she bought Japanese soy sauce, rice, *miso,* and canned goods.[61]

After five years of growing frustration with their lack of independence, she insisted that she and her husband leave and set up their own home. Her in-laws were furious, but Masao and Haruko left, penniless.[62] The young couple were able to borrow money from Iwaasa Matsutarō in Cumberland and set up their own household. In addition, Haruko taught in the Japanese school.

Yokota Kotoma was twenty-one years old when she came to Canada in 1927. Her father was urging her to marry a man recommended by her sister, pointing out that she would be good company for Haruko. By the time her one-year waiting period was over, Kotoma had changed her mind about leaving Japan, but she was persuaded to go anyway. Kotoma and her husband, Kitagawa Kensuke (1894-1974), settled in Duncan, where he had a tailor shop until the outbreak of the Pacific War.[63] Kotoma had no children and worked in the shop alongside her husband. Kotoma's life was fairly comfortable compared to that of earlier arrivals, but in her eyes it had been difficult.

Other immigrant wives became vital to their husbands' businesses. Kumamoto Toshiko (1906-94) was the only child in her family, the Kumamoto, who were the *honke* (principal house) of the Kumamoto family of Kameyama village in Asa county. The family's *yagō* was Hamadaya. Toshiko's cousin, the seventh son of a *bunke,* that is, a branch line of the Kumamoto, was adopted by her father, and this cousin and Toshiko were raised together. This cousin, Kumamoto Jun, became Toshiko's husband.[64] He joined his three blood brothers in Canada in 1917 when he was seventeen, and Toshiko arrived in 1926 at the age of twenty. Before leaving Japan she had graduated from the girls' higher school in Kabe, Hiroshima prefecture. Jun worked at various jobs, in a restaurant, and in lumber camps, while his wife studied sewing. Toshiko earned her room and board at the sewing school by helping with the cleaning and doing odd jobs. Later the couple had a dry-cleaning and alteration establishment on Richards Street in Vancouver. There were many such Japanese businesses in the Vancouver area. Their success owed a great deal to the sewing abilities of the women.[65]

Toshiko had grown up with her cousin Jun, and there was affection if not romantic love between the two of them at the time of their marriage. An emotional bond then developed over the years. In another marriage, there was an obvious early attraction. Takeyasu Nobuichi (1889-1966), who had come to BC in 1906 by way of Hawaii, was a second son of samurai descent, from Yoshina village in Toyota county. He met Shimazu Shizuyo (1889-1988) in a hospital in Hiroshima prefecture, where he had gone for medical care after the First World War. She was a nurse at the hospital. Shizuyo was the daughter of a wealthy importer-exporter in Akitsu town in Kamo county. Her family's *honke* (main branch) was in Onomichi. Takeyasu Nobuichi and Shimazu Shizuyo married in 1919 and left for Canada right away; but they returned to Japan for a time after she became pregnant with her first child. They remained in Hiroshima city until 1927, during which time Nobuichi took training in Japanese medicine while also working as a reporter for *Asahi shinbun,* a major Japanese newspaper. Shizuyo contributed to their finances by running a boarding house for students.

Shizuyo's family begged them to remain in Japan and even offered to build a hospital for Nobuichi.[66] However, they returned to Canada. Nobuichi could have been adopted into the Shimazu family and later inherited the family's wealth, but he preferred life in Canada, and his wife was willing to follow him anywhere. In her later years, when her son, George, asked her why she had come to Canada, she told him that the first time it had been for "romance and adventure" and that the second time it had been because her husband was here.[67] She put her nursing experience to good use in Ocean Falls, where the young couple had first gone on arriving in Canada in 1920. She helped the Aboriginal community there cope with a smallpox epidemic, and they thanked her by making her an Indian princess. She received a letter of commendation from the governor general.[68] Even so, the Shimazu family insisted that Shizuyo return to Japan, and she always told George to study Japanese diligently because he would be going to Japan after graduation from high school to be adopted into the Shimazu family. Shizuyo and Nobuichi also made a great effort in the home to speak "proper" Japanese rather than the Hiroshima dialect. However, the war intervened when George was in grade ten, and as a consequence they could not send him to Japan. Although this strong-willed woman made her own decisions regarding a husband, and although she chose to accompany him to Canada, she also accepted her family responsibilities and agreed to assuage her natal family with the promise that her son would return and continue the family line.

The women described here, and others like them, have not been celebrated by chroniclers of the early twentieth-century Japanese-Canadian community. Instead, articles about the Japanese in Canada during that era extol the virtues of a handful of women who lived more comfortably. As Anne Walthall has similarly concluded about the women who took part in the rice riots and peasant uprisings of the late Tokugawa period, the public praise for women in the Japanese-Canadian community "leaves the reader with the impression that women did nothing but offer support in the shadows." They are "defined not as individuals but in relation to others within the household," and "it would appear that whenever women acted, they did so at least ostensibly on behalf of men."[69] Nakayama Jinshiro's 1921 work included brief biographies of fifty-four women, a number of whom came from Hiroshima. He praised

Satō Matsuyo, her daughter Masae, and Kaminishi Shigeno for their devotion to duty, their feminine modesty, and their activities with the women's association of the Buddhist Church. He lauded Satō's daughter for aiding her mother selflessly and for the many marriage proposals she received.[70] Nowhere did Nakayama mention their exhausting physical labour or their management skills, which kept the boarding houses afloat. Even their activities in the women's associations were presented as means to enhance the social position of their husbands.

In Nakayama and other official and semi-official rhetoric in the Japanese community, some women were depicted as devoting themselves to "service to the community and their families." Women's activities for securing or enhancing family survival were not mentioned. Those who cooked and washed in the camps, and who farmed, canned fish, and worked in white homes, were ignored. We need to search for the stories about these women and to listen to the voices of the ones who struggled so hard to earn a living and to provide stable homes for their children.

Chapter Five
Farmers

Between 1908 and the outbreak of the Pacific War, as economic circumstances thwarted the initial dreams of returning to the homeland, Vancouver's Powell Street district grew into a vibrant Japanese community with shops, schools, churches, temples, and social and sports clubs. Similar albeit much smaller communities emerged in several coastal areas of British Columbia. In this, the third stage in Japanese-Canadian immigrant history, "permanent immigrants established what we now know as Japanese Canadian society."[1]

Some immigrants had always had permanent settlement in mind and had come to Canada to farm; others intended to engage in trade between Canada and Japan; still others were looking for adventure. This chapter deals mainly with those who came intending to buy land and farm. Many achieved this goal in the Fraser Valley, the Okanagan, and southern Alberta. A number of the early farmers became leaders in the rural areas where they settled, inspiring and smoothing the way for later Japanese arrivals. With their encouragement and guidance, newcomers who perhaps had not intended to settle permanently, did so. By starting families whose members were totally committed to the farm, most of these farmers eventually succeeded.

The Pioneers

Most Japanese immigrants were from farming backgrounds and had left their homeland because the Meiji policy to finance the modernization of Japan by taxing the peasants had caused them to lose their ancestral land and fall into debt. Land was precious in Japan, and the immigrants dreamed, as Yamaga Yasutarō did, of becoming "the owner of five thousand acres of golden field in the Canadian Prairies."[2]

In his history of Japanese agriculturists in Haney, Yamaga Yasutarō (1886-1971) noted that the earliest recorded Japanese farmer was a man from Yamaguchi prefecture, who was farming in Pitt Meadows in 1904. It seems that none of the *kusawake* (parters of the grass) pioneers on Yamaga's list came from Hiroshima; however, by the early 1910s many from there were contributing a great deal to farming in the Fraser Valley. Among the most influential was Yamaga, who was born ten *ri* south of Kure, in Toyohama village in Toyota county, on a small island with a circumference of only five *ri* (about twenty kilometres). It is one of many islands in the district. A few of the island's inhabitants farmed; most, though, survived by fishing. Yamaga came to Canada in 1908 with a dream of farming on substantial acreage. While he was working as a labourer in a shingle bolt camp, he read articles in the vernacular press by Inoue Jirō – a Waseda University graduate from Saga prefecture who had bought twenty acres of land in Haney in 1906 – and these inspired him to buy ten acres in Haney.

The relative ease of getting started and the desire for self-employment attracted Yamaga and many other would-be farmers. It was possible to lease five acres of bush with an agreement to clear it within seven years.[3] Lessees could clear small plots, plant strawberry seedlings, and reap a harvest within a year; but they had to supplement their agricultural income with earnings from seasonal labour in the salmon fisheries and the lumber camps. Lessees cleared their land during the winter months. This was slow and arduous work, and often the land was only half-clear after seven years. In these circumstances, the settler forfeited the land because the contract required that the entire property be cleared within seven years. Settlers soon realized that it was more prudent to use their summer earnings to purchase land by instalment. Five or ten acres could be purchased at fifty dollars an acre, with one-quarter down and the rest to be paid within three or four years at 6 percent interest.[4]

Those who were buying land could live rent-free because they built their own homes immediately. Except for windows and nails, building materials could be had for free. Yamaga recalled:

> We could not afford to buy lumber to build our houses so we helped each other by felling large cedar trees and bucking it [*sic*] into three feet lengths to make cedar shakes for the walls and roof of a shack. The unwritten law was for everyone to go to help their new neighbours, carrying their own tools and lunches. We cut out long and straight poles for studs and rafts [*sic*]. Thick shakes were laid on the ground for the floor. Bed and furniture were also made by hand; an apple box for a chair, etc. We used straw for our mattress.

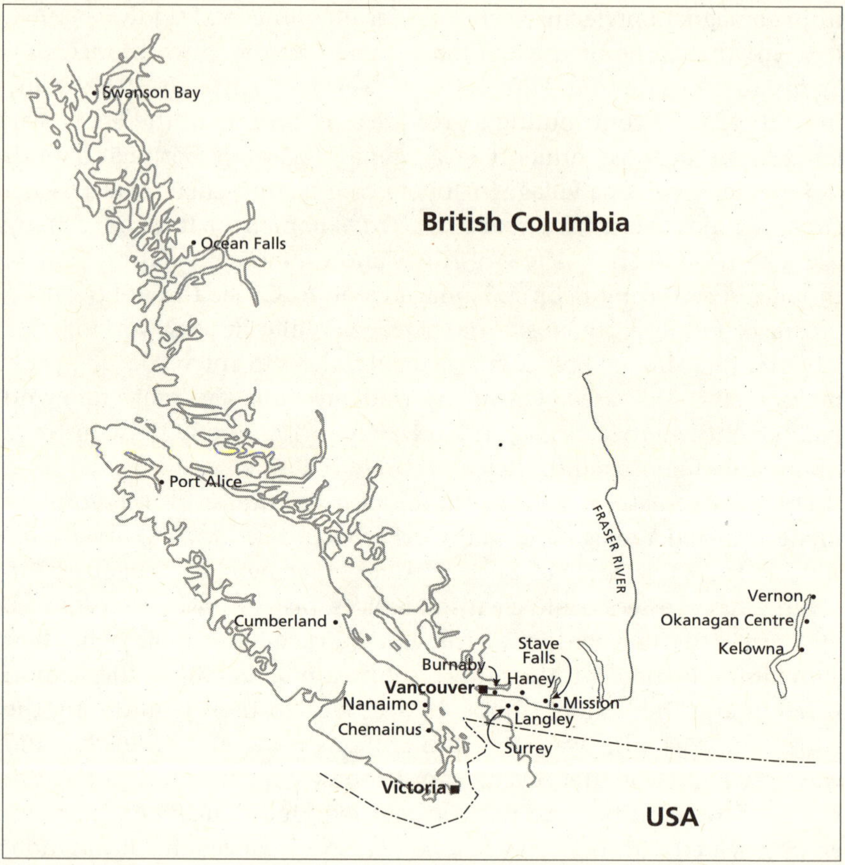

Map 4 British Columbia coast, showing some major Japanese communities pre-1942.

House building and well digging were cooperative ventures. They were also special events that involved a great deal of eating and drinking. Yamaga tells us:

> Money was scarce and our labor was cheap in those days. Often times we could not afford to buy stumping powder so we dug around the stumps of many feet in diameter with a mattock and shovel. In the hole dug underneath we would build a fire and burn it day after day. Some stumps' roots would take two weeks to burn. We planted strawberries as we cleared the land.
>
> We settlers were all husky young men and seldom saw the opposite sex of our own race. We all felt the loneliness and emptiness of this life.

7 Workers posing for a Japanese photographer in a shot showcasing various techniques typically employed in stump removal in British Columbia.

The bachelors found ways of letting off steam. Yamaga vividly recalled some of them gambling, drinking sake, engaging in free-for-all fights, and raucously participating in the Armistice Day parade of 1918, when "we sang at the top of our voices Russo-Japanese war songs which were the only songs we knew."[5]

At about the same time as Yamaga did, another Hiroshima immigrant left Japan with a personal dream to go to a foreign land. In his case, it was not because of family need. Nakashima Teizō (1889-1981) came from the town of Eba, an area where seaweed and clams were abundant.[6] Many from that region near Hiroshima city immigrated to Hawaii and the American mainland. Nakashima's family was quite affluent. They lived in a grand house, fished and farmed, and managed quite well without going overseas as others in the neighbourhood had done. Even so, from childhood Nakashima had dreamed about going abroad. In 1907, when he was seventeen, he and a friend decided to emigrate together. They went to Hawaii, where Nakashima worked for half a year in the sugar cane fields. Then he continued on to Canada.

From the beginning, Nakashima's goal had been to settle permanently as a land-owning farmer. He laboured for three months at a logging camp near Burnaby Lake, then worked at the Christina Lake Resort Hotel as a bellboy for two years in order to learn English.[7] From there, he went to Vernon to investigate the possibility of farming, but he soon returned to the coast. In December 1910 he bought twenty acres of rough land in Mission for fifty dollars an acre. By 1916, when his picture bride came, he had cleared part of the land and was growing strawberries.[8] He became active in the Mission Agricultural Association and in the Japanese Christian church in Mission. He was instrumental in founding the Japanese-language school as well as an English-language kindergarten.

Kudō Minoru, mentioned in the previous chapter, became a leader in the Mission farming community. Because of his command of English, he was especially helpful to his neighbours. He had teachers' training in Japan, and he and his well-educated wife, Hatsue, were in charge of the Mission Japanese Language School.

Some early pioneers who became farmers had left Japan to avoid family expectations. Inouye Zennosuke was from Imuro village in Asa county, very near Hiroshima city (Imuro has been part of that city since 1971). Zennosuke's father was a building contractor in his village and the nearby area and had thirty to thirty-five employees. Zennosuke was expected to carry on the family enterprise, but he was afraid of heights – he would crawl around on all fours on the roofs. Zennosuke's father had little sympathy for what he regarded as disgraceful behaviour and would push Zennosuke around with a pole. This, perhaps, influenced Zennosuke's decision to emigrate in 1900, when he was sixteen.[9] According to his daughter, Beverley, he first went to Cumberland. By 1914 he had learned English and was a Canadian citizen, besides being the first Japanese in Canada with a chauffeur's licence.[10] He worked for a real estate company on Powell Street run by Saeki Tadaichi, who was also from a village in Asa county.[11]

Soon after the start of the First World War, Inouye joined the Volunteer Corps of Japanese Canadians, who trained in Vancouver under Major-General E.A. Cruikshank. The men were hoping to be sent overseas to Europe.[12] Although 227 aspiring Japanese-Canadian soldiers had trained diligently, the Canadian and British governments refused to form a Japanese battalion. Later, hearing rumours that in Alberta they would be allowed to enlist, 174 Japanese men went there. Inouye sold some of his belongings to buy a train ticket to Calgary, where he enlisted in the Thirteenth Canadian Mounted Rifles. On arriving in England, he was transferred to the Princess Patricia's 52nd Battalion (Infantry). He was wounded at Vimy Ridge.[13]

In 1919, through the Soldier Settlement Board, Inouye bought eighty acres of "wild land" in Surrey for $3,200.[14] In 1920 he married Morikawa Hatsuno (1900-93), the daughter of Hiroshima immigrants Morikawa Yasutaro and Tora. Zennosuke and Hatsuno gradually cleared their land, and by 1942 they had tamed thirty-two acres and were producing berries on twenty-five of them. Hatsuno bore five children.

The family was an extended one that kept up some links with Japan. Inouye sponsored his younger brother Otoichi (1891-?), who arrived in 1906 at the age of fifteen, as well as a number of other young men who came as *yobiyose* (sponsored people; literally, "called over") workers.[15] Otoichi married and had three children, but his wife (1900-32) took ill and returned to Japan with her children in 1929. His son George later joined his father in Canada.

Movement into the Okanagan and southern Alberta began a decade or so after the Japanese ventured into farming in the Fraser Valley. Men first went to those inland areas as contract workers in other fields; after that, they gradually turned to agriculture. The first Japanese to arrive in the Okanagan is said to have been a Mr. Katō from Hiroshima prefecture, who was "boss" over thirty-four men at the Coldstream Ranch in Vernon. The manager of this ranch had recruited him in Vancouver around 1900. A few years later, in 1903, a man from Shiga prefecture, Koyama Eijirō, took over from Katō and remained boss there until 1911.[16] It is said that in 1907, the oft-mentioned Nikka yōtatsu kabushiki kaisha (Canadian Nippon Supply Company) supplied men to work on a Coldstream Ranch irrigation project. Japanese men also picked fruit and worked in the ranch's packing plant. During the busy summer months, they were paid $1.40 a day for ten hours' labour. In the late fall and winter they were paid $1.00 to $1.25 per day. They were charged $4.50 per month for room and board. In 1907 a fifty-pound bag of rice cost $2.00, beef was seven cents a pound, and liver was free.[17] By the 1930s, many of the packing houses in the valley had mechanized, but smaller companies still hired Japanese workers. Some of these men apparently could work as fast as and more efficiently than machines.[18]

The Japanese also ventured into southern Alberta as hired labourers for various projects. Some early pioneers had crossed the border from the United States, but most were from BC. After living for a short time on the coast, they "had either been frustrated in their efforts to accumulate wealth or were not satisfied with the restricted situation that existed in [British Columbia] and moved to Alberta."[19] However, many who arrived between 1908 and 1914 were eventually driven out of Alberta by the extreme weather and the harsh working conditions.

The largest number of Japanese workers came in 1907, under contract to the CPR through the Canadian Nippon Supply Company, to work on the railway and on an irrigation system near Gleichan. The Knight Sugar Company also brought in Japanese labourers in 1908 and 1909 to "break land" and to work on the sugar beet farms, but these workers earned only fifteen to sixteen dollars after a whole year, and as a consequence, many left. However, some hardy souls remained and eventually started farming individually or as part of cooperatives. These individuals later formed the nucleus of the Japanese community in southern Alberta. In 1910 some started producing potatoes and other vegetables for market.[20]

Iwaasa Kōjun (1882-1968), a Hiroshima immigrant, was one of these early farming pioneers. He was a relative of Iwaasa Matsutarō, one of the first group of contract workers that had arrived in Cumberland in 1891. Japan's Ministry of Foreign Affairs records note that Kōjun immigrated as a student in 1898 when he was sixteen. He went to Cumberland and worked in Matsutarō's grocery store and in the Dunsmuir mines. Later he went to San Francisco, where he learned English while working as a houseboy. After a stint on the railway in western United States, in 1907 he moved to Alberta. Undoubtedly, his command of English is what enabled him to work as a foreman for a sugar beet work crew. By 1909 he had established himself as an independent farmer in Raymond. In his diaries, he meticulously recorded his early years in Canada.[21]

Family Settlement

In the Fraser Valley, after ten to fifteen years of bringing his land into production, a bachelor would be able to build a frame house and send for a wife. Not only did the wives work tirelessly alongside their husbands, but they also worked at night doing household chores (as described by Yamaga in the previous chapter). They endured pregnancy and delivered babies with little or no medical care or help from family or friends. Unlike in their home villages, where neighbours and family members were close by, or even in other centres in BC, where there were neighbourhood women to offer moral and physical support, childbirth in the Fraser Valley was a lonely and at times frightening experience. These women's lives were grim, and not all of them could endure the poverty and the isolation. At least one that I am aware of committed suicide. The despair that drove this wife and mother to leave her young children behind and take her own life must have been overwhelming.

In the Fraser Valley, as more and more families moved into the area, more support from other women was available. Lives became less isolated as the children began to attend school and contacts were made.

Some women, such as Imada Ito, took on full responsibility for the farm for years while their husbands worked elsewhere. In her memoirs, Imada Ito tells us that it was only through her own persistence and hard work that her family was able to make a down payment on eight acres in Haney in 1922. Her husband was reluctant to take up farming. For years she had gone to lumber and sawmill camps with him to cook and wash for many men, only to watch him spend all her earnings on liquor and gambling. She worked as her husband's partner at a cedar bolt camp at Stave Lake, wielding an eight-foot saw, to save the money they needed to start a farm. For years after that, she worked on the farm alone while her husband remained in the lumber camp; only in the off-season did he return to help clear the bush. According to her, he did not contribute any money to the farm; in fact, he would take money she herself had earned when he returned to the camps. Only much later did he stop logging to stay on the farm year-round.

Imada Ito's story is not unique. Toshi Fudemoto (née Sasaki) (1919-?), who grew up in Haney and attended school with Yamaga's daughter and Imada's sons, related an almost identical story. Her father, Sasaki Tokubei (1878-1949), continued to work at a shingle bolt camp at Stave Lake even after her parents bought five acres in Haney in 1926. When Toshi was seven and it was necessary for her to attend school, her mother, Sasaki Shizu (1892-?), like Imada Ito, settled in Haney. Shizu farmed while tending to the needs of young Toshi and twin sons born in 1923.[22]

On all these farms, land was constantly being cleared and planted with strawberries and raspberries as the farmers struggled to increase their productive acreage. One observer at Mission noted: "The Japanese added an enormous amount of new acreage to the [berry] industry, because they were willing to buy unused, poor or stump-covered land and make it productive through an immense amount of hard work and frugality."[23]

In the Okanagan Valley, the workers at the Coldstream Ranch gradually moved into farming by either leasing land or arranging half-share contracts. Under a half-share contract, one person provided the land, the other (in this case the Japanese) the labour. The costs of fertilizer, seeds, and seedlings were shared equally, and the profit was also divided equally. In 1930, under this system, 109 out of 134 Japanese households in the Okanagan were growing vegetables and tomatoes on land owned by "Canadians."[24] *Kanada Nipponjin nōgyō hattengō* published articles by Japanese farmers in the area, explaining the practical aspects of their agricultural pursuits, including the costs of farming, the long hours, the busy seasons, and the months of unemployment. Some writers called for an emphasis on quality rather than quantity and discussed the advantages of producing ahead of the regular season.

The Okanagan attracted only five Hiroshima people.[25] The largest numbers of Japanese there were from Kagoshima, Shiga, and Wakayama prefectures. However, two Hiroshima men were especially important to the story of the Japanese settlers in the Okanagan: Maehara Takuji (1888-1982) and Peter Cobyace (1895-1975).

Maehara Takuji was the eldest of three sons from Yoshino in Kōnu county in east-central Hiroshima. As a seventeen-year-old he had gone to Hawaii; only later did he continue on to Canada. Maehara, after being abandoned in Saskatchewan by an unscrupulous contractor for the CPR (a story recounted in Chapter 3), arrived in Kelowna in 1907. He remained in the Okanagan and laboured there at a variety of jobs before finding steady work at the Rainbow Ranch in Okanagan Centre.[26]

In 1919 Maehara returned to Japan to marry Tanabe Ayame (1901-92) who had been born in Hawaii but had returned to Hiroshima with her parents. Together, Takuji and Ayame went to the Rainbow Ranch, where Maehara Ayame became the camp cook. They had three daughters, born in 1921, 1922, and 1925. In 1926 the family went to Japan, but Takuji came back to Canada alone after a year. In 1929 Ayame returned, leaving the two eldest daughters behind but bringing Mitsuko, who had refused to stay in Japan. The hard-working Maehara family soon included three sons. They grew fruits and vegetables in Bear Creek (across the lake from Kelowna) for many years on leased land until finally they were able to purchase an orchard in Rutland, where Maehara discovered a variety of apple that was given the name Maehara Delicious in 1956. One day he noticed some "brilliant red apples" on the lower branch of a green apple tree; he proceeded to propagate these, sending samples to experimental stations across North America.[27] Without question, he was a keen and accomplished orchardist. Like many in the farming community, Maehara Takuji became a Christian and an active member of the Japanese United Church in the Okanagan. As an eldest son, he was to have inherited his family's property in Japan, but he chose to settle in Canada.

Kobayashi Peter Takeyoshi (1895-1975), more often known as Peter Cobyace, arrived in Kelowna in 1918.[28] Little is known about his early years except that he was from Hiroshima prefecture and had graduated from Waseda University. While en route to New York on a student visa, he took a spur-of-the-moment detour after meeting a Japanese resident of Kelowna during a stopover in Vancouver.[29]

Cobyace worked at first on a white man's farm in the Kelowna area, but he soon started growing vegetables on leased land. He had a strong command of English and negotiated effortlessly with the white owners of packing and shipping businesses. Soon expanding, he was hiring many Japanese workers. He was described as "one of the first JC [Japanese Canadian] farmers to own his own land, and use modern power equipment, to farm on a large scale."[30]

He was not just a successful farmer. Gaining the confidence of the Japanese community, he became an organizer and an executive officer of the Kelowna *konwakai* (literally, "a gathering for familial talk, a social club"). A colourful character, he drove large and flashy cars even though "he needed a couple of cushions to get himself up high enough to see through the windshield."[31] His wife, Kimi (?-1988), whom Peter married in 1935, also worked, just like the women on the Fraser Valley berry farms. Kimi and Peter were Christians, active in the Okanagan United Church.[32]

In southern Alberta, where the farms were more isolated and the Japanese immigrants were fewer, many women had an extremely lonely life. Iwaasa Kōjun's wife, Ito, who arrived in 1915, felt especially isolated because of the distance between neighbours. Her desire to see smoke wafting from a neighbour's chimney and her husband's suggestion that she bang on the washtub when she thought childbirth was imminent tell us how extreme her isolation was. At least on the Fraser berry farms, husbands were nearby when the women went into labour.

From this lonely beginning, Kōjun's wife, Ito (1893-1983), settled in and became the mother of ten children. She was a cultured and well-educated divorcee and already the mother of two children, whom she had had to leave behind with her natal family when she immigrated. In Canada, nine of her children reached adulthood and became active members of the community. With her help, her husband became a successful farmer and a community leader. He helped build a small credit union among the Japanese; then, in 1914, he helped found the Raymond nihonjin kyōkai (Raymond Japanese Society) as well as the Meirō seinenkai (Meirō Youth Society).[33] Under Iwaasa, its first president, the Raymond Japanese Society had five objectives: to promote the social well-being of the Japanese in Raymond; to create better relations and greater cooperation with white residents; to stimulate progress and development of the Japanese in Raymond; to provide financial assistance to Japanese in need; and to help bring more Japanese farm labourers to southern Alberta. This organization played a key role in the founding of a Buddhist church in Raymond in 1929. Yet in 1944, after his children had already done so, Iwaasa joined the Mormon Church. His activities were not solely within the Japanese community: in the 1920s he served two three-year terms as a public school trustee. He was probably the first Japanese in Canada to hold public office. Iwaasa brought two younger brothers to Alberta as well as other *yobiyose* farm workers, including Kubota Takayuki and Hino Takao.

In contrast to Iwaasa, Kubota Takayuki (1898-1993) was plagued by difficult family circumstances and was able to provide his five children with little more than shelter and sustenance. Yet he doggedly fought poverty and illness and lived to the age of ninety-five. Kubota came from Nishiwa village in Kamo county in central Hiroshima and was the second son in a peasant family with six sons and one daughter. His father had spent six years in San Francisco and had returned with savings, which he used to improve the family property. But those four *tan* (about one acre) could not support them all. An uncle, a Mr. Uyeki, who was a post office clerk, adopted Takayuki, but Takayuki wanted to farm and was reluctant to follow in his uncle's footsteps. In 1917, Kubota Takayuki's reluctance to take up his adopted father's occupation, and his dreams of making a fortune in "Amerika," drew him to Alberta as *yobiyose* to Iwaasa Kōjun.[34] A few years later, Takayuki's brother, Hino Takao (1901-92), who had been adopted into the Hino family, also came to Canada. Hino, however, returned to Japan ten years later. He seems to have done relatively well, because in Alberta he was able to buy property on which he grew potatoes before returning to Japan.[35]

It seems that Kubota Takayuki borrowed his boat fare to Canada from his adopted father. When he arrived, he stayed at the Hiroshimaya, Satō Mohei's rooming house on Alexander Street, before leaving for Alberta. In 1928 he travelled to Japan and married but was unable to bring his wife to Canada; immigration laws had been tightened that year and had effectively barred picture brides, in that women could now represent only half the quota of 150 Japanese immigrants.[36] If Kubota had pushed hard, he eventually might have persuaded authorities to permit his wife to join him in Canada, but probably his dire economic circumstances made it difficult to pursue this end.[37] At any rate, in 1936 he married a young woman of Czech descent and they had five children. The marriage was stormy, for he was a dour, hard-working man, and his wife, who was years younger than he, wanted much more than he could offer. He eventually raised the children on his own. Kubota Takayuki, who had eight years of schooling, kept a diary, and while he was struggling with his wife and later raising his children alone, he poured all his frustrations into it. His next wife, Tamako, whom he married in Japan in 1962, thought it was much too private for others to read, so it is not available to historians.[38]

Anti-Japanese Sentiments Arising from Marketing Problems

During the First World War the market for berries flourished. The price of strawberries soared from four cents a pound to twenty-one cents, and customers swarmed to buy the produce. Many Japanese immigrants went into farming in the Fraser Valley at that time, often borrowing the money to do so. There was little antagonism from the white farmers, since they realized that Japan was an ally whose navy was protecting Canada's Pacific coast.[39] However, prices plummeted after the war and growers were forced to compete in a limited market. The white farmers conceded that their Japanese counterparts were hard-working: they bought cheap land that no one else wanted and within a year were harvesting better crops than their neighbours. The complaint was that "these industrious immigrants would soon squeeze them out of markets."[40] As anti-Japanese sentiment grew, Japanese farmers began to organize, not only to cooperate among themselves but also to improve relations with non-Japanese farmers. Inoue Jirō (dubbed the "Haney Village Headman" by Japanese) worried that an organization of Japanese farmers would only draw attention to them; notwithstanding his concerns, in the spring of 1919 the Haney Agricultural Association was organized.[41]

Soon after this, representatives of the Haney, Mission, Whonnock, and Hammond Japanese Agricultural Associations held a conference to discuss various subjects, including measures to combat frosts, the importing of agricultural labourers from Japan, and the wages to be paid for pickers. More pressing, however, was a search for ways to soften the anti-Japanese feelings that were hardening among whites. The representatives agreed that they would urge everyone to abide by the Lord's Day Act and not work on Sunday, and to conduct themselves in ways that would not inflame public opinion.

The executive of the Haney Agricultural Association met every month. Yamaga noted that the most difficult issue it faced was white animosity against Japanese farmers who worked on Sundays. He described one such example:

> One Sunday, a certain Japanese man was working from early morning clearing his land using blasting powder. A white woman, dressed in her Sunday finery came by on her way to church. She said gently to the man, "Today is Sunday. You should be resting." It seems as if the man thought that only Christians needed to rest so he retorted, "Me Buddhist, you no policeman. I don't care." The lady phoned the police immediately. She must have understood his English babble. A policeman came and gave him a tongue-lashing, "Even Buddhists – everyone in Canada has to obey the Sunday law." He warned the farmer that since this was the first offence, he would be excused, but that next time he would give him a fine.[42]

This incident aroused a great deal of concern among the association's leaders, who realized that it was next to impossible to prevent their fellow Japanese from working on Sundays. They urged their members to work inconspicuously and quietly, away from public view.

Although the policeman had cited the Lord's Day Act, the toiling man had not actually broken the law since the act had been brought in primarily to "regulate Sunday trading."[43] As a criminal law, the Lord's Day Act was a federal statute that applied automatically to all the provinces. Provinces and municipalities could opt out of certain of its sections but could not extend its coverage.[44] Some municipalities in BC debated Sunday store closings, and some editors objected to the "prosecution of culture and music." It is doubtful that a farmer clearing his own agricultural land was prohibited under the act's Regulation 4:

> It is not lawful for any person on the Lord's Day, except as provided herein, or in any provincial Act or law in force on or after the first day of March 1907, to sell or offer for sale or purchase any goods, chattels, or other personal property, or any real estate, or to carry on or transact any business of his ordinary calling, or in connection with such calling, or for gain to do, or employ any other person to do, on that day, work, business or labour.[45]

Whether the policeman believed he was upholding the law is difficult to determine. How is one to interpret the phrase "for gain to do ... work" on one's own land? Yet public opinion surely held the farmer to be breaking the Lord's Day Act. In the Mission area, the white community "viewed their [Japanese] entry into the valley as a threat to Protestant customs and beliefs. Japanese violated the Lord's Day Act by working on Sundays."[46] On 3 April 1928 the *Vancouver Daily Province* reported a complaint against "Oriental farmers":

> We have nothing against them racially, but we want them to live up to our standards. On the second Sunday of July last year I personally counted twenty-six trucks of vegetables in charge of Orientals on the Ladner ferry which was too crowded to carry white men's pleasure cars. When Orientals who ignore the Sabbath are hauled into court they avoid the penalties of the Lord's Day Act by stating that those who labor in their fields are their brothers or partners and not employees.

The "Orientals" depicted in the article were Chinese market gardeners, but the white public did not differentiate between the Chinese and Japanese.

By the mid-1920s, white society's hostility toward Japanese farmers was intensifying. By this time, their Sunday labour was not the only issue: they were also growing in numbers, and in the depressed economy they were widely perceived to be marketing their crops in unfair ways.[47] Yamaga deplored the ignorance of the Japanese farmers, who did not understand the complexities of the marketplace. Some Japanese farmers selfishly refused to think beyond the growing and selling of their own crops. When admonished by a fellow Japanese farmer, they would reply, "I grew it myself so it's my business where I sell it!"[48] Moreover, because they were unable to read English, they were unaware of the growing anger being directed toward them, anger reflected in newspapers and agricultural magazines. For example, on 16 August 1924 the *Vancouver Daily Province* stated:

> The vegetable farmer and small fruit grower of the province is becoming Oriental – the strawberry patches are taking on a yellow tinge ... Agricultural depression favors Oriental farming because the Japan and Chinaman dispense with luxuries in living, work out all daylight, and incur no expense in eating or amusement that is above their income ... [They are] all smiles because living is so much better than in Japan.

Astute farmers such as Yamaga realized that the situation was becoming serious: demands were growing for legislation in BC similar to the Alien Land Act in California (and similar laws in other western states). The 1913 California Alien Land Law prohibited "aliens ineligible to citizenship" from owning land. The US Revised Federal Statues of 1875 had declared that only two types of aliens – namely, those who were white or black – were eligible to become American citizens.[49] In 1882 the Chinese Exclusion Act of the US Congress barred Chinese from citizenship, but since this act did not mention the Japanese, there was confusion in some lower federal courts.[50] In 1920 a further amendment to the Alien Land Law plugged some of the loopholes of the earlier legislation with the intention of "driving Japanese immigrants out of California agriculture."[51]

In BC, the white farmers most affected by Japanese competition were on the Saanich Peninsula near Victoria. Since the late nineteenth century, farmers of British descent had been growing strawberries in the peninsula's Gordon Head district. Since sales in Victoria and Vancouver brought them much profit, they had expanded production, and by 1925 they were sending their berries east of the Rockies on refrigerated freight cars. The Japanese berry farmers in the Fraser Valley had increased their production and had also started shipping their produce to the east; this was reducing the incomes of the Saanich growers. Moreover, since the Fraser Valley season began a week or so ahead of the one on Vancouver Island, Saanich berry growers were missing out on the high prices that producers could demand at the beginning of the season.[52]

By 1925, white farmers in various parts of the province were demanding an alien land law. They were also insisting that people ineligible for the franchise should not be allowed to own land.[53] The Anglo-Japanese Alliance, negotiated between Japan and Britain in 1902 and renewed in 1911, had for a number of years protected Japanese immigrants in Canada, which as a Dominion within the British Empire had its diplomatic affairs controlled by Britain. The non-renewal of the alliance in 1921 and its replacement with the Washington Agreement on Naval Disarmament made the position of the Japanese immigrants more precarious.

An alien land law had the potential to destroy the Japanese farming community. Its leaders, including activists such as Yamaga, decided to meet the problem head on. They consulted with the Japanese consul, Japanese-Canadian journalists, provincial government ministers, and the Canadian Japanese Association.[54] Then they travelled through the Fraser Valley, talking to Japanese farmers and explaining the enormity of this legislation, its impact on Japanese farmers in the United States, and the possible consequences of such a law in BC. More than three hundred Canadian Japanese agreed to form an organization that would include all the Japanese farmers in the Fraser Valley – the Ichigo seisansha rengō kumiai (Union of Berry Producers Association). It sent Yamaga, representing the north Fraser farmers, and Kumatani Jiro, representing the south Fraser farmers, to the 1925 annual meeting of the BC Fruit Growers Association in Kelowna. After the committee campaigning for the adoption of an alien land act delivered its report, Yamaga addressed the meeting. He stated that Japanese farmers realized that through ignorance of the marketplace they had caused monetary losses to themselves and to others. However, now quite aware of their past mistakes, the Japanese farmers were at this moment creating a cooperative and hoping to unite with farmers of all backgrounds in the interest of mutual aid and regulation of the market. Writing years afterwards, Yamaga said that after his address, the assembly's honorary secretary, Dr. Barss, a professor of agriculture at the University of British Columbia, proposed an urgent motion to dissolve the "anti-Japanese resolution committee" immediately. It passed unanimously. To Yamaga, this signalled a tremendous breakthrough in interracial relations.[55]

The Maple Ridge Berry Growers Co-operative Exchange was organized in 1927 by Yamaga, "the dominant figure in the struggle to establish amicable inter-racial relations."[56] Later, the Japanese growers' associations amalgamated into the Consolidated Farmers' Association "and its annual meeting even attracted white growers."[57] Still later, under the Natural Products Marketing Act, white and Japanese groups cooperatively regulated under a local board the marketing of small fruits and rhubarb produced in the valley.[58] The Japanese farmers complained that, although they were responsible for over 80 percent of the produce, the board consisted of two white farmers and one Japanese. But their protests never went beyond grumbling.[59]

In the Okanagan, it appears that the Japanese farmers organized not to counteract but to request representation on marketing boards. As soon as the Vernon *nōkai* (Japanese farmers' association) was organized in January 1935, it asked the federal government to include two "Orientals" [*sic*] on the Interior Vegetable Marketing Board. This request was granted, and at the March meeting of the marketing board, one representative from the Japanese association and one from the Chinese growers were made part of the five-member board. It was the *nōkai* that set wages for its members as well as prices for their produce. For instance, the general meeting in March 1936 decided to ask canners for $12.50 per ton of ungraded tomatoes, or $14.00 for Number One grade and $10.00 for Number Two grade. They also agreed that they would pay their workers twenty dollars a month with room and board from April to June and raise the wages to forty dollars a month with room and board from July to the end of the season.[60]

Bridging the Societies

Although marketing problems and animosities in the farming industry were in this way eased, social and psychological separation remained between the mainstream and the Japanese farming families, especially in the Fraser Valley. Community leaders such as Yamaga made efforts to smooth out these problems. For example, white neighbours disapproved of the conspicuous hard labour of the Japanese farm wives. The long hours the immigrant women spent clearing land, working in the berry fields, and chopping wood – often with babies strapped on their backs – drew much criticism. Since warnings about this at meetings fell on deaf ears, the executive of the Haney Agricultural Association decided that Yamaga should organize gatherings at different sites in the Haney area to alert everyone in the Japanese farming community to the dangers of continuing to fuel such criticism. (It is likely that the men who attended these meetings did not tell their wives about what the white neighbours thought of Japanese women working so hard.) Since the women did stop working so hard, Yamaga gathered that this endeavour had good results.

While Yamaga drove Japanese women to the Parent Teachers Association (PTA) meetings and interpreted for them, he would encourage them to participate in local school activities, especially at Robinson School, which by 1924 had a student population that was half Japanese. The children were pleased to see their mothers working alongside the white mothers at the school functions. What the Japanese women who attended PTA functions thought about this experience, unfortunately we do not know; nor do we know whether their participation involved more than attendance at the meetings.[61]

The Agricultural Association also dealt with innumerable problems that arose owing to parents' ignorance of school attendance regulations. For instance, parents often kept children home from school when their labour was required on the farm. The association reminded farmers that the age of compulsory schooling was seven to fourteen (it was extended to fifteen in 1921). Although Japan did not initially enforce compulsory education, it gradually did so, with the result that school attendance there rose from 45 percent in 1887 to 72 percent in 1899 and 88.1 percent in 1901. The figures for girls were lower – less than 30.0 percent attended school in 1887, 59.0 percent in 1899, and 81.8 percent in 1901.[62] By 1906, elementary school attendance figures had reached 96 percent for boys and 95 percent for girls. The Japanese government's "school enrolment statistics do not tell the full story of school attendance" since "children of poor families were frequently kept out of school to help on the farm and at home to take care of their baby brothers and sisters."[63]

This tradition carried over to Canada. Before the 1920s the Issei in Canada did not always concern themselves with school attendance. Later, they obeyed the law, but they still made maximum use of the daily labour of children. Casual conversation, as well as carefully directed interviews with the children of these pioneer berry farmers, revealed that beginning in early childhood they were working members of their families' enterprises. They weeded, hoed, and picked berries in the early morning before leaving for school, after school, and on weekends. They also chopped wood, hauled water, did the laundry, cooked meals, looked after younger siblings, and did whatever else was required that they were capable of doing.[64]

English Language

Around 1924, some white agitators argued that Japanese students should be segregated in the public schools; they claimed that the Japanese children were taking a disproportionate amount of teachers' time owing to their lack of English. The Japanese consul and concerned Japanese community members conferred with Dr. S.S. Osterhout, director of Oriental evangelization of the Methodist Church. They decided that Japanese children should attend kindergarten so they could learn English in preparation for school. Church-run kindergartens were opened in many Japanese communities, and in January 1927 a kindergarten was started at the Haney Japanese Community Hall under the United Church Women's Association.[65] Misao Yoneyama, who, though born in Vancouver, had spent several years of her childhood in Japan, recalled that after she returned to Haney, she entered the kindergarten with younger children. With the help of Miss De Wolfe, the teacher, she was soon able to enter public school.[66]

The United Church was not the only Christian church to work with Japanese children in Haney. At the suggestion of the "devout Baptist" William Hall and his daughter, Mary, Yamaga helped organize an interracial non-denominational Sunday School in 1917 at the Japanese Hall. It began with about fifteen children. By 1920, eighty children and about twenty adults, both white and Japanese, were participating in the prayer meetings. At Easter, potluck dinners were held, with entertainment for the children. Yamaga noted that as a result of these social events, a close relationship developed between the whites and the Japanese in Haney.[67] These interracial Sunday services were quite unusual at a time when most

Japanese lived in separate communities, had difficulty understanding English, and had little contact with whites. Other Japanese Christian congregations existed, but these had Japanese-speaking ministers.[68]

While the settlers and their offspring were improving their English, there was a need to teach English to the later Japanese male immigrants, the *yobiyose* (literally, "called over"), who had been brought in under the agricultural worker stipulation of the Gentlemen's Agreement.[69] The association arranged twice-weekly English classes for them. It was felt that learning English would help these workers adjust to Canadian life. The host farmers paid the fees for these men, most of whom were relatives or fellow villagers. Each was given room and board and a stipend under a three-year contract. One such immigrant, Fudemoto Chiyoto Frank (1915-93), arrived in Canada in 1934 from Asa county near Hiroshima city. His three-year agreement required him to work for the sponsoring farmer, who was to provide him with room and board and ten dollars a month. In his case, however, he was released from his obligation after two years because the farmer could not afford to pay his monthly stipend.[70]

A *yobiyose* might be brought over not only to help on the farm but also to become a *yōshi* (adopted into the family) husband for a daughter. Itō Gihachi (1875-1962) and his wife, Kikuyo (1896-1962), started farming on fifteen acres in Surrey in 1929 after the closing of the Campbell River sawmill at White Rock, at which Gihachi was working. Okita Yoneso (1919-) arrived on the Itō farm as a *yobiyose* in 1935, when he was sixteen. Since the only son of Gihachi and Kikuyo had died in 1935 at the age of eight and the Itō family worried there might not be a male heir, in 1940 Okita Yoneso and the daughter of Gihachi and Kikuyo, Itō Yeiko (1922-), were married. Okita was to be a *yōshi* husband. Because of the wartime emergency, the marriage was not registered as an adoption into the family, and thus Okita has retained his surname.[71]

Although there were a number of highly successful farmers, and others who unselfishly contributed a great deal of their time to the farming community, many other Hiroshima settlers needed all their energies for their own families' survival. These people included the parents of Zennosuke's wife, Hatsuno. Inouye Hatsuno was the eldest daughter of Morikawa Yasutarō and Tora, who had gone to Hawaii in 1901 through an emigration company. They were from the hamlet of Arashita in Kameyama village in Asa county, near Hiroshima city. They had left behind a baby daughter, Hatsuno, in the care of Tora's sister and parents. Their three years in Hawaii were difficult, and unable to achieve their dreams, they moved on to Canada. In Hawaii they had had another daughter, Asano Essie, born in 1903.

In Canada, Yasutarō worked in a mill in Crofton on Vancouver Island, where Tora bore a son, Katsumi, in 1907. Yasutarō had heard of many Hiroshima people who had settled on farms on the mainland. The couple brought their daughter Hatsuno from Japan to Canada. Soon after, they bought a piece of land with a small house in Port Hammond on the north bank of the Fraser. Hatsuno was then ten years old. Another son, Jitsuo, was born in 1912. Soon after his birth, Tora died. With the help of his two daughters, now eleven and thirteen years old, Yasutarō was able to carry on, and he later bought a ten-acre farm in the same district. The Morikawa family lived in a converted barn for nine years and produced apples, strawberries, and garden vegetables. Morikawa Yasutarō became well known for his *nappa* (Chinese cabbage), which he sold fresh as well as pickled. Jitsuo's widow, Hazel, vividly described the atmosphere in that converted barn:

> A part of what made home such a special place was the mingling of many different smells. There was the pervasive aroma of the father's roll-your-own cigarettes that lingered long in the air over the large open barrels of *nappa* pickling in different stages in the mid-section of the barn. At mealtime meat and vegetables bubbled together in soy and sugar while next to it fish fried in a pan. The added smell from the kitchen would drift in the air, creating a rich mingling of smells to give their home that special appeal of soul food, simple living, a time for rest after work, a table full of people, good friends, the sound of Hiroshima dialect, happy voices, laughter and the contentment of belonging to a loving family.[72]

Yasutarō went to Japan to remarry in 1919. Just after that, in 1920, his eldest daughter, Hatsuno, married Inouye Zennosuke. His second daughter, Asano Essie Morikawa (1903-96), married Shigehiro Otoichi a short while later, also in 1920. Essie and Otoichi farmed in Langley, where they had seventeen children, of whom fourteen survived to maturity.[73]

Hazel Morikawa has painted an idyllic picture of her husband's childhood home. Even so, there clearly was a great deal of poverty and exhausting labour in his life. Life on a farm was difficult for the families, especially the children, who had to work from an early age. Their labour was essential, especially on the Fraser Valley berry farms. They not only travelled long distances to school but also worked in the fields before and after school. The fortunate ones had bicycles; the rest walked to and from school. In the busy season, some children worked in the fields beginning at daybreak and were driven to school just before the bell. As a child, my husband envied his younger sister, "who had to only babysit" while he and his older sister hoed, picked berries, and did other field tasks. Most farmers' sons, once they reached adulthood, left farming to work in lumber camps, sawmills, paper mills, and mines. Yet they were obliged to give their earnings to their families. Few were able to go to university.[74] By the 1940s many of these children, like their elders, were part of flourishing family farming enterprises.

Farming communities benefited from dynamic leadership. That said, all Japanese farming families, by necessity, had to learn to deal cooperatively with the market, one another, and white growers. Still, these families were independent because they worked their own land. Their long hours were their own, and they decided for themselves what they would grow and how they would spend their days. By the 1930s, most of them were at least assured of shelter, and they grew much of their own food. None of this applied to those Japanese who continued to labour in the province's resource industries: they depended much more heavily on others – at work, on their bosses, and in their daily lives, on the Japanese collective. These people had no assurances of either shelter or food. Their jobs were not guaranteed; nor were their wages, and often they were undermined by the bosses whom they considered their benefactors.

Chapter Six

The Divided Urban Community

By the 1930s about half the Japanese in Canada lived in cities of more than thirty thousand, and one-third of Japanese lived in Vancouver. Many of these urban dwellers, though, had links with the hinterland.[1] Japanese tradespeople provided a variety of goods and services: some to the city at large, and others mainly within the community. Many worked in the local sawmills and other labour-intensive industries. A number of families of those men who worked seasonally in the remote areas preferred to live in Vancouver, where schools were better. Families that were headed by women or that required the women to work also lived in the urban centres. Some of the more affluent Japanese – a few doctors and dentists, the labour bosses, the owners of prosperous stores, the managers or owners of lumber camps, sawmills, and fish-processing companies – lived in Vancouver's better residential districts. The Japanese community was not uniform: there were vast economic differences within it. And though its members generally cooperated among themselves, socialized together, and offered one another mutual aid, they also harboured hidden grievances and open animosities.

Tradespeople and Entrepreneurs

Many Japanese operated small businesses. In 1931 one out of every ten Japanese in Vancouver held a trading licence, and 858 of the 12,532 trading licences in Vancouver were in Japanese hands.[2] These tradespeople included dressmakers, cleaners and pressers, and grocers, who were scattered throughout the city and who catered to the community as a whole. In the Powell Street district, lodging-house keepers, fish dealers, bathhouse managers, and proprietors of shops specializing in Japanese goods served mainly fellow Japanese. In Victoria and New Westminster, too, there were a number of Japanese-owned shops with both Japanese and mainstream customers. Wherever there was a concentration of Japanese, as in a mining or lumber town, a Japanese merchant followed to provide Japanese food and goods.

Many of the businesses along Powell Street were small shops and shoestring enterprises. Some had hired help, but most were staffed by family members, who all worked extremely hard to make a living. There were a few large businesses such as T. Maekawa, a dry foods store, and Furuya, which handled dry goods and foodstuffs. The latter was a branch of a Seattle company that not only operated a large store on Powell Street but also sent young men (*banto,* clerks) throughout the province to take orders and make deliveries. Their services were a godsend to housebound women everywhere.[3]

Hiroshima immigrants ran many of the smaller businesses. Kumamoto Jun (1900-85) and his wife, Toshiko (1906-94), had a cleaning and pressing shop in Vancouver's West End. Japanese cleaners were heavily patronized by non-Japanese since the service was very good. They not only painstakingly spot-cleaned each garment but also made alterations and repairs at moderate cost. Most of these businesses were family owned and operated. The husband did the cleaning, pressing, pickup, and delivery, and the wife and adult daughters did the alterations. Many of these enterprises also made dresses. The women's contributions were vital. The Kumamotos relied on white customers; businesses along Powell Street's "Little Tokyo" served the Japanese. Immigrants from Shiga prefecture owned most of these shops, but Hiroshima people ran a few.

One occupation that appealed to many Japanese was barbering, since barbershops required little starting capital. By 1927, fifty-three Japanese held barbershop licences in Vancouver. In 1934, an executive member of the Japanese Barbers' Association explained:

> The first Japanese barber shop was opened about 1907, and by 1910, there were about 15. These shops were all small, but the trade attracted many who wished to settle down, and who liked to live in the city. For about $50 one could take a course at a barber school, and then open a small shop with about $500 to $800. These barber shops were first opened on Powell Street, and were often run by wives, while their husbands worked outside, usually in the saw-mills. Since then, the number of shops gradually increased, and spread to other parts of the city. Before the depression following 1930, there were about 100 Japanese barber shops in the city, each earning an average of $150-200 gross income. At present, there are about 55-60 shops, earning an average of $80-100 gross income.[4]

Among the early barbers was Kumamoto Kasaku (1886-1951), the older brother of Kumamoto Jun. The *Tairiku, 1909* list indicates that his shop was at 207 Powell. The same list includes another early Hiroshima immigrant, Nakagawa Gentarō (?-1938). With two employees, Nakagawa ran a barbershop at 307 Powell.[5] Nakagawa was from Shitami village in Kamo county, now part of East Hiroshima city. His wife, Mine (1884-?), joined him in Vancouver in 1911. Doubtless because they were childless, they adopted a young man, Kuroda (later, Nakagawa) Masashi (1899-1982), the second of five sons in a family in their home village. Masashi immigrated in 1919 when he was nineteen. By then, Gentarō and Mine owned a toy store on Powell. Their adopted son returned to Japan to marry; records show that his wife, Ai (1905-), came to Canada in 1926. Their son, Paul Masaaki Nakagawa, was born in 1930. It seems that after Gentarō died in 1938, there was a major disagreement between the widow and her adopted son, for the store was sold and she returned to Japan.[6] Masashi started working at a sawmill in Port Alice; shortly afterwards, his marriage ended. His wife and son went to Japan; he stayed behind. According to his grandson Paul, Gentarō treated Shishido Masajirō, one of his first employees at the barbershop, more like a son than he did Nakagawa Masashi. Shishido (1881-195?) came to Canada from Takeya district in Hiroshima city in 1908 at the age of twenty-six. His wife, Shō (1888-?), arrived with a three-year-old daughter in 1912. By the time Shishido enlisted in the 192nd Overseas Battalion of the Canadian Armed Forces in the First World War, they had four children.[7] He was wounded on 16 August 1917, when shrapnel struck him near the shoulder blade and penetrated his right breast.[8]

Another barber from Hiroshima was Hayami Kometarō (1868-1950), the adopted son of the Hayami family of Takasaka village in Toyota county, east of Hiroshima city. Hayami married in 1897. Three years later, after a failed business venture in Kobe, he came to Canada with his wife Kise (1879-1953). After working for a white doctor's family in Victoria, the couple went up the coast to work at the Arrandale Cannery on the Nass River. In 1907 they settled in Vancouver, where they operated a barbershop and Western-style bathhouse at 105 Pender Street. During these years, Kise gave birth to six sons, of whom four survived. The businesses must have done well, because Kometarō and Kise went back to Japan in 1911 and Kometarō paid back the money he had borrowed from his adopted father for his failed business venture in Kobe. Hayami and his family returned to Canada in 1913 and started another barbershop in the Powell Street district. By 1930, their eldest son Masato

(1902-92) was well settled; he had taken a bride, Kaoru, from Kuwanashi village in Toyota county in 1928. At that point the elder Hayamis returned to Japan with their fifteen-year-old daughter Chiyeko.[9] The sons who remained in Canada thrived, operating Hayami Radio and Hayami Wood and Coal on Powell Street.[10] So it appears that Hayami Kometarō and Kise achieved their goals and were able to retire in Japan, leaving four adult sons in Canada. It may be that these sons sent money to them regularly. The fourth son, Yoshio, went to Japan in 1936 when he was twenty-seven to care for his parents and to later inherit their property there. He was conscripted into the Japanese army a year later and was killed in action in China in 1940.[11]

The growing Japanese community provided other opportunities for entrepreneurs. Many eventually moved away from Powell Street, but their social life was still focused there. Although some Japanese Canadians bought cars, most relied on taxis. The first Japanese taxi business opened in 1914; by 1920 there were seven, one of which was owned by Yamashita Shintarō.[12] Yamashita was from Ogata village in Saeki county, just west of Hiroshima city. He had come to Canada in 1912.[13] By the 1930s, his company, Yama Taxi, at 205 Gore Avenue, was the largest and best-known taxi company in the Japanese community. His clients were almost all Japanese.

Other urban Japanese worked as gardeners, mainly for white households. Some worked alone; others ran larger operations that arranged gardening contracts and then assigned workers to fulfill them. This was a highly useful arrangement for those who lacked facility in English, like my carpenter father. For him, gardening for a boss sometimes bailed him out of financial difficulties.

A number of Japanese produced and sold sweets, and still others made tofu. Two Hiroshima immigrants launched a more daring enterprise that required much more capital: manufacturing *miso* (fermented soybean paste) and soy sauce. Amano Teiichi (1890-?) was from Yamate village; his brother-in-law, Sakamoto Noriyuki (1906-), was from Fukuyama city. Thus, both were from Numakuma county in the easternmost part of Hiroshima prefecture.[14] Amano came to Canada in 1907 when he was seventeen. According to Canadian government records, he re-entered Canada in 1910 as a "logging camp boss" and his wife, Asano (1891-?), joined him in 1916. The title "logging camp boss" tells us he was an enterprising man. He later amassed sufficient money to buy a truck and carry on a transport business.[15] Then, in Vancouver in the early 1930s, with his brother-in-law he began manufacturing *miso* and soy sauce under the brand name Maruten.[16] Sakamoto, the younger brother of

Amano's wife, Asano, came to Canada in 1926 when he was twenty. Japanese Ministry of Foreign Affairs records list him as a "domestic." After Amano and Sakamoto decided to produce and sell these two very basic Japanese condiments, Sakamoto returned to Japan to learn the manufacturing process for *miso*. They did not need to make a formal study of the brewing of soy sauce, since Amano was from a family of soy sauce producers. Since *miso* can be produced quickly, the would-be entrepreneurs started with it, selling it at ten cents a pound, thereby undercutting imported *miso* by about three cents a pound. Having established a market, they produced soy sauce with soybeans probably imported from Japan as well as Canadian wheat, which they found highly suitable. In less than a decade, they had a booming business with three employees.[17]

Another Hiroshima immigrant who prospered in the food industry was Araki Buemon (1891-1974), a third son, who had trained as a master carpenter in Hiba county in the northeast corner of Hiroshima prefecture. He immigrated in 1908 when he was seventeen. His early years in Canada were not very promising. He spent the first of them building boats in Steveston. Later he also fished. A disastrous fire in the early 1920s left him destitute. Another boat builder, Hisaoka Bunji, also from Hiba county, offered him a temporary place to live in Bidwell Bay on the north shore of Burrard Inlet. There, he joined other shrimp fishermen.[18] The others worked by dragging their nets to shore; Araki was more innovative, inventing traps and, on the advice of a white man, fishing outside the First Narrows, the entrance to Burrard Inlet, which is now spanned by the Lions Gate Bridge. He did very well. By the early 1940s he had a well-established business at 762 Powell. Araki constructed the building himself. It included his store and working area as well as a family apartment. Although it was a family operation, he hired many shrimp peelers in the busy season.[19]

Medical Practitioners and Others

Practitioners of Japanese medicine were popular in the Japanese community. They used massage, *moxa,* and other Asian treatments. One of these practitioners was Takeyasu Nobuichi, whose clientele reached beyond the Japanese community and even into the United States. Takeyasu, whose wife, Shizuyo, had given up a life of luxury to be with him, had studied medicine in Hiroshima city from 1921 to 1926 (see Chapter 4). During most of his time in Canada, he was forbidden by law to practise medicine; but from about 1927 to 1932, he did. His son George recalled that his father had an office overlooking the Powell Street Grounds

(Oppenheimer Park). Takeyasu's treatments attracted many white people. George could not recall much about his father's practice; he did, though, remember the young daughter of a Texas oil millionaire, who had been taken all over the United States to consult with doctors, none of whom had been able to treat her leg problem:

> Since the building did not have an elevator, she had to be carried up by her two attendants. But in the end she was able to walk up by herself. She made quite a lasting impression on my very young mind because on her last visit she gave me a big hug and I remembered how nice she smelled.
>
> Very much later, I was probably in about grade six or so, as I was rummaging through Dad's medical books and correspondence, I came across a letter from a lady in Texas thanking Dad for all he was able to do for her. From the content and the faint scent, I surmised that it was from the same lady. There were [*sic*] a whole apple box of other testimonial letters. Most of them were from all over U.S.A., at least, the English ones were. I don't know what exactly he practised. I know it wasn't acupuncture or herbs ... Whatever it was, it must have been effective. What I can remember about his medical books, they seemed like it was conventional medicine.[20]

Takeyasu may have been forced to close his medical office, because after 1932 the family moved to Ruskin in the Fraser Valley.[21]

One of the first Japanese medical doctors to practise in the Powell Street district was Ishiwara Meinosuke. (A Dr. Kusaka was at the Japanese Fishermen's Hospital in Steveston.) Ishiwara, a graduate of a medical school in Kyoto,[22] practised without a BC licence because his English was inadequate for passing a Canadian examination. Later there were others, who graduated from Canadian or American medical schools but served their internships in Japan.[23]

Harold Mitsugi Shimokura (1904-75) came to Canada in 1915 from Naka village in Saeki county. His father, Sōtarō (1875-1940), who had preceded him, was an early investor in the Royston Lumber Company. Mitsugi supported himself and earned his university tuition by working as a labourer at Royston. As a student he was also a stock boy at Powell Drugs. After attending the Universities of British Columbia and Alberta, he graduated from the University of Toronto Medical School and interned at St. Luke's International Medical Center, Tsukiji, Tokyo. He returned to Canada in 1934 and began his practice. Two years later, he married the daughter of Ishiwara Meinosuke.[24]

Powell Drugs was the only drugstore in Japantown that had a Western pharmacist.[25] However, a number of shops in the district sold Japanese cosmetics, herbal medicines, and other traditional remedies, which probably had been suggested by practitioners of Japanese medicine.

Not all Japanese entrepreneurs were in Vancouver. At Gorge Park in Victoria, Kishida Yoshijirō, from Kanagawa prefecture, and Takata Hayato, from Hiroshima prefecture, established a popular spot for family entertainment. Their Japanese Tea Garden was a rather unusual enterprise; it comprised a beautiful Japanese garden, a pavilion that served English tea, and access to boats that families could paddle in the Gorge waterway. The completion of a streetcar line to the park in 1905 made it readily accessible to Victoria residents. Kishida was the "idea man"; he summoned his father, Isaburō, a landscape gardener, to BC to design and landscape the garden. Kishida was later commissioned to plan Japanese gardens at Butchart Gardens as well as Hatley Park, the estate of James Dunsmuir.[26] Takata looked after the daily management of the popular teahouse.

Takata Hayato was from Niho village in Aki county, whose inhabitants depended almost entirely on the sea for their livelihood since there was very little land suitable for growing rice. During the Tokugawa era his family had hired workers to harvest seaweed and make *nori* (laver). Their ships ventured through the Strait of Shimonoseki as far as Tsushima Island to catch squid (see Map 1). During the Meiji era the prosperous Takata family, like many others, fell on hard times when the building of a deep-sea port at Ujina near Niho village destroyed oyster and seaweed beds and the livelihood of fishers.[27]

Takata Hayato was the second son of a branch of the Takata family. The three eldest of this family of four sons emigrated, although the eldest, Naoto, eventually returned to Japan. Hayato, who immigrated to Canada in 1899, learned English by working in white homes and hotels for several years before starting the Tea Garden with Kishida. The third Takata son, Kensuke (1884-1979), immigrated in 1903. He joined his brother Naoto at Rivers Inlet, where he fished in summer and worked in a sawmill in winter before joining his brother Hayato's enterprise in Victoria after Kishida left in 1923. By the time Kensuke became his brother's partner, the business was not doing as well as it had been. Many families had acquired motor cars by the 1920s, which meant they could travel farther afield. Nevertheless, the two brothers continued to operate the teahouse until they, along with all people of Japanese descent, were removed from the coastal area in the spring of 1942. In an interview in Hiroshima, the daughter of the fourth Takata son – the only one who remained in Japan – recalled that her father used to go to Miyajima, a popular island for tourists near Hiroshima city, to buy trinkets to sell at the Tea Garden.[28]

The Takata Kensuke family was the only Japanese-Canadian family in Esquimalt. Kensuke had promised his wife that she would not have to work outside the home in Canada.[29] He kept his promise; but it was a lonely life since she rarely met other Japanese women. She devoted herself to her children and their Japanese-language education. At one point she returned to Japan with her children; finding life with her husband's family difficult, she returned to Esquimalt, choosing loneliness in Canada over the difficulties of living with an autocratic sister-in-law who had returned to her natal home after a failed marriage. Takata Kensuke had more contact with other Japanese because he went every Saturday to the Ozawa Hotel at 820 Fisgard Street, Victoria, to play Japanese card games with other Japanese men.[30]

Bosses, Labourers, and the Union

The tradespeople who ran their small businesses worked long, hard hours and rarely had any time to rest. Still, they were independent, the services they provided were needed and wanted, and they probably received some satisfaction from their efforts. In contrast, the vast majority of the urban residents and labourers in remote company towns and camps were dependent on the bosses who had recruited them. These bosses supplied food, tools, and clothing to the camps; undoubtedly, the stores offered them commissions on sales, and as a consequence they became among the most affluent members of the Japanese community. The bosses had the power to hire and fire the workers. Beneath the Japanese community's peaceful, cooperative, and united facade was internal strife and an unequal struggle for power, rewards, and social status.

The wealthiest and most powerful men in the Japanese community were the ones who owned lumber companies. Two of them were Hiroshima men: Kaminishi Kannosuke (1881-1933) and Sasaki Shūichi (1891-1986).[31] In 1917, Kaminishi and eleven others formed the Royston Lumber Company. Kaminishi owned 60 percent of the shares. Two Hiroshima minor shareholders were Iwaasa Matsutarō, one of the first Japanese Cumberland miners, and Shimokura Shōtaro, father of Dr. Harold Shimokura.[32]

Sasaki Shūichi came to Canada from Hiura village in Asa county in 1907 with a "dream of one day playing a part in promoting trade between Canada and Japan." To this end, he learned English and eventually – in partnership with a firm in Japan – formed the Canadian Lumber

Company. He also formed the Cameron Lake Logging Company, which had a logging operation and sawmill in Coombs.[33] Both Kaminishi's operations and Sasaki's hired Japanese labourers – about two hundred in total. In April 1943 their enterprises were confiscated and sold for a fraction of their worth.[34]

Much more numerous than these lumber magnates, but still influential, were the bosses (i.e., recruiters) who did the hiring for both Japanese and white enterprises. Many of them had their offices on Powell Street; others conducted business in company towns and remote lumber camps. The large employers and bosses constituted an elite; the hundreds of labourers who depended on them were at the bottom of the social and economic pyramid. The labourers sought a decent living; the company owners, to maximize profits; the boss-recruiters, to keep their lucrative positions.

This is, of course, only part of a very complex story. Much of what passed between those who were hired and those who did the hiring was rooted in customs and perspectives brought from Japan. Those who provided the jobs were viewed as the *onjin* (benefactors) of those who received the positions; thus, the labourers owed the bosses their allegiance. In addition, the Japanese consulate in Vancouver played a major role in the lives of Japanese immigrants and, as part of this, was heavily involved in employer-employee relations. Contract labourers, such as those who were exploited at Cumberland in 1891, could appeal to the consulate.

Furthermore, the consulate was sensitive to Japan's image in the world and kept a watchful eye on anti-Japanese legislation. For example, when the BC legislature added "and Japanese" to the British Columbia Coal Mines Regulations Act, which excluded Chinese from underground mining, the consulate passed the information to the Japanese embassy in London, which protested to Britain's Colonial Secretary. Britain was anxious to improve relations with Japan, so it pressed the Canadian government (which lacked autonomy in its external relations) to disallow such laws. Thus, for "imperial reasons," Ottawa disallowed such legislation; or it allowed the courts to rule that these laws exceeded the powers of the provincial government, even though this upset politicians in Victoria.[35]

Invoking the Anglo-Japanese Alliance of 1902 and the Anglo-Japanese Treaty of Commerce and Navigation of 1906 (renewed in 1911 for another ten years), Japan would later complain to Britain about the many pieces of anti-Japanese legislation passed by the BC legislature in the early twentieth century. [36] No doubt it was national pride that drove the

Japanese government and its representatives in Canada to make demands on behalf of the Japanese in Canada. Nonetheless, the Japanese in BC sometimes did benefit from the consulate's actions. Immigrants appreciated the consulate's help and felt indebted to its officials.

Similarly, they felt beholden to the Canadian Japanese Association (CJA), founded in 1897 to help Japanese immigrants find jobs and learn English. Perhaps it began as an altruistic group whose leaders were dedicated to assisting their fellow immigrants, but as the years went by, and its leaders grew wealthy, the CJA evolved into a club for wealthy businessmen, employers, and bosses. After the Japanese consulate officially recognized the CJA in 1909, immigrants had to go through that group in order to conduct consular business – for example, to acquire a passport, secure a deferment from military service, or register a birth, marriage, or death.[37] In 1934 the CJA tried to seize even more power by claiming that all Japanese organizations ought to be under its umbrella. Its official newspaper, *Tairiku nippō* (Continental Daily News), had three thousand subscribers.[38]

The CJA's leaders were among the elite of Japanese-Canadian society and fully intended to stay that way. So their loud protests when Suzuki Etsu organized the Japanese Labour Union of Canada were not surprising. Many labourers were also lukewarm about the union because their obligations to their "benefactors" – the men who had hired them and who sometimes provided them with a home away from home – were often stronger than their concerns about discriminatory wages.

Prefectural ties also complicated matters. Many felt that loyalty to their regional "family" took precedence over personal gain. Through prefectural connections, new arrivals received lodging, familiar food, and jobs. Among their *kunimono* (literally, "fellow country people"), who spoke the same dialect and shared their customs and tastes, they could relax. Prefectural ties alleviated some of the stress of leaving home and village. Japanese from the fiefs of Aki and Bingo, which the Meiji government had merged to form Hiroshima prefecture, met in 1902 to form the Geibidōshikai (Association of Geibi Friends). (This name took the Chinese characters Ki from Aki and Bi from Bingo, and gave the former the more common reading of *Gei,* to form the name Geibi.) This was the first prefectural association organized in BC. Later, similar organizations were formed.[39] In 1906 the Geibidōshikai was reorganized and renamed the Hiroshima kenjinkai (Hiroshima Prefectural Association). The leaders of the prefectural associations were in large part also active in the CJA.

8 Cars belonging to Hiroshima people are all lined up and ready to depart for the annual Hiroshima kenjinkai picnic.

The prefectural associations provided solace and companionship. This is evident in the enthusiasm with which Kazuta Kiyoso (1899-2000) talked about the Hiroshima kenjinkai.[40] Kazuta was active in the Hiroshima prefectural organization on Powell Street. The youngest of four sons, born in 1899, he came to Canada in January 1917 from Hesaka village in Aki county. An older brother Sentarō, who arrived in 1907, had arranged his passage. Kazuta was well educated for his time and circumstances, with higher elementary and higher vocational education. Even at the age of ninety-six, he wrote a beautiful Japanese script; the minutes and records of the Hiroshima Prefectural Association he had kept, and the letters he wrote for the association, were the works of an educated man.[41]

Kazuta was especially active in the kōryō seinenkai (Hiroshima Young Men's Association). The two Hiroshima prefectural associations helped organize picnics and sports days, cared for children, made hospital visits to the sick, and provided funerals for the deceased. The association also facilitated return passage to Japan for the old, lonely, and destitute.[42]

When I interviewed Kazuta in 1995, he showed me a copy of the 1937 Hiroshima Prefectural Association's constitution, which carefully laid out rules for every contingency. Details of hospital visits, the amount of *kōden* (money gifts) given to the family of a deceased, and occasions for which flowers were to be sent were all carefully stipulated according to whether the person concerned was an association member, the number of years that the person had been a member, and the person's activities in the organization. There was to be no room for accusations of favouritism.

One cultural support system utilized by Japanese Canadians "permitted the immigrants to bypass white credit and lending institutions that often discriminated against them." This was the *tanomoshi* (mutual financing association or rotating credit association).[43] The cash was most often used to obtain capital for developing a small business and was not restricted to people of the same prefecture. Sometimes a *tanomoshi* was held for purchasing what might not be considered a necessity, such as a suit of clothes. These were referred to as *yōfuku tanomoshi* (*tanomoshi* for Western-style clothes). These groups chose their participants carefully. *Tanomoshi* meetings were also social gatherings: "The members ... met regularly and used these occasions as opportunities to build social bonds with one another ... If an individual was not known to the other members of the group s/he had to be appropriately introduced by someone known to the group who was willing to vouch for the stranger."[44]

These associations reinforced bonds among people of similar interests and status; they also excluded many, including common labourers. Most Japanese in the community were unskilled labourers who depended on labour contractors for jobs. Whether the job was in a Vancouver sawmill or a remote lumber camp or paper mill, the language barrier meant that Japanese labourers could obtain work only through the Japanese bosses. Yoshida Ryūichi, a labour activist, told interviewers that "the boss ... could give promotions and better and worse jobs or fire men if they did not work hard enough. He also negotiated on the workers' wages with white employers. So much for this 'boy' so much for that 'boy.' The wages at logging camps were not standardized." Moreover, "many Japanese working outside of town would not be able to find a job without the help of a Japanese boss." Yoshida added that some unscrupulous bosses not only overcharged for food but also received commissions from the stores that sold it to them.[45] The food suppliers also profited, so several people took portions of a labourer's pay.

In the negotiations for jobs outside the Japanese community, contractors volunteered to accept low wages for their men. The white companies that hired the Japanese workers were pleased with the "split labour market," in which wage rates varied according to the racial origin of the labourer.[46] Eager to maximize profits, employers were only too happy to hire reliable workers as cheaply as possible. The Japanese bosses, in turn, were eager to provide as many labourers as the companies wanted so that they, too, could increase their gains. This "racialization of labour" understandably led to bitterness among the labourers themselves, both white and Japanese.[47] The whites resented the fact that their jobs were being threatened by cheap Japanese labour; the Japanese resented the fact that even though they worked just as hard and produced just as much, they were receiving less pay. Yet still they felt grateful to the Japanese bosses who gave them work, and generally they did not blame their "benefactors," who in fact were exploiting them. Japanese labourers, naively trustful of their fellow countrymen, attributed the imbalance in wages entirely to racism.

As noted in Chapter 3, labour recruiters were not exclusive to the Japanese community. Employment agencies for white male workers, "employment sharks," also operated in Vancouver and were a barrier to organizing unemployed and unskilled immigrant workers.[48] Union leaders accused recruiters of splitting fees with camp foremen and forcing high employee turnover.[49] A much greater threat were unscrupulous agents who provided scab workers to undermine strikes. These agents used such perks as "the shark's 'den' [where] unemployed men could play cards (for real money), play pool (for more money) and drink whatever they wished."[50] The economic depression that began in 1913 drove the employment sharks out of business, since these outfits could function only when there was a strong demand for labour. In the absence of these unscrupulous operations, unions could organize workers more readily. However, most unions at this time wanted to exclude Asians. They were seeking "protection from cheap labour competition and strike breakers" and were trying to raise their members' standard of living and job security through collective bargaining rights that would weaken the power of capitalists in the province.[51]

Compared to the "sharks," Asian labour contractors were more permanent fixtures on the labour scene, since they "were not seen to be in conflict with their worker clients,"[52] owing to the complex traditions and social relationships in the Japanese community. Indeed, the bosses were firmly entrenched in the social fabric of the Japanese community. The bosses were often in executive positions in the prefectural organizations – the same groups that came to the aid of workers in times of financial, social, and personal crisis. Though some Japanese workers harboured doubts as to the real motives of the recruiters, many struggled with their feelings of loyalty, gratitude, and indebtedness.

But others did have a better comprehension of the situation. Suzuki Etsu (1886-1933) devoted two decades to trying to change the thinking of Japanese labourers in BC. A charismatic journalist and a graduate of Waseda University, he had been recruited by the *Tairiku nippō* newspaper. He arrived in Vancouver in May 1918, to be joined in October by his companion, Tamura Toshiko (1884-1945), a "modern" Japanese woman and a highly acclaimed novelist.[53] Suzuki, who translated Tolstoy into Japanese, was a strong advocate of Taisho democracy. Journalists in Japan were taking the lead in organizing rallies and opposing the government. Suzuki had been a reporter on the *Asahi shinbun,* which, with another newspaper *Mainichi shinbun,* had been at the forefront of this movement. He began to write articles in *Tairiku* to raise the consciousness of Japanese labourers. Beginning in November 1919, Suzuki, and sometimes even the Japanese consul in Vancouver, Ukita Gōji, wrote columns urging Japanese labourers in the province to think in terms of becoming permanent immigrants, and to cooperate with their white co-workers to improve their situation.[54]

These exhortations had an effect. On 3 May 1920, at a lumber and pulp mill at Swanson Bay, white loggers went on strike against the lowering of wages. On 10 May, Japanese and Chinese mill workers joined them.[55] The seventy-nine Japanese employees declared that in order to combat racial discrimination and promote mutual understanding with their white co-workers, they would stand together with the Chinese and white workers.[56]

They would show solidarity with the Chinese and white workers by finding work elsewhere. The steamship to Vancouver had space to take only thirty Japanese men from Swanson Bay; so the others, from Mie and Shiga prefectures, agreed to go to Prince Rupert to another job.[57] As soon as the thirty men left, several white men, forty Chinese who were under contract, about sixty management people, and the Japanese who were supposed to be leaving for Prince Rupert, faced with coercion from their bosses, went back to work. On 26 May 1920 the Maekawa Department Store advertised in *Tairiku* for strikebreakers for Swanson Bay. This illustrates the close relationship between store owners and bosses – in this case, both were from Shiga prefecture.[58] The strike had lasted fifteen days.

Meanwhile, the strikers who had travelled to Vancouver consulted Suzuki. At a meeting of more than fifty Japanese labourers held on 1 July at the Japanese Language School, Consul Ukita and leaders of the Japanese community congratulated the men for uniting with white workers.[59] Kanada nihonjin rōdō kumiai (the Japanese Labour Union of Canada) was formed that night, with Suzuki Etsu as its advisor. Within a short time, 120 of the 5,000 Japanese labourers in the lumber industry joined the union. In *Tairiku,* Suzuki wrote articles urging everyone to join the union, but many advertisers and readers disagreed with his views. As a consequence, *Tairiku* dropped Suzuki's columns; however, on 11 August 1920 it began publishing *Rōdō shuhō* (Labour Weekly), with Suzuki as editor. The weekly was distributed in Vancouver and remote areas; readers sent in donations, many anonymously.

The Japanese Labour Union was officially recognized on 24 August 1920; however, the Vancouver Trade and Labour Council refused to accept it as an affiliate.[60] One of the union's first battles began in February 1921, when more than eighty Japanese workers at the Alberta Mill in Vancouver, after being forced to accept a gradual reduction of wages from forty cents an hour to thirty, were told by the foreman that their wages would be further reduced to twenty-five. They consulted the Japanese Labour Union. Sada Shōji, its leader, discussed the situation with the company, but it refused to back down, so the Japanese mill workers struck. White war veterans quickly replaced them. The all-white Lumber Workers International Union picketed in support of the Japanese workers – a breakthrough in interracial relations. In spite of contributions by the Japanese community and the "borrowing" of five hundred dollars from the treasury of the Fukushima Prefectural Association by a member of the union executive, who was also treasurer of that association, the Japanese union was defeated. It simply did not have the funds to support the strikers and their families. Suzuki finally called on the strikers to return to work.[61]

The union's difficulties were largely due to the "place-specific social ties" involved in the recruiting of workers. This increased "the level of solidarity among workers since they would often have been recruited from the same prefecture or village; on the other hand the level of activism is likely to have been reduced by the groups' dependence on the goodwill of the boss."[62] At Hastings Mill, for instance, all two hundred Japanese workers were from Shiga prefecture, and they had their own separate "union." Although it was called a "union," it was more like an association of mill workers. One of its advisors was Yoshiye Saburō of *Nikka jihō* (Daily News), a rival conservative newspaper. Yoshiye was also closely connected with the Nikka yōtatsu kabushiki kaisha (the Canadian Nippon Supply Company), which had monopolized the hiring of workers for the CPR Railway. The conflict between Yoshiye and Suzuki split not only the labourers but also the entire Japanese community.[63]

The Canadian Japanese Association was the single-most influential organization in the community. However, it had been taken over by the

Japanese consulate and forty-three "big store owners" on Powell Street and had been entrusted with a great deal of power by the Japanese consul.[64] Suzuki and his group decided they would have to reform the conservative CJA from within. They got themselves elected to the executive in 1922 but found they could do nothing there, since neither the labour nor the business faction had a majority.[65]

Meanwhile, *Labour Weekly* continued to publish articles against the boss system and to promote the Japanese Labour Union. Yoshida Ryūichi launched a series of articles exposing the actions of the Canadian Nippon Supply Company. He accused the Furuya Company, the supplier of foodstuffs and miscellany to this company, of skimming profits from the labourers by charging double the actual cost of the foodstuffs. Yamasaki Yasushi, the publisher of *Tairiku,* ordered Yoshida to stop these articles that condemned the two companies. Yoshida complied, but a week later, Yamasaki informed Suzuki that *Labour Weekly* could no longer use the facilities of his paper.[66] This created a crisis, since no other printing presses were available. Realizing that they had to become self-sufficient, the labour group bought a used press; after a brief interval, on 21 March 1924, the first issue of *Nikka minshū* (Daily People) appeared. It operated on a shoestring. Its monthly costs were seven hundred dollars. A subscription cost forty-five cents per month, but only about half the readers paid for their subscriptions.[67] It survived on donations and volunteer help. Suzuki and Yoshida were to have been paid a hundred dollars and seventy-five dollars a month, respectively, but were unable to draw their salaries.[68] Yoshida, plagued by family responsibilities, eventually left, but Suzuki continued to work full-time for the labour cause.

The New Westminster Trades and Labour Council finally accepted the Japanese Labour Union in August 1927 as the Japanese Camp and Mill Workers' Union, Local 31 (henceforth referred to as the CMWU), after the "patient lobbying of the C.M.W.U., the continual efforts of men like Ernest Winch and Angus McInnis." The "declining power of organized labor during the 1920s" may have been a factor.[69] Even so, this was a triumph for Suzuki and the Japanese Labour Union.[70]

Many ignored the union, yet its membership steadily increased, from 644 in 1926, to 936 in 1927, to 1,009 in 1928.[71] Japanese businesses refused to advertise in the newspaper, which struggled on with unpaid workers, surviving on donations and as a sideline publishing educational pamphlets, Japanese books, and magazines. It also served as an employment agency, the brainchild of some women. They believed that by offering free ad space, they could undermine the boss system. On 20

March 1925, an announcement in the paper asked readers to send in details about available jobs so that it could publish them. Also, job applicants were asked to provide their name, address, and telephone number and to designate their work experience, the type of work desired, and preferred location. In 1925, 1,018 employment opportunities and 771 applications for jobs were listed in *Daily People*.[72]

To survive, the labour newspaper also experimented with a cooperative food store that cost its members fifty dollars per share. The store was opened in 1928; the following year it was declared a failure. Doi Hajime (1906-9?), who immigrated in 1924 from Nagatsuka village in Asa county (now South Asa ward in Hiroshima city), was manager of this enterprise. He recounted his experiences in 1990 to a reporter with *Chūgoku shinbun*.[73] Soon after arriving in Vancouver, having found work in a sawmill, he encountered the harsh realities of a Japanese immigrant's life: he was being paid only twenty-five cents an hour even though his white co-workers were earning forty. The province's Male Minimum Wage Law had set the minimum wage at forty cents, but this did not help the Japanese. In fact, that law was intended to drive Japanese labourers out of the industry, and in this it largely succeeded – 986 Japanese subsequently lost their jobs. The law was later modified to set the general rate at thirty-five cents, while stipulating that one-quarter of the workers in the sawmill industry might be paid twenty-five cents an hour; this meant that once again, lower wages were paid to the Japanese.[74] Fired from the mill, Doi survived by digging potatoes on a farm (which was probably owned by a white man). He was sharing a room with four other men in a boarding house on Powell Street when he read the first issue of *Daily People*. Persuaded by Suzuki Etsu's argument that the Japanese labourers were not Japanese of Japan but Japanese of Canada and thus should become active members of the labour movement, Doi became active in the Japanese Labour Union. When Kōbai kumiai (the cooperative store) opened in 1928, he became its manager. He was married by then, and his wife had to go work as a waitress in a noodle shop in order for them to survive.[75]

According to a memoir written by a self-professed "socialist," Takahashi Genshichi, the co-op store was doomed from the start. Takahashi believed that "the co-op was an idea created by those who knew how to earn their bread with a pen but not with a scale ... It was childish to think that a business could be set up in such a simple way."[76] This reflected the sharp difference of opinion between the followers of Suzuki and the young "red" group of which Takahashi was a member. The Japanese Labour Union had among its membership people who were "not exactly labourers ... like laundry store operators."[77] The union felt that small business operators and tradespeople were also workers, who, if they joined with contract labourers, could fight against discrimination – an endeavour that the young "radicals" felt was beyond the scope of the union. The union itself labelled these dissenters "red." These internal disagreements did little to improve opinions of the union held by some sections of the Japanese community.

Opposition to the union was increased as well by developments in Japan during the 1930s. Following the Manchurian Incident of 1931 and Japan's departure from the League of Nations in 1933, ultranationalism rose in Japan along with state repression of the left.[78] The conservative newspapers in the Vancouver Japanese community reported sympathetically on these developments and on the sentiments underlying them. Many readers came to view the union members as "reds" and "radicals" and even accused them of disloyalty to Japan. *Daily People* opposed Japan's aggressive activities in Asia, infuriating those who could not tolerate criticisms of this kind.

In spite of these problems, there is no doubt that Suzuki Etsu and his followers had a tremendously positive impact on the Japanese community. Although not entirely destroying the power of the bosses and their

9 The Japanese Women's Association in Ocean Falls, 1 July 1937. In many company towns such as Ocean Falls, the Japanese lived in segregated communities. They formed organizations like the women's association shown here and met to socialize and help at funerals and social events.

partners, they gradually weakened the influence of the food suppliers. By 1935 the CMWU had eight locals even though "some of the largest concentrations of Japanese sawmill workers remained under local benevolent societies or Japanese bosses, as at Ocean Falls, Woodfibre, Fraser Mills and Royston."[79] According to Yoshida Ryūichi, at the start of the Second World War the membership in the CMWU was 1,200; others, though, have stated that it was 1,000.[80] At that time, 1,839 Japanese worked in the lumber industry; a total of 8,321, including women, were in the workforce.[81] All in all, membership in the CMWU was surprisingly strong, given the resistance to it.

In this milieu, the Nisei were beginning to enter the workforce. Many worked alongside the Issei, but their attitudes were different from those of their parents. Imbued in varying degrees with traditions of Canada as well as Japan, and, unlike their elders, able to converse easily in English, they viewed the injustices of the boss system through a less rosy lens than did the Issei. But in the 1930s, the Nisei were relatively powerless junior partners whose time was yet to come.

Chapter Seven

Nisei, the Second Generation

When the Hiroshima immigrants first arrived, their main concern was personal survival; their second, earning sufficient funds to return to Japan with a nest egg. Later, with marriage and children, their attention turned to economic and social stability. Many of the Issei learned and adopted only enough Canadian ways to survive. Within their families and the Japanese community, they continued to practise the customs they had brought with them from Japan. Faced with public intolerance and discriminatory wages and laws,[1] they turned to their own group for solace and support and to Japan for dignity and respect. In Hawaii and in Canada as well, "the Japanese sense of superiority helped them maintain pride in themselves ... and helped them overcome many difficulties."[2]

Did the Issei believe that the difficulties their children faced in Canada could be eased if they developed pride in their Japanese heritage? Is this why they carefully enculturated their children with Japanese customs and traditions?[3] Undoubtedly, many tried to raise their children just as they themselves had been raised, because they knew no other way; but some made deliberate efforts to make their offspring realize they were "Japanese."[4]

Generally, the Japanese came to accept Canadian customs. Even so, as long as the hope of returning to Japan was strong, they made a careful point of raising their children to be Japanese, and community organizations such as schools and Buddhist churches promoted this indoctrination.[5]

At first, parents felt that moral instruction was more important than doctrinal differences, so they encouraged their children to attend Christian churches and Sunday schools. Many parents felt obligated to the Christian missionaries who had helped them. Many others, though, were not so accepting of a foreign religion.[6]

10 Japanese-Canadian community float participating in the Silver Jubilee of the City of Vancouver in 1936.

Most Japanese in Canada belonged to the Pure Land Sect of Buddhism and felt a strong need to conduct proper rituals for their deceased compatriots.[7] Twelve leaders of the community, including at least two Hiroshima men, Satō Mohei and Nakanishi Kanekichi, formed the Buddhist Church in Canada in 1905.[8] It began as a room in the Ishikawa *ryokan* (hotel) at 330 Powell Street. By 1921 there were Buddhist churches in many other locations.[9] That year, these churches made a concerted effort to attract young people, forming Sunday schools and Bussei (Young Buddhists' Associations; YBAs), which were organized much like YMCAs. By 1941 the YBAs had eight hundred members. They held socials and organized sports activities. Especially popular was the Bussei Baseball League, formed in 1933. Its teams played among themselves and also took on other leagues.

The largest Buddhist church was founded in 1934. It was built at the corner of Cordova and Princess Streets by Japanese-trained carpenters, my father and Uyeno Ritsuichi among them. On 17 November a *chigo* procession led by the elders and the ministers left the old church on the 500 block of Cordova Street and proceeded to the new hall.[10] Although

11 Michiko Ishii (left) and a friend, all dressed and prepared to participate in the *chigo* parade, a Buddhist procession of children, November 1934. The parade celebrated the completion of the Hompa Buddhist Church at Princess and Cordova Streets.

I had no idea of the parade's significance, I recall my excitement in participating in it.

The Methodist (later United) Church, the Salvation Army, the Four Square Gospel Church, and the Anglican Church attracted many Japanese immigrants and their children. The youth were especially drawn to the United Church at Jackson and Powell Streets. It offered a student dormitory, a basketball court, and music groups. Some parents would probably have preferred that their children participate in Buddhist church activities, but mostly they surmised that "they won't learn anything wrong" if their activities were connected with a Christian church.

It is impossible to generalize about families' goals regarding enculturating children in the ways of Meiji and Taisho Japan, or about their feelings regarding assimilation, since there was such a wide range of attitudes among them. Some families, in their efforts to be Canadian, lived completely apart from Japanese society except for brief trips to Powell Street; other families lived in the Powell Street community or in similar ones and emphasized "proper Japanese behaviour." Rose Kutsukake (1918-2003) attended Japanese-language school for thirteen years. She was the youngest daughter of Satō Mohei and Matsuyo, proprietors of the Hiroshimaya boarding house. Her father had insisted: "First and foremost you must be Japanese."[11] Some parents sent their children to Japan to be educated, as did Kaminishi Kannosuke with his son, Kōichi (Kaye).[12] At times, considerable sacrifices were made in order to do so. Okimura Mataichi (1880-1951) and his wife, Shizuno (1884-?), came from an impressive samurai background.[13] They sent their eldest daughter, Shizuye (1921-), to Japan in 1935 to attend teachers' training school. However, when Mataichi retired, Shizuno was determined to continue supporting her daughter and to do so she worked as a rag-sorter.

Some parents, especially those who hoped some day to return permanently to Japan, raised their children to fit into the society they thought existed in Japan. Some parents strongly emphasized "proper Japanese behaviour" and lived that behaviour themselves; others, who cherished the same dream of returning to Japan, taught "Japanese behaviour" and ways of thought only through occasional verbal injunctions.

The variation in the amount of traditional Japanese behaviour taught at home was mentioned in a journal kept by an inmate in the Angler internment camp during the Second World War, himself a *kika nisei* (literally, a "returned to Canada Nisei" – that is, someone born in Canada but raised and educated in Japan). He had returned to Canada when he was fifteen in the mid-1930s. He concluded that the Nisei, interned because they were Japanese, did not bear any allegiance to Japan,[14] because their parents had been so busy with their working lives that they had neglected home training in Japanese morality and tradition. This may have been so, but he obviously did not consider that some families believed that children learn "naturally" by the example of their parents or that some preferred to raise their children as Canadians. Nor did he realize that most Nisei had grown up in a completely different environment from the one he knew and, that, though incarcerated because they were Japanese, they did not necessarily feel Japanese.[15]

Many fathers involved themselves deeply in their children's upbringing and with a few stern words saw to it that their views were understood and that their wishes were followed. This picture of the taciturn, uncompromising father may be common in many other societies as well, but the young Nisei believed that it was a uniquely Japanese trait. A Japanese study associated the patriarchal father with modernization in Japan during the Meiji era, in which urbanization rapidly nuclearized the Japanese family:

> The father heading a household in the loneliness of the city separated from the extended family of the village, had to strengthen the authoritarian side of his character to shore up the family's morale and fortify it for the struggle to survive. By the same token, the mother took on stronger features of family guardian.[16]

In the everyday lives of the second generation, from infancy, women's influence was undoubtedly strong. What has been noted about Japanese Americans is also true of the Japanese in Canada:

> In many cases, the father was simply unavailable except for major disciplinary issues, and many everyday problems were handled by the mother. In some families, both parents were unavailable because they worked, or because a language barrier made communication too difficult.[17]

Most Japanese women were isolated in their homes or, at best, in the confines of their community. Wives were less exposed than their husbands to mainstream society; many lived entirely within the Powell Street neighbourhood or within their rural community, mining camp, or segregated company town. All they knew about the Anglo-Canadian community was what their growing children told them. So isolated were they within their ethnic group, one can understand why they tried to mould their children to their own familiar ways. Yet many went beyond that – they tried to teach their children what they perceived to be the "upper class" behaviour of contemporary Japan. Thus, the Nisei were enculturated by their parents from childhood into a non-existent culture, one that their mothers had imagined or – if it had ever existed – had already vanished.

Elementary school was often a Japanese child's first introduction to people of other cultures. Where Japanese children were numerous, mainstream culture was a minimal influence, since they continued to socialize with one another and to talk to one another in Japanese – often to the chagrin of public school teachers.[18] In some parts of the country, however, attending a Canadian school meant a sudden leap into an alien world. The eldest children in families were often the most distressed, since many had never been exposed to the English language or

12 Grade six class, Strathcona School, spring 1941. The majority of the students were of Asian descent. No class photos were taken in 1942 because Japanese families had been removed from their homes.

associated with white children.[19] When my eldest brother entered grade one in 1930 at Seymour School in Vancouver, where there were few Japanese, he spoke no English and had never played with white children. He was so timid that my mother had to sit with him in class for a few days. At least, this is what I have been told![20] But by the time I entered school six years later, I had been speaking English with my elder brothers and had been playing with neighbourhood children of various ethnic backgrounds. The problems my eldest brother encountered would probably not have occurred had our family lived closer to Powell Street, where English-language kindergarten classes had been set up in the Buddhist and Christian churches.

Japanese-Language Schools

Once children reached school age, the great purveyors of Japanese tradition were the Japanese-language schools. The impact of these schools on Nisei children depended on individual teachers, the frequency of attendance, the philosophy of the school's *gakumuiinkai* (governing board), and the emphasis parents placed on Japanese education.[21] Moreover, some children were more acquiescent than others to the additional demands these schools made on their lives. Even within one family there could be differences. My two older brothers resented every moment they spent at Japanese school, and although they were promoted regularly, they learned very little. I found it a challenge to memorize the Chinese characters, yet I enjoyed writing compositions; besides, I was driven by the parental pride that my annual "firsts" in class generated.

By the time my siblings and I attended Japanese-language school, it was offering only after-school language classes. In the earlier sojourning period, however, that school (and similar ones) had offered a full curriculum taught in Japanese. These schools met the needs of those Japanese parents who planned to return to Japan with their children. Some sent their children to their home villages in Japan to be raised by relatives (usually grandparents), but not all could afford the sea passage and the other associated costs. Others could not bear to part with their children. So an acceptable alternative was to provide an education believed to be the equivalent of what the children would have received in Japan.

The first school was an informal one that was begun in a home in Vancouver in 1897.[22] The first official institution, the Kokumingakkō (Vancouver Japanese National School), opened in 1906 under the auspices of the Japanese consul. The curriculum followed that prescribed by the Japanese Ministry of Education, the only difference being that English-language courses were included. The teachers' salaries and other costs were borne by the parents and the Japanese community.[23] A few years later, similar schools opened in Steveston and Cumberland.

Gradually, with the increase in Canadian-born children, changes came. As many Nisei began attending Canadian public schools, Japanese schools evolved into language-only schools held after regular school hours. For a time, the two curricula – the Japanese-based elementary courses and the Japanese-language training programs – coexisted in the Japanese schools in Steveston and Vancouver; that is, regular Japanese school subjects all day and an after-school Japanese-language-only curriculum. Thus, some children received all their early education in Japanese, whereas others attended local public schools and studied the Japanese language only as an extra. By the 1920s, wherever there were centres with a sufficient number of Japanese children, there were language schools, but these offered only supplementary language training.

Many parents felt that Japanese-language education was necessary for their Canadian-born children.[24] Often, because of the parents' poor command of English, it was only through the Japanese language that the children could understand their parents. Later, once the children grew up and left home, they needed to be able to keep in touch by writing letters. The Japanese-language schools charged fees, but the parents did not begrudge this expenditure or the time this education took. By 1940 there were fifty-one Japanese-language schools in BC.[25]

Some Nisei lived in areas where Japanese-language education was unavailable. In the 1930s, for example, Roy Honda lived in White Rock, where at one time there was a fair-sized Japanese community, mostly the families of the men who worked at the Campbell River Sawmill. The community had company houses for families, a boarding house for single men, and a Japanese-language school.[26] After the sawmill closed in 1929, many Japanese left and the school closed, so Roy and his siblings did not receive any Japanese-language education. His mother, Honda Tami (1889-1980), remained there with her children while the father, Honda Genichi (1889-1972), left to work in Englewood on Vancouver Island.[27]

In outlying areas, parents established schools on their own initiative. The school year began on 1 April, following the school calendar in Japan, even though the BC school year began in September.[28] Since children had to travel long distances in the rural areas, classes were held on two or three weekdays and on Saturdays.

In Haney, Japanese schooling began with informal classes in a family home in 1913. By 1915 the school had moved to the Haney Japanese Community Hall. All the other Japanese schools in BC used textbooks issued by Japan's Ministry of Education; the school in Haney was unique because, once they became available in 1926, it used books developed for Japanese-language schools in California.[29] These American books taught Japanese without attempting to inculcate Japanese nationalism. They were chosen for the Haney school in the hope that the students would become good Canadian citizens. Ariga Chōkichi, the school's principal beginning in 1933, believed strongly in this.[30] A Nisei who attended that school remembered the textbooks:

> The major difference was in the setting ... they would be American rather than Japanese, street scenes, classrooms, etc. I also recall stories of American heroes, George Washington and the cherry tree, Abraham Lincoln and the slaves, etc. And Ariga would supplement these text books with articles he had written himself about Canadian heroes. His approach was not above criticism. In my own home, my father thought that anything not approved by the *Monbusho* [Japan's Ministry of Education] was faulty. My mother tended to be less critical.[31]

Ariga also held classroom discussions on the moral codes and laws of Canada and arranged inter-Japanese school activities, recitations, and mothers' groups. He made a great effort to implant in his Nisei students an awareness of their Canadian roots. Yet some families did not take much interest in the education their children were receiving in the Canadian public schools and wanted the Japanese school to provide moral training and to teach proper behaviour – that is, Japanese ethics and ideas.[32]

In Cumberland, the Japanese lived in two closely knit Japanese communities called Number One Jap Town and Number Five Jap Town. The children there spent more than twenty hours a week in Japanese school, and as a result many achieved solid proficiency in the language.[33] Two Hiroshima Nisei, Harold Hirose (1918-94) and Hiroshi Okuda (1914-94), who grew up in Cumberland, became leaders in the Japanese Canadian Citizens League and later similar organizations. Their ability to converse in both Japanese and English was invaluable when it came to presenting the Nisei perspective to the Issei as well as to the public at large.[34]

Satō Tsutae was principal of the Vancouver Japanese Language School on Alexander Street from 1917 until it closed in December 1941, and again from 1952 to 1966. His was the largest school of its kind in BC. He

13 Japanese school play at the Alexander Street language school. Every year *gakugeikai* (school concerts) were held and each grade (there were usually two classes per grade) put on a play. Centre front in the rabbit costume is the author.

always maintained that the goal of his school was to produce loyal Canadian citizens.[35] Yet despite efforts to at least claim the goal of westernizing children by preparing alternative textbooks, the schools were closely modelled on the elementary schools in Japan and had the same strict routines and demands for proper etiquette. All the teachers at these schools were expected to be graduates of Japanese teacher training schools or women's higher schools.[36]

Notwithstanding that they followed Japan's curricula, used textbooks published in Japan, and conducted many classes in the Japanese "style," the Japanese schools had little success in indoctrinating Nisei children in Japanese nationalism. Although experiences in the wider world had embittered some, causing them to turn to Japan for solace and to ease their wounded pride, to many Nisei who attended Japanese-language schools, the stories of the gods who descended from the heavens to rule Japan and the divine wind that saved the country from the invading Mongols were nothing more than interesting tales.[37] Once, at the Alexander Street Japanese school, after his return from Japan, Satō shared with his pupils the special ceremonial cakes that had been presented to him by Emperor Hirohito. As he did so, he solemnly declared that everyone should appreciate the honour that the emperor had bestowed upon the school. He instructed the children to receive with humility and gratitude the pink and white crumbs they were to take home to share with their families. After Japan went to war with China, the students were asked to line up and sew knots for the *senninbari* (thousand-stitch belt), which was believed to be a talisman to save the life of a soldier. In composition class, students were told to write letters to soldiers. In spite of such events and the desires of at least some adult members of the community, the school generally failed to produce Japanese nationalists.[38]

Despite his patriotic fervour, Satō did insist that the school remain autonomous. In November 1925 he objected strongly to the proposal by the Japanese consul, Kawai Tatsuo, that the planned Japanese school building and hall on Alexander Street be placed under the administration of the Canadian Japanese Association, over which the consul had strong influence.[39] Satō and the school's governors felt that this action would not be beneficial and insisted on autonomy.[40]

Some schools were anxious to retain their autonomy; even so, representatives of all the Japanese schools met regularly to discuss matters of common concern. On 19 April 1935, for instance, at a meeting of the Nihongo gakkō kyōikukai (Japanese Language School Educational Society) held at the Marpole school, in a detailed written "aim," the members in attendance reiterated that the main goal of Japanese-language education was to supplement the public school curriculum with the teaching of the Japanese language.[41]

In spite of these public protestations that the schools taught language only, "the Japanese language school was ... an institutional device for reaffirming traditional Japanese values that attempted to perpetuate these values in the growing children."[42] The teachers insisted on pupils' "proper" behaviour – at school but also at home, in the Japanese community, and in mainstream society. Shameful words and actions, we were told, reflected on the family, the school, and the entire Japanese community. Certainly for the students, the daily routine was quite unlike what they encountered in the Canadian public schools. There were strict procedures for lining up, bowing, and marching to classrooms. Reading and writing postures, public speaking styles, and classroom deportment were very different from what was learned in the public schools. The academic demands were heavy – hours of homework every night, reading, memorizing the Chinese characters, and preparing for compositions that were to be written the next day in class.

The language readers, much like the ones used in Japan, contained tales of ancient heroes and their legendary deeds, which were meant to teach students Japanese morals. After the mid-1930s, under pressure from the BC Ministry of Education, the Japanese Language School Educational Society attempted to produce textbooks more suitable for children living in Canada.[43] A series of disagreements within the book committee slowed progress toward this goal. A few primary textbooks were ready by 1941 in Vancouver, and Satō went to Japan to arrange for their publication, but when war between the United States and Japan appeared imminent, he rushed back in November 1941 on what would be the last ship to sail for Canada before the bombing of Pearl Harbor.[44] The books had still not been published when the schools were closed in December 1941.

In 1940 the provincial government changed the School Act to place all language schools in BC under direct control of the Department of Education. In the spring of 1941, owing to accusations of subversion made by members of Vancouver City Council and escalating public antagonism toward the Vancouver Japanese schools, representatives from the Japanese community went to City Hall to explain the importance of the Japanese language. Because of racial discrimination in the Anglo-Canadian community, there were few employment opportunities for Nisei. Many were forced to work as labourers in the primary industries. To obtain a position within the ethnic community, facility in Japanese was absolutely necessary. Among the delegates to City Hall was Thomas K. Shoyama, editor of *The New Canadian,* a Nisei newspaper, who spoke from personal experience. He had degrees in both commerce and economics from the University of British Columbia, yet because of discrimination he had not been able to obtain a position with any Anglo-Canadian firm. At the same time, his lack of Japanese proficiency precluded him from employment with any Japanese-Canadian firm.[45]

Since Japanese was the only language that most Issei spoke, Nisei needed to learn Japanese to communicate with their elders. But few Nisei were able to meet the linguistic expectations of their parents and educators. Many attended language school reluctantly, resenting the hours "wasted" there.[46] It annoyed the Nisei that attending Japanese-language school made it impossible for them to participate in after-school activities such as sports. I recall that in the spring of 1941, my seatmate in Japanese school was a softball star at Strathcona School. Since he missed some Japanese school classes and was often late, the teacher berated him as soon as he walked in. The class tried to ignore the commotion, but many secretly admired their fellow student for his courage. The goal of parents for their children was fluency in two languages; unfortunately, many Nisei "were genuinely and instinctively at home with neither language."[47] This lack of fluency in Japanese led to misunderstandings within families, with the result that many Nisei tried to avoid interaction with their elders.[48]

In Japan, except among the well-to-do in the countryside, most young Japanese chose their own marriage partners. The Issei, however, were strongly influenced by the samurai culture of the Meiji era; they insisted that marriages were between families and that they as parents had the right to choose their children's marriage partners. Most Nisei wanted to emulate their white peers and could neither understand nor sympathize with their parents' fears and demands. A study conducted in Winnipeg in the 1980s found that most of the women who had started families before 1942 had had their marriages arranged, and that many had married Issei.[49]

These arranged marriages often crossed generations. Some of my Nisei interviewees had married Issei. In 1939, Toshi Sasaki, a Nisei who grew up in Haney, married Fudemoto Chiyoto Frank, who had immigrated in 1934 as an agricultural worker. Toshi, like many other young Nisei women, had studied sewing and was a skilled seamstress. The couple operated a dry-cleaning and alterations shop in Vancouver. In 1940, Yeiko Ito, also a Nisei, was married at the age of eighteen to Okita Yonesō, who had immigrated in 1935. Following Japanese custom, the parents carefully checked the background and character of the potential mate. Occasionally, where two families had been close for many years, their Nisei children married. More often, though, Nisei women were forced to marry Issei men and Nisei men had marriages with women from Japan arranged for them. For example, Masao, the eldest son of Kobayakawa Giichi, one of the first Hiroshima immigrants in Cumberland, went to Japan to marry Yokota Haruko. Hayami Masato also travelled to Japan to marry.

But there were also love matches, the truly fortunate of which gained the acceptance of both families. It was especially fortuitous if both families were from the same prefecture. Such was the happy situation for Nisei Suzue Enomoto (1911-2006) and Issei Inouye Takuo (1904-69). Suzue Enomoto, the daughter of Enomoto Tsunetaro and Mume, had lived in New Westminster with her elder brother, her mother, and her stepfather, Miyagawa. After completing grade eight, she did housework in New Westminster and later in Vancouver, where she was a live-in maid for a superintendent of the BC Electric Company in Shaughnessy Heights. On her Thursday afternoon off she would meet friends on Powell Street. There she met Inouye Takuo, the brother of a friend. The son of Inouye Takuichi, a barber on Powell Street, Takuo had been born and educated in Japan. Suzue and Takuo married in 1936 and "lived happily ever after."[50]

Many Issei feared that dating, dancing, and close associations between the sexes would lead to premarital sex and perhaps even pregnancy. Their abhorrence of such close relations between young people was in sharp contrast to the acceptance of intimate relationships and premarital pregnancies among youth in the Japanese villages where many Issei grew up. A detailed study of a village in a remote area of Kumamoto prefecture in the 1930s richly documents the "sexual looseness" that was an accepted part of the villagers' lives.[51] The society depicted in this particular village, called Suye Mura, was similar to that in the home villages of Hiroshima immigrants who came to Canada in the 1910s and later.

Clearly, Issei parents expected their children to follow the mores and traditions that they believed to be the practices of upper-class Japanese. For example, my own father, who had lived in a remote mountain village in a family that could barely feed itself, insisted that I take lessons on the *koto,* a harp-like instrument played only by the elite and the wealthy, and certainly by no members of any of the families in his native village.

The Nisei were caught in a tug-of-war between the ideas of their parents and the Japanese community at large and the social customs of

Anglo society. That made it difficult for them to relax outside their own Nisei groups: "Neither comfortable in the larger society nor in the Japanese society, they developed their own particular subculture."[52] The children of Hiroshima immigrants combined various aspects of their two cultures. Nisei participated in concerts organized for the Japanese community. I remember attending Hiroshima Prefectural Association concerts held at the Japanese Language School, where Nisei performed in both Japanese-language plays and English-language skits. George and Lily Shishido, the adult children of Shishido Masajirō, sang modern Japanese songs, and Nisei Roy Kumano and his harmonica band entertained the audience with both Japanese and American popular songs.[53] The program featured Japanese dancing as well as Western tap dancing by young children.

Hiroshi Okuda had enough ability to play soccer at the University of British Columbia; Akira Okimura shone in rugby at Britannia High School. Most Nisei, however, participated in sports only within their community.[54] Japanese martial arts such as judo and kendo (sword fighting) were practised. Thomas K. Shoyama, the editor of *The New Canadian,* attributed his paper's strong circulation to the regular sports columns reporting on badminton, basketball, bowling, and baseball. The most popular game was baseball. Almost every company town fielded a Japanese baseball team, but the famous Asahi players were the dazzling stars.

> The [players in the] Asahi Baseball Team were the local heroes in Vancouver. Possible recruits came not only from the hometown but from every surrounding town, village and farming area and even from south of the border. Wearing the Asahi uniform and being part of this illustrious group of ball players was the dream of every boy.[55]

Some sons of Hiroshima immigrants were members of this "top gate attraction." Tom Matoba, said to be the first Nisei born in Cumberland, was on the first team in 1914. Celebrated as a "slugger" and an excellent fielder, he was often said to be the Babe Ruth of Japanese-Canadian baseball. Gakuto Hayami (1904-93), the second son of Hayami Kometarō and Kise, and Mickey Shigeru Satō (1908-67), the son of Satō Mohei and Matsuyo, were on the Asahi team in their youth. George Shishido was well known not only for his singing voice but also as an athlete who played second base and shortstop for the Asahi team.[56]

The son of Kaminishi Kannosuke, Kōichi (Kaye) (1922-), who had been sent to Japan as a child, also made the team. When he returned to Canada at the age of eleven after the sudden death of his father, he was a misfit. Only when he joined the Asahi at age sixteen did he feel comfortable with his fellow Nisei:

> Playing against the tall Caucasian opponents did not faze him. There was no discrimination in baseball. Wearing the Asahi uniform for the first time made him so proud he was unable to sleep at night.[57]

The Asahi baseball team was the pride of the Japanese community. It provided hours of entertainment for men and women whose lives were bleak and difficult.[58] For the sons and daughters of Hiroshima and for other Japanese Canadians, a gratifying aspect of the team was that it earned the respect of the white community. Here was something in which the Japanese could hold their own – and even outdo the whites. The Asahi played against other Japanese teams in BC, the United States, and Japan; it also at various times played in the Vancouver leagues such as the Terminal, the Burrard-Commercial, and the Burrard, often winning championships. They thrilled Nisei, Issei, and white spectators "with their brilliant fielding, pitching and spectacular running games."[59]

Roy Kumano's harmonica band and another instrumental band provided a focus for the musically minded. There were also Nisei groups affiliated with Christian and Buddhist churches. The University of British Columbia had a Japanese Students' Club where Nisei met and socialized, although some believed that all-Nisei groups encouraged too much insularity. A 1939 editorial in *The New Canadian* expressed concern that Nisei clubs were "tending much too strongly towards an increasing isolation of the Nisei from the community as a whole. Instead of aiding the process of contact and assimilation, these social functions, by monopolizing the entire interest of an individual definitely retards this process."[60]

But not all second-generation Japanese Canadians were comfortable within Nisei society. Some had experienced little exposure to other Nisei except perhaps within a Japanese school setting and thus felt alienated from fellow Nisei. Others, from overwhelmingly strict traditional families, could not adjust to the dual culture of the Nisei. The Nisei were not a homogeneous group.

The burden of the Nisei was that they were told that delinquent behaviour would bring shame "not only to themselves ... but to their parents, the family, the community, and finally by extension, to the entire race."[61] This teaching was a potent method of control. Parents exhorted children to follow proper Japanese social protocol so that the family would not be shamed. Yet this "proper behaviour" was much stricter than what the parents themselves had experienced in Japan. In Canada, obedience to parental wishes was stressed above all else. In the face of this, some Nisei gave up their romantic attachments and reluctantly agreed to marry partners chosen by their parents. Others rebelled in a variety of ways; for example, some eloped. But actions like these aroused gossip and damaged the reputations of the principals as well as their families.

The family was meant to be paramount. Nisei children who had jobs were expected to add their earnings to the family coffers. Most complied, but a few refused, especially if their fathers were squandering the family income on gambling and liquor. George Inouye (1921-) spent a few years in Japan, between the ages of eight and eleven, where he helped his mother struggle to survive on an inadequate remittance from his father. He picked pebbles from a riverbed and gathered firewood for mere pennies. When he was eleven, his mother died, and his father called him back to Canada, where he lived with a foster family and attended school. When he was fifteen he went to a camp at Stave Falls to cut cedar bolts. He worked with his father until he was seventeen and then left to become independent, tired of how his father always took his earnings and spent them on his own pleasure and on medical care. George's father had always complained of stomach ulcers and rheumatism, but his ill health was probably the result of years of imbibing. At any rate, George was not sympathetic to his father and chose to free himself from parental control. It took courage to ignore what would naturally be the negative opinion of the Japanese community.[62]

A number of Nisei males, when they were old enough, worked in labouring jobs alongside Issei men and maintained close family ties. Frank Ohno, son of Ohno Keizo¯ (1894-1985), who had joined his cousin Nakashima Teizo¯ in Mission, left the farm in 1938 to work at Britannia Mines and later at Ocean Falls.[63] Also, the Imada brothers, Toshio and Katsumi, left home to work at a sawmill in Englewood, BC, where the Japanese boss was reputed to control the behaviour of the young Nisei by not allowing any gambling. Most of these young men gave their wages to their parents. Parents ruled their lives – Toshio Imada was called back to the farm to run it while his parents went on an extended trip to Japan in 1939-40.[64]

Among the Nisei, the same enculturation to be "Japanese" that caused confusion during childhood later induced ambivalent feelings and at times resentment over their dual identity as both Canadian and Japanese. Toyo Takata (1920-2001), who grew up in Esquimalt, was the only Japanese in his high school in the late 1930s. Although he socialized freely with his non-Japanese classmates, he never dared date any of them and wished he were white.[65]

In *The New Canadian* from 1938 to 1949, young Nisei women expressed the same desire to be like their non-Japanese contemporaries. They wrote eloquently about their confusion and frustration as well as their eagerness to gain social acceptance as Canadians. Many authors of these articles before mid-1942 were students at the University of British Columbia at a time when few Nisei, especially women, were able to receive a university education. These young women were deeply anxious to shed the restraints of parental control and racism and live freely as Canadian citizens in an Anglo-Canadian milieu.[66] A number of young Nisei women wrote poetry to express their Canadian self-identity. A literary scholar explained:

> One way for the nisei to try and resolve the tension of being discriminated against by their fellow Canadians was to erase the difference they believed lay at the root of discrimination. Thus they integrated even more the symbols of the dominant rejecting culture, in this case poetic forms, into their cultural memory. These nisei poets reveal a strong conviction, or hope, that they share an identity more with their non-Japanese Canadian classmates than with their very "Japanese" parents.[67]

A study of Nisei women living in Winnipeg after the Second World War found that over the years, Japanese enculturation gradually decreased. Nisei women born in the 1910s had spent "their childhood, adolescence, and early adulthood in institutionalized ethnic communities."[68] Of the three age groups studied, this is the one that had been most heavily influenced by traditional Japanese culture; all of these women spoke fluent Japanese. Most of them had had marriages arranged for them, some to Issei men. Because of the economic situation of their families and the limited occupations open to them, most of them had left school after grade eight. After marriage, most of them had worked at home and on the farm:

> I washed my younger sisters' diapers, when I was still nine years old. I went through all these hardships. Although everybody says that the oldest is lucky. It's not true. We could not finish school. The older one had to help look after little ones at even exam time.[69]

These women had not had the "privilege" of being exposed to the dominant Anglo society that the younger ones who were attending university had experienced; at the same time, though, they were spared the dilemma of the younger Nisei, who found themselves caught between the Japanese and Canadian communities. Their problems were summarized accurately on 22 December 1939 in an editorial in *The New Canadian:*

> In the years to come ... the Nisei will find himself caught between two crossfires – between the Japanese community and the rest of Canadian society. It will require the utmost in moral courage and sincerity to battle criticism and prejudice on two sides.[70]

Elders at home and at the Japanese-language schools had made considerable efforts to instill pride in belonging to a "worthy people with a centuries-old cultural heritage," but with varying degrees of success.[71] In many respects the Nisei – reluctantly or otherwise – accepted their parents' customs and demands, because they wanted their parents' approval. When they did not give in to their parents' wishes, they felt they were being selfish and self-serving. Try as they might to accede to their parents' wishes, their behaviour was often condemned. Some Issei thought they understood the problem and tried to address it. In the 15 March 1941 issue of *Daily People,* published by the CMWU, a member of the union executive, Sada Shōji, bemoaned the low morality and the high crime rate among Nisei. He attributed what he saw as a breakdown in public morality and discipline to the confusion wrought by the two ideologies of Japanese familism and Canadian individualism.[72] The CMWU launched a campaign to provide wholesome entertainment and educational seminars and services; the goal in this was to "not aggravate the antagonism of the white populace" – an antagonism that Sada and others feared would be triggered by Nisei immorality and crime.[73] It is unclear what positive measures, if any, were actually taken by the CMWU.[74]

In their efforts to master an impossible balancing act, many Nisei developed an inferiority complex in relation to the white community. This was reinforced by the second-class citizenship that was their lot in BC. Public segregation in movie theatres, exclusion and discriminatory practices in public facilities such as Vancouver's Crystal Pool, racism that denied them the franchise and that barred them from certain careers and professions, the "racialization of labour" that permitted only menial, lower-paying positions – all of these had a serious effect on their feelings of self-worth. Add to this, the Male Minimum Wage Law passed by the BC legislature in 1925 was modified so that Asians would receive lower rates.[75] Yet not all Nisei cowered: there were also determined young people who took positive steps to make fresh beginnings in what they hoped would be less restrictive environments. Several young men and women travelled east to Toronto and Ottawa; some, like Kazuma Uyeno, the eldest son of Uyeno Ritsuichi, went to Japan to work for an English-language newspaper in Tokyo.

In light of the individualistic actions by some Nisei, it is obviously not possible to generalize about the ultimate impact of attempts to enculturate the Nisei to their Japanese heritage. In the 1990s a study of the leaders of Nisei organizations such as the Japanese Canadian Citizens Association – founded in 1932, re-formed in 1936 as the Japanese Canadian Citizens League, and re-formed again in 1947 as the National Japanese Canadian Citizens Association – concluded that the early Nisei organizations were in the main for university graduates and did not represent the majority of young Nisei, who were labourers and whose concerns had more to do with wages, hours of work, and survival than with gaining the right to vote. Also, though "the Nisei leaders were ready to assert themselves among their own people ... they were ill-prepared to do the same in the wider community." Lacking self-confidence, they "abdicated their responsibilities." It was argued that in the struggle against the Canadian government concerning repatriation of the Japanese Canadians and better compensation for the sale of Japanese-Canadian properties during the war, the Nisei leaders allowed white middle-class liberals in the Cooperative Committee on Japanese Canadians (CCJC) to make all the decisions, in the belief that "without the aid of the CCJC they would be politically powerless."[76] These criticisms, however, are much too harsh: they do not consider the attitudes of that era. A more realistic observation is that of Roberto Perin, who claims that defenders of minorities such as Japanese Canadians "were effective only insofar as they could recruit Canadian opinion makers to their cause."[77] This is clearly so, since in the struggle by the National Japanese Canadian Citizens Association in the 1980s for redress for wartime injustices, the "powerful unifying voice" of Canadians from all backgrounds was required for its success.[78] In the late 1940s with regard to the property claims, the Japanese-Canadian community was riven with disagreements. For this reason, the NJCCA's decision to heed the advice of the CCJC was an extremely difficult one. It was not that the leaders lacked the self-confidence to question the CCJC; rather, they were making the most practical decision at that time.[79]

Rather than bringing to light the weakness of the Nisei, the struggles of the late 1940s emphasize the fact that they were not all alike, that they varied in opinions and behaviour. Some were strongly outspoken;

others wanted to halt the entire appeal process so as not to attract undesirable attention or criticism from white Canadians. If there was such a wide variety of reactions and behaviour among the Nisei, and if we attribute it to the degree of enculturation, can we then say that Asian and European cultures differ in their values?[80] It has been claimed that family responsibility, personal sacrifice, and spirituality are Asian characteristics, and that individual freedom, pursuit of happiness, and materialism are European characteristics. Many Canadian and American scholars of the lives of Japanese immigrants in North America have drawn up similar lists of Japanese and non-Japanese characteristics. I provide here ten qualities to which the Japanese immigrants to Canada are said to have been socialized and to have passed on to the Nisei: a sense of the group or communality; a strong sense of obligation and gratitude; a sense of sympathy and compassion for others; a strong sense of "we" versus "they"; an underlying emotionality and excitability, which is controlled by a somewhat compulsive attention to details, plans, and rules; a willingness to work and to persevere toward long-range goals; devotion to parents, and an especially strong and long-enduring tie to the mother persisting in almost its childhood form; an emphasis on self-effacement and a tendency to avoid taking responsibility for the actions of oneself or others; a tendency toward understanding and an emphasis on non-verbal communication; and a pleasure in the simple things of life.[81] Are we to assume that all Canadian Nisei have these "Japanese" characteristics? Clearly, we cannot.

Is there such a large difference between Japanese and Western cultural behaviour? A few decades ago, owing to the worldwide business success of Japanese companies, speculating about "the Japanese way" and "the Western way" was a popular pastime, with Westerners and Japanese alike talking about Japanese "group society." Over the years, though, the scholarly and analytical literature has thoroughly debunked that idea. Some theorists have declared that it is wrong to treat the Japanese as "a homogeneous whole," to create stereotypes, and to emphasize differences between peoples rather than similarities.[82] One scholar has argued that individualism, long theorized as a European trait, had always existed in Japan, especially in merchant societies. Even within agricultural society, peasants have always been eager to embrace technical innovations.[83]

The above arguments – that Japanese and Western society do not differ so radically, and that common Japanese stereotypes are misleading – may be valid. Yet my personal experience of the Japanese-Canadian community, and especially of Nisei characteristics, compels me to acknowledge that certain qualities *are* common among the Nisei, who *do* have behavioural and cultural characteristics that they themselves judge to be Japanese. An American Nisei journalist with Hiroshima roots noted that American Nisei in the 1930s undeniably

> lived under unusual cultural, social and economic pressures ... Their Japanese cultural heritage demanded respect of elders, filial piety even to the point of sacrificing one's personal desires and ambitions, unquestioning respect of authority, a deep sensitivity to the opinions of one's peers, a sense of group rather than individual responsibility.[84]

Yet the degree to which the Nisei manifested these characteristics definitely varied, depending on the degree of their enculturation into Japanese behaviour brought about by the family and community environment in which they were raised, as well as disparities in individual personalities.

Conclusion

The Hiroshima immigrants' story began in 1853 when Commodore Perry precipitated the Meiji Restoration of 1868. The new regime's policies of rapid modernization led to severe social and economic problems. In Meiji times the peasants, most of whom for centuries had barely eked out a living, were further burdened with increased taxation and the loss of cottage industries. *Dekasegi* emigration, which began in 1885 to Hawaii, was a possible solution – not only to improve the lot of the impoverished peasants but also to bring foreign currency into the country.

Japanese immigration to Canada may have started in 1877, but it was a mere trickle until the 1890s. The first sizable group from Hiroshima prefecture arrived in Canada in 1891, as contract labourers for the Union Colliery in Cumberland. The difficult experiences of these one hundred "miners" did not deter others from following. In fact, many others from Hiroshima gravitated toward the Cumberland area. Some had been invited by the early immigrants; others had sought the help of fellow villagers who had gone to Canada. Most of the Hiroshima immigrants came from the environs of what today is Hiroshima city, from Aki, Asa, and Saeki counties (see Map 2). In the middle years of the Meiji era, those three counties were heavily populated, the farms were small, and the peasants were suffering the consequences of industrialization: loss of markets for cash crops and the destruction of cottage industries. The building of the deep-sea port of Ujina caused havoc in the coastal waters on which many depended for their livelihood. Young men in these areas had to make a fresh start in some other endeavour if not somewhere else.

The Japanese immigrants to BC formed communities not unlike Japanese villages, where people socialized and assisted one other. These communities were scattered along the BC coast in company towns. The

Powell Street district in Vancouver, with its Japanese shops, boarding houses, and labour contractors' offices, became the focal point of Japanese settlement. From Powell Street, people and goods left for the remote areas. That district was also the headquarters for organizations such as the Canadian Japanese Association as well as for the prefectural associations, which the Japanese could approach for aid and companionship.

Powell Street was the social and economic centre for the Japanese in Canada. It was also a refuge from the overt hostility of white mainstream society, which forced Japanese immigrants to associate with and take solace from one another. Anti-Asian prejudice had led to institutionalized racism; as a consequence, Japanese immigrants and their children suffered under second-class status. They did not meekly accept that state, and they responded in the pattern identified by sociologist James C. Scott, who investigated how the dominated resist those who dominate them by "a hidden transcript," a "backstage discourse," "by engendering a subculture and by opposing its own variant form of social domination against that of the dominant elite."[1] One way in which this "hidden transcript" operated was through the retention of cultural identity, for "culture [is] a medium in which power is both constituted and resisted."[2] Away from the white society, the Japanese tried to enculturate the Nisei with pride in their heritage so that their offspring would not cower before Anglo society. The Nisei were exhorted to outperform their classmates in public school and in the workplace and were taught that the Japanese were morally and intellectually superior to their persecutors. But at the same time, the Issei and Nisei also hoped to improve the Japanese Canadians' marginal status.

In their quest for political enfranchisement, the Issei cited their service in the Canadian army during the First World War. This worked to some extent: in 1931 the Japanese-Canadian veterans were finally allowed to vote. However, fewer than eighty men were so affected.[3] Since the Japanese were not permitted to work on Crown land, some bought tracts of forest that were privately owned and developed large enterprises, as did Kaminishi and Sasaki. When the white farmers began to agitate for an alien land law such as existed in the United States, the Japanese farmers acted quickly to block this measure. Whenever Japanese in Canada believed that their dignity was being assaulted, they called upon the Japanese consul in Vancouver for support.

According to Michel Foucault, "Power is simply what the dominant class has and the oppressed lack ... It is a strategy, and the dominated are as much a part of the network of power relations and the particular social matrix as the dominating. As a complete strategy spread throughout the social system in a capillary fashion, power is never manifested globally, but only at local points as 'micro-powers.'"[4] The power of the white capitalists over the Japanese labourers was clearly manifested in remarks made by Richard H. Alexander, the manager of the Hastings Mill, to the 1902 Royal Commission on Chinese and Japanese Immigration. He argued that for the company to compete in the markets of the world, "they [Japanese labourers] should be here to supply that proportion of cheap labour in order that we may employ a larger number of whites." Yet the idea that white capitalists were exploiting Japanese "cheap" labour is too simplistic: the negotiators for this "proportion of cheap labour" were the Japanese bosses, who maximized their own profits by recruiting a large number of Japanese workers to work for low wages. In remote areas these bosses increased their income by skimming percentages from the food and goods they provided. In this, they worked closely with the suppliers, who also profited. This linkage was apparent during the 1920 strike in Swanson Bay, when the bosses coaxed half the Japanese strikers back to work and the supplier of goods, the Maekawa store on Powell Street, advertised for strikebreakers. When the Japanese Labour Union was organized, Powell Street's "elite" fought hard to undermine it by refusing to advertise in its "voice," *Daily People*. The newspaper countered by operating a free employment agency.

Whenever the provincial legislature passed discriminatory laws, the Japanese consul appealed to Japan for help.[5] Japan would then petition Britain on the basis of the Anglo-Japanese Alliance. Britain would contact the federal government, and the latter would order the provincial legislature to repeal the discriminatory law. In 1925 the consul, Kawai Tatsuo, tried to increase consular power over the Issei by moving to control the Vancouver Japanese Language School. He succeeded in securing control over the Canadian Japanese Association and ousting from it the labour leaders who had been using that organization as a power base. He did not, however, gain control over the school. As this suggests, the Japanese community was not internally united. There was conflict between capitalists and labourers and between Issei and Nisei as well. While the Nisei were young or few in number, the Issei elders had the upper hand and demanded strict obedience, be it in marriage arrangements, social relationships, or claims on earnings. They controlled the Nisei by emphasizing strict adherence to Japanese social behaviour and customs as well as through blackmailing comments such as, "What will others say?"

The white-owned companies continued to perpetuate the "split-labour market." The strike at the Alberta Mill (see Chapter 6) indicates the lengths to which white companies would go to preserve their advantage over the Japanese workers. The mill repeatedly lowered the wages of the Japanese workers until they struck in desperation; the company then hired white veterans to break the strike. Clearly, there were tiers of power throughout the society in which the Japanese Canadians found themselves. Some gains were made, but there was still a long way to go.

My research supports the power theories of Scott and Foucault, which explain the directions the pioneers took. The immigrants encountered many obstacles in BC but did not always submit meekly to unfair treatment by the dominant society. Instead, they actively shaped their own lives, making modifications, trying new approaches, at times boldly facing antagonists (as Yamaga and the berry farmers did), and never giving up.

As dreams of returning home with a nest egg had faded, men sought wives from Japan and the picture brides began to arrive. These adventurous women had no conception of what their future held. Some immigrated just to go to "Amerika," others because they were obedient daughters and did as their parents requested, some to avoid spinsterhood, others to escape a mother-in-law. None expected the hard lives that they would have to endure. These women may have been escaping the friction of in-laws, but they were also losing the kinship system that would have supported them in their homeland. Yet they endured, for the sake of the children that inevitably were born.

As the years went by, the immigrants modified their hopes and habits. Isolated from the mainstream, at first they clung to their old ways, dreaming of returning to Japan and registering their children's births with the Japanese government. A 1935 survey revealed that 85.8 percent of Nisei held dual citizenship.[6] The Issei tried to give their children the upbringing of those raised in Japan, but the image of Japan they presented to their children was not the one they had experienced in Japan. Instead, they dreamed of a better life with a bigger farm, a grander house, or a prosperous business, so they tried to mould children who would fit into the well-to-do stratum in Japan. They were enculturating their offspring in what they believed would be the lifestyle of the family when it returned to Japan with its savings.

As the decades passed, the Issei were forced to accept the inevitable – that in spite of all their efforts, their dreams were out of reach and their children were becoming westernized. Many of them would probably not fit into society in Japan, so the family's future was perhaps to be in

14 Ishii family in 1940. The author found this photograph among those that the Ishii, her ancestral family in Hisayamada, Onomichi, had in their collection when she visited in 1983.

Canada. Yet the Issei also realized that because of prejudice in BC, the path ahead would be rocky for their children. So they tried to instill in the Nisei a pride in their Japanese heritage. Thus, the enculturation at home and in the Japanese schools continued, though for different reasons than before.

For all the efforts of the Issei, they did not succeed entirely in instilling Japanese culture in the Nisei. Many young Japanese were confused regarding appropriate behaviour in both Western and Japanese societies and never developed fluency in either English or Japanese. As a result, many of them were uncomfortable in both societies: they felt self-conscious, or they felt inferior to mainstream Canadians.

The Nisei were still considered *namaiki* (brash, impertinent) by the Issei, who clung stubbornly to their power. By this time, a number of university-educated Nisei were expressing themselves in *The New Canadian;* they were making it clear that they were Canadians first and foremost. In 1941, the power in Japanese-Canadian society was still in the hands of a small, well-established elite, but the working classes were gaining strength through the CMWU. Meanwhile, large numbers of Nisei worked as labourers, like their fathers and mothers before them, hoping for a bright future but unable to see it. No doubt, the community would have changed gradually as the Issei aged and the Nisei grew to adulthood. But then, on 7 December 1941, the Japanese bombed Pearl Harbor.

Soon afterwards, the Japanese Canadians were expelled from the west coast, an act that destroyed this society by scattering its members across Canada and back to Japan.

To a considerable extent, this study of immigrants from Hiroshima prefecture is also a portrait of the prewar Japanese society in BC, but it is by no means the whole story. There were many other regional groups besides the Hiroshima people, and their reasons for immigration varied. Moreover, the lives that immigrants led in Canada were influenced by which home prefecture they came from in Japan.

Epilogue

As the years passed, prefectural differences gradually blurred as close friendships developed among neighbours, fellow workers, and community associates. Moreover, the maturing Canadian-born children saw themselves as Japanese Canadians, not as belonging to certain prefectures. As far as the Canadian government was concerned, however, the Japanese in Canada were all "Japanese," whether they were immigrants, naturalized Canadians, or Canadian born. This became evident when Japan's aggressive activities in Manchuria and China in the 1930s increased anti-Japanese feelings in British Columbia. Between March and August 1941, the RCMP registered all persons of Japanese origin over the age of sixteen – about 14,700 of them – and issued them registration cards, which they had to carry at all times.[1] The RCMP also compiled a dossier of Japanese nationals believed to be "dangerous to national security."[2]

After Japanese forces attacked Pearl Harbor on 7 December 1941, war was declared. Almost immediately, under the blanket of national security, political and business opportunists seized the chance to destroy the social and economic base of the Japanese Canadians.[3] Thirty-eight Issei on the RCMP's list of security risks were picked up within hours; within days, all Japanese-language newspapers and schools were closed and the community's fishing boats were impounded. By a number of Orders-in-Council issued under the War Measures Act, the government proceeded to dismantle the Japanese-Canadian community. After designating all lands within one hundred miles of the BC coast a "protected area," the Canadian government sent able-bodied Japanese men to road camps. Those who protested were incarcerated behind barbed wire at Angler, Ontario. By the end of April, the federal government had gathered Japanese families from the coastal towns and Vancouver Island at the Pacific National Exhibition buildings in Hastings Park, Vancouver.

All able-bodied men had already been removed; women, the young, and the elderly had to arrange the safekeeping of family assets and pack what little they were allowed to take.

By the fall of 1942 all Japanese Canadians were living in refurbished buildings in old mining towns, in hastily built shacks on grazing land in the West Kootenays, in "self-supporting" communities in the Cariboo, on prairie sugar beet farms, in road camps, or in prisoner-of-war camps in Northern Ontario. A few, the more adventurous ones, moved on their own to Ontario and Quebec. An Order-in-Council passed in January 1943 gave the custodian of enemy property the right to sell without the owners' consent all properties held "in trust." All Japanese-Canadian properties and businesses were sold for a fraction of their true value. In early 1945 all Japanese Canadians sixteen years and over were ordered either to sign papers renouncing their Canadian citizenship and to agree to "repatriate" to Japan, or to move east of the Rockies immediately. Ten thousand signed to go to Japan. Many soon realized the enormity of this move and attempted to cancel their signatures.

The war ended in August 1945. By the end of December 1946, some 4,000 Japanese had been deported to Japan, 5,871 were in the prairie provinces, 7,880 lived in eastern Canada, and only 6,776 remained in the BC Interior.[4] The federal government did not remove restrictions on Japanese Canadians until April 1949, by which time most had already settled down and rebuilt their lives east of the Rockies.[5] There was no stampede to return to the BC coast.

Most Japanese immigrants were aging in the immediate postwar years. Furthermore, their dynamism had been eroded since they could no longer function without the community they had built up over the years. Because they lacked fluency in English, they found it impossible to make their own way again. The Issei were again reduced to manual labour, but they now lacked the exuberance and stamina of their youth. Those who had been exceptionally wealthy and successful, like the Kaminishi and Sasaki families, had lost everything they had accumulated over the years; the farmers had lost their property; and business people had nothing left. The Issei were now dependent on their children, the Nisei, who became the principal wage earners for their families. Older Nisei made inordinate sacrifices during those years, forgoing their own education and their own pleasures in order to provide for their parents and younger siblings by labouring in the factories of eastern Canada.

The elite of Powell Street, the lumber magnates, the former successful farmers, and the former gardeners and labourers, all now struggled. Kaye

Kaminishi, who had inherited from his father a large share of the Royston Lumber Company, was reduced to picking tomatoes for a farmer in Kamloops. Sasaki Shūichi, who had completed a multimillion-dollar business deal between a BC mine and a Japanese company a few days before Pearl Harbor, and who also owned a lumber company in Coombs on Vancouver Island, became a night watchman. His son Fred, who had completed his bachelor of commerce degree with the University of British Columbia by mail in 1942 while living in Calgary, struggled to provide for his parents and sisters.[6] Most of the money – paltry sums – that the government had passed on to farmers, fishers, and shopkeepers after the sale of their property had been spent during the war on mere survival.

As they struggled to rebuild their lives, the Japanese Canadians were silent. Few talked to their children about their wartime ordeal. Not until the community was preparing to celebrate the centenary of the arrival of the first Japanese immigrant in 1877 did the younger generation begin to ask questions. Most had grown up in a relatively non-racist environment; because of the protective instincts of their elders, they had no knowledge of what their families had endured during the war. The Redress Movement followed, led primarily by Sansei (third-generation Japanese), who had not been negatively affected by the racism the others had suffered.

With the achievement of redress and the government apology in September 1988, the rebuilding began. The Japanese-Canadian community now bears very little resemblance to the prewar one. In 1967, immigration regulations were changed and a point system was established, one purpose of which was to "abolish discrimination" while "pay[ing] more regard to the claim of family relationship." Since then, Japanese immigrants have been trickling into Canada.[7] Most of the *shinijūsha* (new immigrants) are well-educated urbanites and thus very different from the earlier immigrants, who arrived in Canada mainly from fishing and farming villages. By 1996, postwar immigrants accounted for 25 percent of the 77,000 Japanese Canadians.[8] According to the 2001 Canadian census, there are now more than 85,000 Japanese Canadians. This increase is undoubtedly a result of the birth of children of intermarriages. Today, over 95 percent of Japanese Canadians marry into other ethnic groups.[9] This trend is likely to continue, so Japanese Canadians may well disappear as a distinct ethnic group. These changes may have been inevitable as the generations matured, but the events of 1941 to 1949 undoubtedly accelerated the trend.

A Note about the Sources

Few books have been written about the history of the Japanese in Canada. In their works, Peter Ward and Patricia Roy focused on the hostility of the whites in the province toward Asian immigrants, the actions of white supremacists, Anglo-Saxon race hatred, and xenophobia.[1] Even Ken Adachi's history, *The Enemy That Never Was,* focused mainly on white racism and the discrimination against Japanese Canadians, presenting Japanese Canadians as passive victims of mainstream paranoia.[2]

The two main records of the early history of the Japanese in Canada are by Nakayama Jinshirō: *Kanada dōhō hatten taikan* [Encyclopedia of the Japanese in Canada] and *Kanada no hōkō* [Treasures of Canada]. Original copies of these are very scarce, but in 1995 they were reprinted together with a few other rare books in an extremely expensive volume.[3] Both these books, published in 1921, were written while the pioneers who contributed to these volumes were still present to write or relate their stories. In spite of inaccuracies, these two works are valuable. They are written in highly stylized literary Japanese. They contain lists of all the Japanese in Canada in 1920, divided into the prefectures from which they had come, and they give the names of home villages and all family members. They also contain extremely laudatory short biographies of many prominent people in the community. Another old book, published in 1920 by *Nikka jihōsha hōkō* and titled *Kanada zairyū dōhō sōran* [General Survey of Compatriots Resident in Canada], was reprinted in 1993. It contains short biographies with accompanying photographs of a number of Japanese in Canada.[4]

A major source of information on the history of the Japanese berry producers is Yamaga Yasutarō's history of the Haney farmers, *Hene'e nōkaishi* (History of the Haney Agricultural Association). Fortunately for non-readers of Japanese, a large part of it is available in English in the Yamaga Yasutarō Papers at the University of British Columbia Library

Special Collections and the book has also recently been translated by William T. Hashizume.[5]

Owing to an awakening of interest in Japan and Japanese immigrants, Japanese authors have recently been contributing to the literature on Japanese Canadians. This awareness of those who emigrated was brought about by the "U-turn" – that is, the temporary immigration to Japan of Nikkei (people of Japanese descent) labourers in the industries of Japan. This trend started in 1990 with Nikkei from the Philippines and South America.[6] By 1992, some 150,000 had gone to Japan. Curiosity about these "Japanese" who are *gaijin* (foreigners) has led to academic and popular books about them. *Chūgoku shinbun* (Central Area News; *chūgoku* refers to southwestern Honshu), a newspaper published in Hiroshima city, commemorated its one hundredth anniversary by publishing *Imin* [Emigrants] in 1992. The newspaper sent reporters throughout the Western Hemisphere and Southeast Asia in search of immigrants from Hiroshima prefecture.

Even before the 1990 "U-turn," the limited scholarly interest in Japan regarding emigrants had produced work that was useful for studying Hiroshima immigrants in Canada. Four volumes on Hiroshima prefecture published in 1976, 1980, 1981, and 1991 involved some top academics in Hiroshima city. Ishikawa Tomonori, Irie Toraji, and Sasaki Toshiji also have written well-researched articles about the emigration of Japanese. Sasaki wrote a series of papers on the Kobe Emigration Company, which carried contract workers to Cumberland, BC. These are invaluable contributions to the early history of the Japanese in Canada. The studies of Tamura Norio on Suzuki Etsu, the Japanese-Canadian labour union (Camp and Mill Workers' Union) and his newspaper, *The Daily People,* were important sources of Japanese-Canadian labour history.[7] Tamura's Japanese books were good supplements to Rolf Knight and Maya Koizumi's *Man of Our Times.*[8]

To locate the actors in my study, living and dead, I started with the database that Audrey Kobayashi had created at McGill University with the financial support of the National Association of Japanese Canadians. In September 1992, at my request, she printed out the names of all Hiroshima immigrants to Canada that were in her listings. These lists consisted of the following: *Tairiku nippō*'s *Kanada dōhō hattenshi* [History of Japanese Progress in Canada], 1909; Nakayama Jinshirō, *Kanada dōhō hatten taikan* [Encyclopedia of Japanese in Canada], 1921; Canada, Department of Labour, *Immigration Records,* 1908-20, "Returning Immigrants from Japan"; Canada, Department of Labour, *Immigration Records,* 1908-20, "New Immigrants from Japan"; Japan, *Gaimusho* [Ministry of

Foreign Affairs] Records; and *Tairiku nippō*'s *Kanada zairyū hōjin jinmei* (Japanese Residents in Canada), 1941.

Unfortunately, a number of errors were made in the database when information was transcribed and when place names were translated as well as in personal names; even so, the lists were helpful. I also used a copy of the BC Japanese phone directory of June 1941, which I received from an interviewee, Reginald Hayami, in October 1992. Nakayama Jinshirō's list was much more useful in the original Japanese, which gave home village addresses and names of family members, than in the translated version. *Nikka jihōsha hōkō*'s *Kanada zairyū dōhō sōran* [Compatriots Resident in Canada], 1920, provided additional names and information on more prominent men. From these lists, I selected people whose names I recognized and contacted them. Suggestions from friends were helpful; others in the Japanese community were of great assistance in arranging some interviews. Hiroshima descendants sometimes approached me and asked that their families be included in my research. I did some interviews by telephone, but the majority were carried out in person. I conducted about eighty interviews in Montreal, Ottawa, Toronto, Hamilton, Lethbridge, Taber, Salmon Arm, Kamloops, Barriere, Vancouver, Surrey, Victoria, Tokyo, and Hiroshima, usually in the interviewee's home. These interviews of elderly Issei and Nisei, and also of Japanese who did not emigrate, were conducted over a period of six years, with occasional ones later.

The fact that I was a Hiroshima descendant helped open many doors for my research, which was based largely on the lives of individual Japanese, many of whom have passed on. The descendants, as well as many who had known the pioneers, appreciated the prefectural connection and agreed to lengthy and repeated interviews. During pauses in our conversations, names and events I recalled from my childhood awakened latent memories. Also, from my advance preparations, I was able to provide information to many Nisei on when their parents had immigrated and on the names and locations of their home villages. There was strong variation in the amount of knowledge they had of their roots, and many were grateful for what I could provide. Mutual feelings of sympathy and understanding often prevailed. As Peter Rose put it, "Acquaintance with something is very different from true understanding ... There is a wide chasm between KENNEN and VERSTEHEN. Outsiders might know a bit of another person's history and some cold facts, but it is much more difficult for them to feel the undertones."[9] My insider's knowledge was often necessary in analyzing the information received. Memory is not always infallible, and people tend to "rewrite" history in their own mind. Many prefer to put the best face on past events and to deny actions that in present times might be judged unacceptable.

Oral evidence was a challenge. Fortunately, a large network of independent witnesses to events developed over the course of the research, and this helped me evaluate oral testimony. Even so, I had to constantly remember my role of historian-as-detective.[10] Even when written materials existed, there could be different interpretations; for instance, regarding conflict within the community, different factions told different stories.

It was important for me to be mindful always of the need to respect the interviewees' privacy. Family secrets were sometimes revealed inadvertently; when they were, I used my discretion and judgment and did not write about them. A few times, comments that I thought were harmless and even humorous were objected to when I showed them my written materials. Some upsetting topics were avoided. There is always a danger of unintentionally or otherwise submitting to an interviewee's censorship, the motives of which may not always be unselfish. The interviewee and I were always aware of the profound effects of the racism we had experienced in our lives. Since painful memories inhibited answers to questions about racism, I have perhaps neglected or understated parts of the story. Being an insider can be a difficult as well as a privileged position.

Notes

N.B. For most Issei, both in the Notes and the Bibliography, the surname precedes the given name, following the Japanese convention. Western name order is used for Nisei and/or authors who have published primarily in English.

Prologue

1 See Yuji Ichioka, *The Issei: The World of the First Generation Japanese Immigrants, 1885-1924* (New York: Free Press, 1988), 67-69.

2 According to the Division of Immigration, Department of Manpower and Immigration, the number of Japanese who entered Canada suddenly rose from 354 in 1904-05, to 1,922 in 1905-06, to 2,042 in 1906-07, to 7,601 in 1907-08. Ken Adachi, *The Enemy That Never Was: A History of the Japanese Canadians* (Toronto: McClelland and Stewart, 1976), 412.

3 Roberto Perin, "Themes in Immigration History," in *Encyclopedia of Canada's Peoples*, ed. Paul Robert Magocsi (Toronto: University of Toronto Press, 1999), 1259.

4 Richard K. Beardsley, John W. Hall, and Robert E. Ward, *Village Japan* (Chicago: University of Chicago Press, 1969 [1959]), 14-15.

5 Mikiso Hane, *Modern Japan: A Historical Survey* (Boulder: Westview Press, 1986), 24, 50-52.

6 Alan Takeo Moriyama, *Imingaisha: Japanese Emigration Companies and Hawaii, 1894-1908* (Honolulu: University of Hawaii Press, 1985), xviii, 10, 158-59.

7 Audrey Kobayashi, "Emigration from Kaideima, Japan, 1885-1950: An Analysis of Community and Landscape Change," PhD diss., University of California, Los Angeles, 1983.

8 Ibid., 219.

9 Nitta Jiro, *Mikkōsen, Suianmaru* [Stowaway Ship, *Suianmaru*] (Tokyo: Kōdansha, 1982). See also David Sulz, "Japanese 'Entrepreneur' on the Fraser River: Oikawa Jinsaburo and the Illegal Immigration of the *Suianmaru*," MA thesis, University of Victoria, Department of History, 2003.

10 Nishihama Hisakazu, "Kanadaimin no chichi, Kuno Gihei" [The Father of Canadian Emigrants, Kuno Gihei], *Ijū kenkyū* [Migration Research] 30, 3 (1993): 170-84. See also Tsurumi Kazuko, *Sutebusuton monogatari* [Tales of Steveston] (Tokyo: Chūōkōronsha, 1962), 147-79; and Daphne Marlatt, *Steveston Recollected: A Japanese Canadian History* (Victoria: Aural History, Provincial Archives of British Columbia, 1975).

11 Nakayama Jinshirō, *Kanada dōhō hatten taikan* [Encyclopedia of Japanese in Canada] (Tokyo, 1921), 133-57.

12 Hiroshimaken, *Hiroshima kenshi, kindai I* [The History of Hiroshima Prefecture, Modern Period I] (Hiroshima: Toppan insatsukabushikigaisha, 1980), 1025.

13 Kodama Masaaki, *Nihon iminshi kenkyū josetsu* [Introduction to the Study of the History of Japanese Emigration] (Hiroshima: Keisuisho, 1992), 110-11.

14 Yoshida Tadao, *Kanada no imin no kiseki* [The Situation of Immigrants in Canada] (Tokyo: Chūō shinsatsukabushikigaisha, 1993), 179.

15 Sumida Rigenda, "The Japanese in British Columbia," MA thesis, University of British Columbia, 1935, 55. Early Hiroshima immigrants did fish, according to my research, but in all cases just long enough to earn sufficient money for other ventures such as boatbuilding, farming, or starting a business. It is interesting that in the San Pedro fishing community near Los Angeles, there were no Hiroshima fishers. John Modell, *The Economics and Politics of Racial Accommodation: The Japanese of Los Angeles, 1900-1942* (Chicago: University of Illinois Press, 1977), 21.

16 Michiko Midge Ayukawa, "The Memoirs of Imada Ito: A Japanese Pioneer Woman," BA essay, University of Victoria, 1988, 17-19, 61-64.

17 My father usually worked as a carpenter, building boats as well as building and renovating houses. When such jobs were not available, he laboured in sawmills or as a gardener and even set pins in a bowling alley. His only recreation was watching the games of the Asahi baseball team and its junior teams (see Chapter 7).

18 Michiko Midge Ayukawa, "Japanese Pioneer Women: Fighting Racism and Rearing the Next Generation," in *Sisters or Strangers: Immigrant, Ethnic, and Racialized Women in Canadian History,* ed. Marlene Epp, Franca Iacovetta, and Frances Swyripa, (Toronto: University of Toronto Press, 2004), 233-47.

Chapter 1: The Hiroshima Homeland

1 Richard K. Beardsley, John W. Hall, and Robert E. Ward, *Village Japan* (Chicago: University of Chicago Press, 1969 [1959]), 14.

2 Mikiso Hane, *Modern Japan: A Historical Survey* (Boulder: Westview Press, 1986), 23. Hideyoshi, who preceded Ieyasu in trying to unify the land, had ordered men to choose between being warriors or peasants.

3 Satō Tsuneo, "Tokugawa Villages and Agriculture," in *Tokugawa Japan: The Social and Economic Antecedents of Modern Japan,* ed. Nakane Chie and Ōishi Shinzaburō, trans. Conrad Totman (Tokyo: University of Tokyo Press, 1990), 38.

4 Before the 1600 battle, both Bingo and Aki had been part of the vast domain of the Mōri clan. The "carp castle" built by Mōri Terumoto became Asano's. A replica stands today on its former site in what is now the city of Hiroshima. The Mōri clan had been one of the leading contenders for national hegemony and had extended its domain from the southwestern end of Honshu as far east as Bitchu (the present-day area around Okayama city). Since they had opposed him, Ieyasu seized Bingo and Aki and confined Mōri to what is now Yamaguchi prefecture. Beardsley, Hall, and Ward, *Village Japan,* 44-46. See also Nakane and Ōishi, eds., *Tokugawa Japan,* 22.

5 E. Papinot, *Historical and Geographical Dictionary of Japan* (Rutland, VT: Charles E. Tuttle, 1996 [1910]), 830. *Kokudaka* was a system of land assessment based on the estimated yield of rice. A *koku* – "a measure of volume approximately 5.2 bushels traditionally, a standard allowance of rice for one person for one year." See also Beardsley, Hall, and Ward, *Village Japan*, 487.

6 Hiroshimaken, *Hiroshima kenshi, kindai I* [The History of Hiroshima Prefecture, Modern Period I] (Hiroshima: Toppan insatsukabushikigaisha, 1980), 775.

7 Thomas C. Smith, *The Agrarian Origins of Modern Japan* (Stanford: Stanford University Press, 1959), 68-69, 72.
8 Ibid., 5, 144-45, 179.
9 Kodama Masaaki reminds us that *dekasegi* (going out to work) flourished in late Edo and early Meiji. For example, in Ansei 5 (the year 1859), nineteen of the twenty-nine employees (that is, 65.5 percent) at a Bitchu plant that produced *bengara* (red-ochre rouge) were from Aki. According to the 1871 records of Mitsugi county in Bingo, seventy-one of the residents were working in other areas such as Shikoku, Fukuyama, and Tsuyama. Kodama Masaaki, *Nihon iminshi kenkyū josetsu* [Introduction to the Study of the History of Japanese Emigration] (Hiroshima: Keisuisho, 1992), 56.
10 E. Patricia Tsurumi, *Factory Girls: Women in the Thread Mills of Meiji Japan* (Princeton: Princeton University Press, 1990), 19, 15.
11 Peter Duus, *The Rise of Modern Japan* (Boston: Houghton Mifflin, 1976), 60-62.
12 Marius B. Jansen, *Sakamoto Ryōma and the Meiji Restoration* (Princeton: Princeton University Press, 1961), 312-33; Conrad Totman, *The Collapse of the Tokugawa Bakufu, 1862-1868* (Honolulu: University of Hawaii Press, 1980), 238.
13 Baroness Ishimoto Shidzue, *Facing Two Ways: The Story of My Life* (1st ed., 1935; repr., Stanford: Stanford University Press, 1984), 362. A number of books have been written about these "experts." Two of them are Edward R. Beauchamp, *An American Teacher in Early Meiji Japan* (Honolulu: University of Hawaii Press, 1976); and Richard Rubinger, ed., *An American Scientist in Early Meiji Japan* (Honolulu: University of Hawaii Press, 1989).
14 Fukutake Tadashi reports that it was the land tax that "provided the basis for a capitalist state." Fukutake Tadashi, *Japanese Rural Society,* trans. R.P. Dore (Ithaca: Cornell University Press, 1967), 5. In the early 1870s, deeds were issued to the farmers who had worked the land for generations. They were also granted the right to buy and sell land. Hane, *Modern Japan*, 93.
15 Hiroshimaken, *Hiroshima kenshi, kindai I,* 338, 339.
16 Hane, *Modern Japan*, 93-94, 99.
17 The effect on farmers was expressed very vividly by Stephen Vlastos. "All farmers suffered to some extent as a consequence of the Matsukata deflation. However, small-scale producers of cash crops, and especially farmers who customarily relied on short-term debt, were hit the hardest. Caught between the government and the local money-lender, saddled with drastically reduced income but high fixed costs, such farmers struggled to stave off bankruptcy. Even moderately well-to-do farmers caught in the same predicament often had to mortgage their land ... Bankruptcies soared." Stephen Vlastos, "Opposition Movements in Early Meiji, 1868-1885," in *The Emergence of Meiji Japan,* ed. Marius B. Jansen (Cambridge: Cambridge University Press, 1995), 256.
18 Hane, *Modern Japan*, 99-100.
19 Kodama, *Nihon iminshi,* 14; Hiroshimaken, *Hiroshima kenshi, kindai I,* 340, 343.
20 Ishikawa Tomonori, "Setonai chiiki kara no (shutsu) imin" [Emigrants from the Inland Sea Area], *Shigaku kenkyū* [History Research] 126 (1975): 68.
21 Hiroshimaken, *Hiroshima kenshi, kindai I,* 359, 418-29.
22 Kodama, *Nihon iminshi*, 67.
23 *Bingo-gasuri* is described as "a variety of pre-dyed cotton cloth with patterns predetermined by the spacing sequences given the weft thread before weaving. Warf (or lengthwise threads) are also dyed and expertise of the weaver brings

them to perfect matches creating two-dimensional designs." Amaury Saint-Gilles, *Mingei: Japan's Enduring Folk Arts* (Union City: Heian International, 1983), 73. Amy Sylvester Katoh notes that "*kasuri* was widely used in Japan for farm clothing, carrying cloths and bedding." Amy Sylvester Katoh, *Blue and White Japan* (Boston: Tuttle Publishing, 2002), 105.

24 Hiroshimaken, *Hiroshima kenshi, kindai I,* 840-43. It is valued as a folk art.

25 My mother once mentioned that after she was betrothed to my father, she occasionally went by *riksha* to her future in-laws' home and helped weave *tatami-omote* (top covering of the *tatami*) from *igusa.*

26 Hiroshimaken, *Hiroshima kenshi, kindai I,* 462-88. The port at Ujina was planned in 1878 as a means to employ *shizoku,* but it was also thought necessary for promoting foreign trade. Although the planners estimated that it would take thirty months, it required five years and three months, and cost over 300,000 yen – more than three times the estimate. However, it proved to be very useful to the military during the Russo-Japanese War of 1904 and 1905, and during the Pacific War it had the dubious distinction of being the port from which troops sailed to Southeast Asia.

27 There are ten *rin* in one *sen* and one hundred *sen* in one yen. One yen was equivalent to 0.78 American dollars in 1891, according to Kodama, *Nihon iminshi,* 226.

28 *Sakamachi kaigai katsuyaku shi* [History of the Overseas Activities of Sakamachi] (Hiroshima: Nakamoto sōgō insatsukabushikigaisha, 1985), 29.

29 In 1882, Aki county provided the third-highest number of Hokkaido settlers in the country (330 people); in 1883, the highest (492); and in 1884, the second highest (635). Kodama, *Nihon iminshi,* 15. Ichihashi Yamato also noted that "between 1869 and 1884 some 105,593 persons left their homes and emigrated to that northern island." Ichihashi Yamato, *Japanese in the United States* (Stanford: Stanford University Press, 1932), 6.

30 Yuji Ichioka notes that Robert Irwin was a "special agent of the Immigration Bureau of Hawaii and Hawaii consul in Yokohama." Yuji Ichioka, *The Issei: The World of the First Generation Japanese Immigrants, 1885-1924* (New York: Free Press, 1988), 41. See also Kodama, *Nihon iminshi,* 11; and Yukiko Irwin and Hilary Conroy, "R.W. Irwin and Systematic Immigration to Hawaii," in *East across the Pacific,* ed. Hilary Conroy and T. Scott Miyakawa (Santa Barbara, CA: Clio Press, 1972), 40-55.

31 Ichioka, *Issei,* 41. The "Japanese officials concerned above all with national dignity, [were] willing to have an outlet for Japan's economically depressed agricultural population but only if it would not sully the national image."

32 Ishikawa, "Setonai," 60, 62.

33 Ichioka, *Issei,* 44; Alan Takeo Moriyama, *Imingaisha: Japanese Emigration Companies and Hawaii, 1894-1908* (Honolulu: University of Hawaii Press, 1985), 13.

34 Ishikawa Tomonori, "Hiroshimawangan Jigozenson keiyakuimin no shakaichirigakuteki kōsatsu" [A Socio-Geographic Study of Contract Emigrants of Jigozen Village, Hiroshima Bay], *Jinbun chiri* [Social Geography] 19, 1 (February 1967): 75-91. According to Ishikawa, living facilities were provided in Hawaii and the only monthly expenses were for food – approximately $6.00 (7.06 yen) for men and $4.00 (4.70 yen) for women.

35 Jigozen, the village discussed by Ishikawa, has been called Amerika-mura (America village) by the local people and is well known as a village from which a large number went overseas. I visited there in April 1993. My guide, a reporter from

Chūgoku shinbun whose special interest was emigration from Hiroshima, showed me the temple that had been rebuilt with donations from overseas villagers after it had been devastated by a storm. He told me that since the turn of the century, many the homes in the area had been built with Western-style rooms and kitchens, and that when villagers met on the street, they greeted one another with "Aloha" rather than "Konnichiwa."

36 Ishikawa, "Setonai chiiki kara no (shutsu) imin" [Emigrants from the Inland Sea Area], *Shigaku kenkyū* [History Research] 126 (1975): 65.

37 Smith, *Agrarian Origins,* 213, also notes that Hiroshima people had gone to work in the Kyushu mines. Kodama, *Nihon iminshi,* 56.

38 Tsurumi, *Factory Girls,* 59-67.

39 Ichioka, *Issei,* 46. "By December 1891, Hiroshima emigrants had remitted a total of $732,000 from Hawaii. Of this amount, $220,500 went into savings, $172,000 went towards the purchase of real property and household goods, $270,000 was earmarked for repayment of debts, and $67,500 went for miscellaneous expenses."

40 Hiroshimaken, *Hiroshima kenshi kindai gendai shiryōhen III* [The History of Hiroshima Prefecture, Modern Period, Present-Day Documents III] (Hiroshima: Hiroshimaken, 1976), 103-4, and idem, *Hiroshima kenshi, kindai I,* 1001.

41 Moriyama, *Imingaisha,* 29, 48.

42 Sasaki Toshiji, "Kanada-Yunion tankō to Kobe imingaisha" [Canada-Union Colliery and the Kobe Emigration Company], *Han* [Pan] 6 (September 1987): 177.

Chapter 2: The First Ones

1 Sasaki Toshiji, "Kanada-Yunion tankō to Kobe imingaisha" [Canada-Union Colliery and the Kobe Emigration Company], *Han* [Pan], 6 (September 1987): 174.

2 Ken Adachi, *The Enemy That Never Was: A History of the Japanese Canadians* (Toronto: McClelland and Stewart, 1976), 412.

3 Nakayama Jinshirō, *Kanada dōhō hatten taikan* [Encyclopedia of Japanese in Canada] (Tokyo, 1921), 337-38.

4 Audrey Kobayashi, *Memories of Our Past: A Brief Walking Tour of Powell Street* (Vancouver: NRC Publishing, 1992), 12.

5 Roy Ito, *Stories of My People: A Japanese Canadian Journal* (Hamilton: Promark Printing, 1994), 18. Ito translates the term as "the helping hand company," but I prefer "saviour company" because of the honorific "o."

6 Alan Morley, *Vancouver: From Milltown to Metropolis* (Vancouver: Mitchell Press, 1961), 32. "Kanaka" refers to Hawaiian pioneers in British Columbia. See Tom Koppel, *Kanaka: The Untold Story of Hawaiian Pioneers in British Columbia and the Pacific Northwest* (Vancouver: Whitecap Books, 1995), 92-93.

7 Allen Seager, "Introduction," in Working Lives Collective, *Working Lives: Vancouver 1886-1986* (Vancouver: New Star Books, 1985), 9.

8 Morley, *Vancouver,* 78.

9 Kobayashi, *Memories,* 12.

10 "Working for a cannery" was a phrase that included fishing.

11 Gillian Creese, "Class, Ethnicity, and Conflict: The Case of Chinese and Japanese Immigrants, 1880-1923," in *Workers, Capital, and the State in British Columbia,* ed. Rennie Warburton and David Coburn (Vancouver: UBC Press, 1988), 66.

12 Nakayama, *Kanada dōhō,* 337-38. Ueda's name does not appear in the "home" listing in Nakayama nor in any of the immigration records. In the *Tairiku, 1909*

list, however, Ueda Minoru appears as the owner of a restaurant at 116 Westminster in Vancouver, with four employees, a wife, and two children. (Westminster later became Main.)

13 Communication by mail, 11 February 1993. It appears that Raye, the granddaughter of Matoba Toyokichi, may have had wrong information. According to death records (BC Archives, microfilm reels B 13101 and B 13103), the elder son of Matoba Toyokichi, Kaku, was born on 1895 and died on 12 September 1915 in Vancouver of pulmonary tuberculosis. He had been a clerk. Toyokichi, the father, a sawmill hand, died on 4 July 1918, about two months after he was injured. Cause of death was listed as an intracranial hemorrhage resulting from the injury.

14 Information about the son's birth was received from George Doi in an interview in Surrey, 27 September 1992.

15 Since the only survivor of the family, the second son, rarely spoke to his children about his early days or his family, there is little further information available – not unusual among many Japanese immigrants. According to a July 1996 letter from the granddaughter, Raye Shin, her father "was reunited with his mother on his first trip to Japan as a member of the Seattle Baseball Club. After that, he was in constant touch with her until her death" (see Chapter 7).

16 Adachi, *The Enemy,* 26; Toyo Takata, *Nikkei Legacy* (Toronto: NC Press, 1983), 82; Sumida Rigenda, "The Japanese in British Columbia," MA thesis, University of British Columbia, 1935; D.E. Isenor, W.N. McInnis, E. G. Stephens, and D.E. Watson, *Land of Plenty: A History of the Comox District* (Campbell River: Ptarmigan Press, 1987), 32.

17 Sasaki, "Kanada-Yunion," 164-88; idem, "Yunion tankō: dainiji keiyaku imin" [Union Colliery: Number Two Contract Emigrants], *Han* [Pan] 7 (December 1987): 170-98; idem, "Meiji imingaisha ni yoru jiyūtokōsha no okuridashi" [Meiji Emigration Company and the Sending of Independent Voyagers], *Han* [Pan] 8 (April 1988): 156-81.

18 Lynne Bowen, *Three Dollar Dreams* (Lantzville: Oolichan Books, 1987), 174, 292. Although Bowen refers to the Union Pacific Railway, it was the Union Pacific Railroad.

19 Alan Grove and Ross Lambertson, "Pawns of the Powerful: The Politics of Litigation in the Union Colliery Case," *BC Studies* 103 (Autumn 1994): 11.

20 Lynne Bowen, *Boss Whistle: The Coal Miners of Vancouver Island Remember* (Lantzville: Oolichan Books, 1982), 45.

21 Bowen, *Three Dollar Dreams,* 251.

22 Grove and Lambertson, "Pawns of the Powerful," 18, 21.

23 Sasaki, "Kanada-Yunion," 182.

24 Grove and Lambertson, "Pawns of the Powerful," 12.

25 Bowen, *Three Dollar Dreams,* 307. A Chinese head tax of fifty dollars was levied in 1885; it was raised to one hundred dollars in 1900 and to five hundred dollars in 1904.

26 Sasaki, "Kanada-Yunion," 176-80.

27 Alan Takeo Moriyama, *Imingaisha*: *Japanese Emigration Companies and Hawaii, 1894-1908* (Honolulu: University of Hawaii Press, 1985), 34.

28 Ibid., 35.

29 Sasaki, "Kanada-Yunion," 186.

30 *Nanaimo Free Press*, 19 December 1891.
31 Ibid., 9 January 1892.
32 *San Francisco Examiner*, 13 January 1892.
33 Sasaki, "Yunion tankō," 171.
34 Bowen, *Three Dollar Dreams*, 243.
35 Stephen Vlastos, *Peasant Protests and Uprisings in Tokugawa Japan* (Berkeley and Los Angeles: University of California Press, 1986), 171.
36 Sasaki, "Yunion tankō," 174.
37 Sasaki is extremely critical but he does not appear to be aware that the Dunsmuirs had provided the passage money. D.E. Isenor and colleagues state that "Canadian Collieries' notes indicate that passage money of Japanese miners was advanced by Dunsmuir, probably in 1890 or 1891." D.E. Isenor, E.G. Stephens, and D.E. Watson, *One Hundred Spirited Years: A History of Cumberland, 1888-1988* (Campbell River: Ptarmigan Press, 1988), 32. If this is correct, the actions of the Kobe Emigration Company were even more unprincipled and avaricious than Sasaki has argued.
38 Sasaki, "Yunion tankō," 193.
39 Ibid., 194.
40 Sasaki, "Meiji imingaisha," 157.
41 Yuji Ichioka, *The Issei: The World of the First Generation Japanese Americans, 1885-1924* (New York: Free Press, 1988), 53.
42 Sasaki, "Meiji imingaisha," 164, 158, 169. Moriyama, *Imingaisha,* 153, and Ichioka, *Issei*, 47, also discuss the activities of emigration companies and their misrepresentations.
43 Sasaki, "Meiji imingaisha," 169.
44 It has been possible to learn about him and his descendants. Doi's nephew, Manabu Doi, has been a long-time friend of mine, and a grandson, George Doi – the son of Umatarō's eldest son, Kenichi, now retired – has been delving into his family's past. Moreover, the descendants of the Doi brothers who immigrated to North America had a family reunion in August 1989 in Surrey. The shared stories have added considerably to the Doi family memoirs. They were shared generously with me.
45 The suffix "ichi" often appears in Japanese place names. It means "market" and was thus a place where farmers went regularly to buy and sell produce and other goods.
46 Records of the Ministry of Foreign Affairs confirm this information received from George.
47 The third son, Chiyojirō, born in 1879, went to the United States; another son, Yūji (1887-1964), went to Mexico and later the United States. The story of Yūji was related and taped by his son. While still a teenager, Yūji eloped to Mexico with his wife, who had been betrothed to another. They made a difficult escape from their work camp, walking at night and sleeping during the day, and depending on the generosity of the Mexicans during their flight into Texas (1911-?). A copy of the tape is in my possession.
48 Manabu did not know when this had happened.
49 He does not appear on Sasaki's list. Nakayama Jinshirō states that he was among the first contract miners and that he arrived in August 1892. Nakayama, *Kanada dōhō hatten taikan,* 332.
50 Sasaki, "Kanada-Yunion," 185.

51 Nakayama, *Kanada dōhō,* 366.

52 Roy Ito refers to Nakanishi in *Stories of My People:* "Tadaichi Nagao ... [sold] cigarettes and newspapers in Hotel Vancouver. A Cariboo mine owner staying at the hotel asked Nagao if he could hire Japanese workers for him. Nagao with Kanekichi Nakanishi recruited ten men. Nagao found the work too hard and returned to Vancouver. Nakanishi prospered as the 'boss' of the mine workers." Ito, *Stories of My People,* 39. In October 2005 I met a grandson of Nakanishi Kanekichi, Nakanishi Teruo, who was in Vancouver seeking information about his family roots. He was the son of Nakanishi Hajime, who was born in Vancouver on 11 August 1908. On Hajime's birth certificate, the parents' home address was given as 118 Main Street, Vancouver. The Nakanishis had another son, Ken, who later played baseball on the Asahi baseball team (see Chapter 7). Both Hajime and Ken went to Japan with their mother in the 1930s. The father stayed behind and died in 1954. Throughout the years, he kept in touch with the Kaminishi family.

53 *Nikka jihōsha hōkō, Kanada zairyū dōhō sōran* [General Survey of Compatriots Resident in Canada] (Tokyo, 1920; repr., Tokyo: Nihon tōsho senta, 1993), 328.

54 Interviews with Hiroshi Okuda in Montreal, by phone in June 1991 and again, in person, October 1992. Interview with Harold Hirose of Winnipeg in Toronto, October 1993.

55 The first mine in which the Japanese worked was Number One Mine. The men and their families lived in what was called Number One Jap Town. Number Five was a mine that opened in 1895, and the adjacent living quarters were referred to as Number Five Jap Town. Bowen, *Boss Whistle,* 77-79.

56 Isenor, Stephens, and Watson, *One Hundred Spirited Years,* 32; Cheryl Maeva Thomas, "The Japanese Communities of Cumberland, British Columbia, 1885-1942: Portrait of a Past," MA thesis, University of Victoria, 1992.

57 Bowen, *Boss Whistle,* 68-78.

58 Nakayama, *Kanada dōhō; Nikka, Kanada zairyū.*

59 Nakayama, *Kanada dōhō,* 328.

60 Ibid., 321-22.

Chapter 3: Sojourning and Beyond

1 Allen Seager, "Introduction," in Working Lives Collective, *Working Lives: Vancouver 1886-1986* (Vancouver: New Star Books, 1985), 9.

2 *British Columbia Magazine* (April 1911): 311-12.

3 Robert McDonald, "Working," in Working Lives Collective, *Working Lives,* 26, 35.

4 Yuji Ichioka, *The Issei: The World of the First Generation Japanese Immigrants, 1885-1924* (New York: Free Press, 1988), 57.

5 Royal Commission on Chinese and Japanese Immigration, *Report* (Ottawa: King's Printer, 1902; repr., New York: Arno Press, 1978), 382.

6 Ibid., 103.

7 Ibid., 393-94.

8 Audrey Kobayashi and Peter Jackson, "Japanese Canadians and the Racialization of Labour in the British Columbia Sawmill Industry," *BC Studies* 103 (Autumn 1994): 42-43.

9 Uyeno died in 1994 at the age of 104. Until his final few years he was very alert, so his recollections are quite reliable. This letter was written to a later immigrant, Kazuta Kiyoso (1899-2000). A copy is in my possession.

10 Ichioka, *Issei,* 57.

11 Ken Adachi, *The Enemy That Never Was: A History of the Japanese Canadians* (Toronto: McClelland and Stewart, 1976), 28.

12 In *Japanese Education,* K. Yoshida and T. Kaigō state: "From the eighteenth century on, common education in the form of Terakoya schools (writing school) flourished widely. In these Terakoya schools the teachers gathered the children of the neighbourhood and focussed their teaching upon the simple requirements of everyday life, reading, writing and arithmetic." K. Yoshida and T. Kaigō, *Japanese Education* (Tokyo: Japan Travel Bureau, 1937), 14-15. See also Tsurumi Kazuko, *Social Change and the Individual: Japan before and after Defeat in World War II* (Princeton: Princeton University Press, 1970), 215. For a thorough description of *terakoya* schools, see R.P. Dore, *Education in Tokugawa Japan* (Berkeley and Los Angeles: University of California Press, 1965), chaps. 8, 9.

13 *Nikka jihōsha hōkō, Kanada zairyū dōhō sōran* [General Survey of Compatriots Resident in Canada] (Tokyo, 1920; repr., Tokyo: Nihon tōsho senta, 1993), 239.

14 Mrs. Imada wrote in her memoirs that in November 1918, when she went to Stave Falls with her husband and family, Miyake was the "boss." Michiko Midge Ayukawa, "The Memoirs of Imada Ito: A Japanese Pioneer Woman," BA essay, University of Victoria, 1988, 64.

15 Telephone interview with Miori Mayeda, oldest daughter of Miyake Ryūkichi, in October 1992. The Canadian Japanese Association was established in 1897, mainly as a support group for Japanese immigrants. In 1934, it was reorganized and became the coordinating agency for all Japanese associations. Adachi, *The Enemy,* 123.

16 Sandra O. Uyeunten, "Struggle and Survival: The History of Japanese Immigrant Families in California, 1907-1945" PhD diss., University of California, San Diego, 1988, 36.

17 In Japan, for generations there had been little movement outside of immediate village areas except for *dekasegi* (as noted in Chapter 1). Thus, the regions had developed their own dialects. The standard Japanese that is universally employed in present-day Japan had not yet become widely used.

18 In my own family, because my parents did not have any siblings or relatives in Canada, another immigrant from Hiroshima, Uyeno Ritsuichi, was our surrogate relative, like an older brother to my father.

19 *Chūgoku shinbun, Imin* (Hiroshima: Chūgoku shinbunsha, 1992), 125.

20 Ibid.

21 I interviewed him in the fall of 1995. At the age of ninety-six he was hard of hearing and had just recently stopped driving. But he was still very alert and well. His recollections and written records of the Japanese-Canadian community of the 1920s and 1930s are invaluable. His earliest days in Vancouver were spent in the boarding houses.

22 *Nikka, Kanada zairyū,* 202.

23 There is a 1890 photograph of the Imperial Hotel, an imposing three-storey building on a corner lot. It was interesting to discover that it was formerly the Secord Hotel, a boarding house for single men and workers at Hastings Mill. See Working Lives Collective, *Working Lives,* 94.

24 The information Uyeno gave about the difficulty finding work at Hastings Mill unless one was from Shiga prefecture, mentioned earlier, related to a later period, 1907, when hordes of Japanese immigrants were arriving from Japan and

Hawaii. Presumably with so many men to choose from, preference was given to those from Shiga.

25 Ichioka, *Issei*, 164.

26 *Chūgoku shinbun, Imin*, 138.

27 *Vancouver Daily Province,* Woodward's store advertisement, February 1912.

28 Sasaki Toshiji, "Kanada-Yunion tankō to Kobe imingaisha." [Canada-Union Colliery and the Kobe Emigration Company] *Han* [Pan] 6 (September 1987): 186.

29 The term "average" was used by Sato's daughter, Rose, in an interview in Toronto in October 1993. The first contract immigrants to Hawaii from the area close to Hiroshima city owned less than 1.5 *chō* (1 *chō* = 2.45 acres). Fukuyama and Hiroshima cities had been castle towns; thus, they were heavily populated and the nearby landowners owned smaller plots. As a result, farmers in Fukuyama would be in a situation comparable to that of the first contract immigrants. In other words, the family probably owned at least five acres of land.

30 Tamio Wakayama, *Kikyō: Coming Home to Powell Street* (Madeira Park: Harbour Publishing, 1992), 15.

31 Nakayama Jinshirō, *Kanada dōhō hatten taikan* [Encyclopedia of Japanese in Canada] (Tokyo, 1921), 360. A photograph of his inn has been described incorrectly by Kobayashi as the Takahashi boarding house. Audrey Kobayashi, *Memories of Our Past: A Brief Walking Tour of Powell Street* (Vancouver: NRC Publishing, 1992), 16.

32 Ayukawa, "The Memoirs of Imada Ito," 25.

33 Imada Ito used the term *ryokan,* which is often translated as "hotel."

34 Ayukawa, "The Memoirs of Imada Ito," 25.

35 Rolf Knight and Maya Koizumi, *A Man of Our Times: The Life-History of a Japanese-Canadian Fisherman* (Vancouver: New Star Books, 1976), 20.

36 Vic Satzewich, "Racisms: The Reactions to Chinese Migrants in Canada at the Turn of the Century," *International Sociology* 4 (September 1989): 313.

37 Robin John Anderson, "Sharks and Red Herrings: Vancouver's Male Employment Agencies, 1898-1915," *BC Studies* 98 (Summer 1993): 83.

38 In the Nakayama listing of Hiroshima immigrants, Katō was listed as from Kawamoto village in Toyota county, with a wife, Naka, second, third, and fourth sons, Hideo, Kazuo, and Gunji, and a second daughter, Yoshiye. Since the eldest son and eldest daughter are not mentioned, presumably they were in Japan. Japanese Ministry of Foreign Affairs records show that Tōsaku immigrated in 1899 at thirty-three, and Naka in 1899 at twenty-one, but also again in 1905 at twenty-seven. It appears that she may have had two children, taken them to Japan, and returned without them in 1905.

39 Royal Commission on Chinese and Japanese Immigration, *Report* (Ottawa: King's Printer, 1902; repr., New York: Arno Press, 1999) , 370.

40 Ibid., 371.

41 Tamura Norio, *Suzuki Etsu: Nihon to Kanada o musunda jaanalisuto* [Suzuki Etsu: The Journalist Who Linked Japan and Canada] (Tokyo: Liburopōto Publishing, 1992), 195; Knight and Koizumi, *A Man of Our Times,* 38.

42 Ayukawa, "The Memoirs of Imada Ito," 29.

43 Ichioka, *Issei*, 78-80.

44 Knight and Koizumi, *A Man of Our Times,* 35.

45 Interview with Mitsuko Ito, daughter of Maehara Takuji, October 1993, in Hamilton; Gordon G. Nakayama, *Issei* (Toronto: NC Press, 1984), 89-101.

46 Ayukawa, "The Memoirs of Imada Ito," 42, 58-59.

47 Interview with Sunada's second son, Masato, Lethbridge, October 1993. The resolution in the BC legislature of 15 April 1902 pertaining to the use of Asian labour on Crown land – section 50 of the Crown Lands Act – is difficult to study because the legislation is so hard to unravel. This law seems to have been enforced on and off after 1903. See Adachi, *The Enemy,* 139-42; and Norman MacKenzie and Lionel H. Laing, eds., *Canada and the Law of Nations* (Toronto: Ryerson Press, 1938), 265-68.

48 One Issei, Kado Shizuo (1904-2000), from Kawauchi village in Asa county, said that his father, Kado Toramatsu, and his father's brother, Kado Junjirō, were two of the ten men brought to Canada by Nakanishi in 1900 to work in a North Vancouver rock quarry. Kado said that the rocks excavated there were used to build Vancouver's roads. Toramatsu returned to Japan after three years, but his son Junjirō stayed behind. Another son, Gunjirō, later also went to Canada, and Shizuo followed in 1927. Interview with Kado Shizuo, November 1992, in Vancouver.

49 Nakayama, *Kanada dōhō,* 316-17; *Nikka, Kanada zairyū,* 340.

50 When Uyeno Ritsuichi was in his senior years, his third son, "Mori," spent many hours with him trying to trace his early years in Canada. With the help of the dates on Vancouver poll tax receipts, Burnaby and Delta road tax receipts, British Columbia revenue tax receipts (Vancouver, Comox, Golden), and other items, "Mori" managed to gather much information from his father.

51 In 1913 there was considerable activity around the Atlin Lake gold mines.

52 Mining reports mention water flumes as long as 800 feet and 1,200 feet. John D. Galloway, Provincial Mineralogist, *Placer-Mining in British Columbia,* BC Geological Survey Bulletin 1933-1 (Victoria: British Columbia Department of Mines, King's Printer, 1933), 19, 20.

53 They celebrated their seventy-first wedding anniversary before she died in 1989 at the age of ninety-three. Uyeno died in April 1994 in his 105th year.

54 See *Nikka, Kanada zairyū,* 95. *Gaimusho* records and *Nikka* do not agree on his birth date or when he arrived in British Columbia, but the former may be more reliable. According to information received in March 2006 from Roy Kawamoto, Hoita married Kuwabara Misao (see Chapter 4) and joined the armed forces (143rd battalion) on 15 November 1915 in Kamloops. However, he was left behind because he was too short, and was sent to Victoria to join the BC Bantams. He was wounded twice, awarded two medals, and medically discharged on 31 May 1918.

55 Ministry of Foreign Affairs records note that he left Japan in 1900 when he was thirty-two.

56 Nakayama, *Kanada dōhō,* 312-14. Inquiries to people who had lived in Chemainus have not been fruitful.

57 According to Catherine Lang, Nakashima Giichi sold this "store and surrounding property" to Kawahara Gihei in 1924. Catherine Lang, *O-bon in Chimunesu* (Vancouver: Arsenal Pulp Press, 1996), 62. Lang also notes that Nakashima Giichi owned a number of "shacks along Oak Street and a 'ranch' past the railway station" (246).

58 Nishimoto Masami, the reporter to the *Chūgoku shinbun* who has been very helpful in my research, confirmed that at one time this park existed.

59 Sumida Rigenda, "The Japanese in British Columbia" (MA thesis, University of British Columbia, 1935), 77.

Chapter 4: The Women Come

1 Audrey Kobayashi, "For the Sake of the Children: Japanese/Canadian Workers/ Mothers," in *Women, Work, and Place,* ed. Audrey Kobayashi (Montreal and Kingston: McGill-Queen's University Press, 1994), 55.
2 Ibid., 53-55.
3 Charles H. Young and Helen R.Y. Reid, *The Japanese Canadians* (Toronto: University of Toronto Press, 1938), 10.
4 Yuji Ichioka, *The Issei: The World of the First Generation Japanese Immigrants, 1885-1924* (New York: Free Press, 1988), 51-58.
5 Patricia E. Roy, *A White Man's Province: British Columbia Politics and Chinese and Japanese Immigrants, 1858-1914* (Vancouver: UBC Press, 1989), 190.
6 Ibid., 90-95. See also Ken Adachi, *The Enemy That Never Was: A History of the Japanese Canadians* (Toronto: McClelland and Stewart, 1976), 73-75.
7 See Roy, *A White Man's Province,* 207-13.
8 Adachi, *The Enemy,* 81.
9 Ibid.
10 In 1923 another change in the Gentlemen's Agreement reduced the number of male immigrants from 400 to 150. In 1928, a further modification included wives and children in the 150 immigrants, and the picture bride system of marriage was terminated (Adachi, *The Enemy*, 137-38).
11 Ichioka, *Issei,* 164. The first conscription law, in 1873, granted exemptions to "heads of families, sole sons and grandsons, adopted sons, and others" or to those who paid a fee of 270 yen in lieu of military service. But amendments in 1879, 1883, and 1889 made every male subject to conscription.
12 Ichioka, *Issei,* 165.
13 Makabe Tomoko, *Picture Brides: Japanese Women in Canada,* trans. Kathleen Chisato Merken (Toronto: University of Toronto Press, 1995), 131.
14 Inouye Jūkichi, *Home Life in Tokyo* (London: KPI, 1985 [1910]), 118.
15 Ibid., 112. My mother often spoke with pride of how her hairdresser used to praise her abundant tresses.
16 When Ishikawa Yasu was dreaming of becoming a doctor, in the early 1910s, the Tokyo Women's Medical School had been open for about ten years. In 1908 its students were allowed to write medical examinations, and in 1912 it became the Tokyo Women's School of Medicine (Tokyo joshi igaku semmon gakkō). Until then it had been extremely difficult for women to obtain proper medical training, since women were excluded from the male-only higher schools. Shibukawa Hisako, *Kyōiku: kindai nihon josei shi–1* [Education: History of Women in Modern Japan–1] (Tokyo: Kashima kenkyūjo shuppansha, 1970), 194-214.
17 Makabe, *Picture Brides*, 108.
18 Ibid., 107. She did not mention Canadian law, but stated only that it took that long to remove her name from her husband's family register.
19 Interview in Hamilton with Masao Kuwabara, the eldest son of Bunpei and Masano, summer 1991. For more information on Hoita, see Chapter 3.
20 There is a photograph of the Immigration Building in an article by Chuen-yan David Lai. It was built in 1908 and used as a "detention hospital" for Asian

immigrants until 1958. It was demolished in 1977. Chuen-yan David Lai, "A 'Prison' for Chinese Immigrants," *Asianadian: An Asian Canadian Magazine* 2, 4 (Spring 1980): 16-19.

21 Shigeno's husband, Kuwabara Bunpei, from Miiri village, Asa county, had immigrated in 1898, disappointed and angry when he was not accepted into law school because he had a cleft palate. In Victoria, he studied English at night school while working first on a potato farm on the Saanich Peninsula, and later in a Japanese general store owned by Nagano Manzo – purportedly the first Japanese immigrant in Canada. Later, when Bunpei worked for the Department of Immigration, to supplement his income he fished for rock cod in the waters near Albert Head and Oak Bay, selling his catch to Chinese restaurants. He moored his fifteen-foot boat with a four-horsepower engine in a boathouse at the foot of Fisgard Street. His son, Masao, born in 1910, recalled helping him after school. Interview in Hamilton with Bunpei and Masano's eldest son, Masao, summer 1991.

22 Sharon Nolte noted that "throughout the twentieth century fewer than one percent of Japanese women remained single for life." Sharon H. Nolte, "Women's Rights and Society's Needs: Japan's 1931 Suffrage Bill," *Comparative Studies in Society and History* 28, 4 (1986): 695.

23 The revised Japanese Ministry of Education Normal School Ordinance of 1897 and an amendment to it in 1907 specified that a male student could enter a normal school after graduation from middle school if he was recommended by a local official. There were different rules for women. Only 20 to 25 percent of normal school applicants were accepted, however. Since the successful entrant received room and board, he was obligated to teach where assigned for seven years if he received a stipend while a student, or three years if he had not. A graduate from eight years of higher elementary school could also enter normal school, but the number of years of study for such students was longer. Kudō had graduated from middle school, and if he had also attended normal school, he must have had to put in his years of obligatory service before immigrating. Kudō's daughter Kathleen wondered whether he had been a qualified teacher. See Baron Dairoku Kikuchi, *Japanese Education* (London: John Murray, 1908), 282-96; and Aso Makoto and Amano Ikuo, *Education and Japan's Modernization* (Tokyo: Japan Times, 1983), 19.

24 Interviews with Roland Kudo, Owen Sound, Ontario, August 1992; Jack Kudo, Vancouver, August 1992; Alice Kudo, Montreal, October 1992; and Kathleen Kudo Merken, Montreal, October 1992.

25 Anne Walthall, "Devoted Wives/Unruly Women: Invisible Presence in the History of Japanese Social Protest," *Signs* 20, 1 (Autumn 1994): 130.

26 Interviewed in the 1990s by Catherine Lang for her book on the Japanese community in Chemainus, *O-bon in Chimunesu* (Vancouver: Arsenal Pulp Press, 1996).

27 According to information received in February 2006 from Ray Iwaasa and Hanae Iwaasa-Robbs, children of Iwaasa Kōjun and Ito, Ito had only one son from her first marriage. She was forced to leave him with her husband's family when she was divorced.

28 David Iwaasa, "Canadian Japanese in Southern Alberta, 1905-1945," in *Two Monographs on Japanese Canadians,* ed. Roger Daniels (New York: Arno Press, 1978), 31.

29 Ibid., 32.

30 They had the *yagō* of Okaneya. In 1870 the Meiji government gave "permission" for commoners to assume family names, and in the 1871 house register law prescribed every household to be registered in the local government file. "In addition to the newly acquired and legally registered family name many households retained an old *yagō*, the legally unrecognized but often better known house name." Takie Sugiyama Lebra, *Japanese Women: Constraint and Fulfillment* (Honolulu: University of Hawaii Press, 1984), 21.

31 Mikiso Hane, *Peasants, Rebels, and Outcasts: The Underside of Modern Japan* (New York: Pantheon Books, 1982), 82. Sharon Nolte and Sally Ann Hastings have also noted that the "good wife and wise mother was rarely privileged to live in a situation where she could care for only her husband and her children." Sharon Nolte and Sally Ann Hastings, "The Meiji State's Policy toward Women, 1890-1910," in *Recreating Japanese Women, 1600-1945,* ed. Gail Lee Bernstein (Berkeley and Los Angeles: University of California Press, 1991), 174.

32 Furuki Yoshiko, *The White Plum: A Biography of Ume Tsuda* (New York: Weatherhill, 1991), 102-3.

33 Ibid., 102.

34 K. Yoshida and T. Kaigō, *Japanese Education* (Tokyo: Japan Travel Bureau, 1937), 55.

35 My mother attended *jogakkō* in Onomichi. She and another girl – only two from the entire village – walked two kilometres each way dressed in their long Japanese skirts (*hakama*) and Western shoes.

36 Government-sponsored normal schools for women produced mainly primary school teachers. The school founded by Umeko Tsuda in 1900 (now Tsuda College) offered a course for teachers in secondary schools. A private medical school for women was founded in 1900. The following year the Japan Women's University was opened by Jinzo Naruse. The education offered women at most colleges was equivalent to junior college. After 1913 a few women were admitted at Sendai, Fukuoka, and Sapporo, but admission to the most prestigious imperial universities – the ones in Tokyo and Kyoto – was still denied. Joy Paulson, "Evolution of the Feminine Ideal," in *Women in Changing Japan,* ed. Joy Lebra, Joy Paulson, and Elizabeth Powers (Stanford: University of Stanford Press, 1976), 16.

37 Michiko Midge Ayukawa, "The Memoirs of Imada Ito: A Japanese Pioneer Woman," BA essay, University of Victoria, 1988, 21-65. A copy of Mrs. Imada's memoirs (written in Japanese) is in Special Collections, University of British Columbia.

38 The previous three paragraphs are drawn from Ayukawa, "The Memoirs of Imada Ito," 24-33.

39 Iwaasa, "Canadian Japanese in Southern Alberta," 32.

40 Ayukawa, "The Memoirs of Imada Ito," 34.

41 Though she was at the advanced age of ninety-five when she told me, this recollection of her first years of motherhood still gave her shivers.

42 F. Henry Johnson, *A History of Public Education in British Columbia* (Vancouver: UBC Press, 1964), 56.

43 Imada Kaichi, Ito's husband, did not share her views about the value of education. Kaichi had promised his eldest son, Toshio, that he would allow him to go to high school if he did well in elementary school. Yet eight years later, he refused to allow him to do so even though "the principal wrote to us twice urging us to send him to high school." Ayukawa, "The Memoirs of Imada Ito," 73.

44 Yamaga Yasutarō, "My Footsteps in BC," UBC Special Collections, Yamaga Yasutarō Papers, Box 1.1.

45 Quoted in Makabe, *Picture Brides,* 137-38.

46 Telephone interview with Joe Horibe, husband of eldest daughter, Ruth, in Montreal, October 1993.

47 Inouye, *Home Life,* 24-26.

48 Kyōshi Shimizu, who lived in a *nagaya* in the Heaps district of Vancouver for close to ten years as a child, provided me with this interesting information in a letter, June 1995.

49 The family was "repatriated" in 1946 to Mrs. Shibata's family home in the Tenma district of Hiroshima city. Owing to family need and language difficulties, few Nisei who were repatriated in their teens were able to graduate from Japanese universities, yet all the Shibata sons did. Henry became a medical doctor. He attributes his success to his mother's strength of character. Interview in Montreal, October 1992.

50 Ayukawa, "The Memoirs of Imada Ito," 62.

51 Ibid., 61.

52 It has been a custom in Japan to adopt a husband for a daughter if there are no sons in the family. The husband takes the wife's family name and takes on the responsibilities of a household head, although most often his wife is "the boss."

53 Her second and third sons returned to Canada in 1929 and 1928, respectively. Her husband joined her in Japan in 1935. Interview with the second son, Niiya Yukio, in Montreal, October 1992. It appears that the marriage had not broken down; it was a practical move.

54 Telephone interview with her granddaughter, Chieko Endo, in Montreal, October 1993.

55 Interview with Tom Kaga in Taber, Alberta, October 1993.

56 The record at the BC Archives (microfilm reel B 13119) states that his death was reported at Queensborough. He was a sawmill labourer and died on 8 August 1921 at the age of fifty-three. Cause of death was "asphyxia by drowning."

57 Ichioka, *Issei,* 164.

58 Inouye, *Home Life,* 181.

59 The memoirs are now in the Japanese Canadian National Museum in Burnaby, Haruko Kobayakawa Collection.

60 Interview with Kitagawa Kotoma in Vancouver, September 1992.

61 UBC, Special Collections, Japanese Canadian Citizens Association collection, Tape 23:83.

62 In her 1982 interview, Kobayakawa Haruko did not give many details of why they left the farm. Her sister, Kitagawa (Yokota) Kotoma, was more candid in her interview with me.

63 The wartime writings of Kitagawa Kensuke have been published in Keibo Ōiwa, ed., *Stone Voices: Wartime Writings of Japanese Canadian Issei* (Montreal: Vehicule Press, 1991), 93-113.

64 That is, Jun became a *yōshi* husband.

65 When I interviewed Kumamoto Toshiko in August 1992, she was widowed and wore a pacemaker but was very alert and eager to share the story of her life. She said that she and her husband had been repeatedly asked by her family to return to Japan, but that they had chosen to remain in Canada. She said that she learned to drive a car when she was sixty-eight years old after her husband's Parkinson's

disease prevented him from driving. In the living room of her home were her paintings of her place of birth and her husband. In 1992 she still attended Japanese brush painting (*sumie*) classes every two weeks.

66 This is not unusual – small private hospitals are often established this way.

67 Letter from George Takeyasu, October 1993.

68 Letter from George Takeyasu, July 1995.

69 Walthall, "Devoted Wives," 131, 137.

70 Nakayama Jinshiro, *Kanada dōhō hatten taikan* [Encyclopedia of Japanese in Canada] (Tokyo, 1921), 562, 568.

Chapter 5: Farmers

1 Audrey Kobayashi, "For the Sake of the Children: Japanese/Canadian Workers/Mothers," in *Women, Work, and Place,* ed. Audrey Kobayashi, (Montreal and Kingston: McGill-Queen's University Press, 1994), 55.

2 Yamaga Yasutarō, *History of Haney Nokai,* trans. W.T. Hashizume (Toronto: 4Print Div. of Musson Copy Centres, 2006), 69. Michiko Midge Ayukawa, "Yasutarō Yamaga: Fraser Valley Berry Farmer, Community Leader, and Strategist," in *Nikkei in the Pacific Northwest: Japanese Americans and Japanese Canadians in the Twentieth Century,* ed. Louis Fiset and Gail Nomura (Seattle: University of Washington Press, 2005), 73.

3 Investigations have led me to believe that these leases were with private individuals and must have involved some sharecropping arrangement; see below, with regard to Okanagan Valley land.

4 Yamaga, *History of Haney Nokai,* 12.

5 Yamaga Yasutarō, "My Footsteps in BC," 1958, UBC Special Collections, Yamaga Yasutarō Papers, Boxes 1-7.

6 Eba, on the delta of a branch of the Ota River, adjacent to the Inland Sea, was about one *ri* (five kilometres) from the centre of Hiroshima city.

7 Communication from Miyoshi Tanaka, Nakashima Teizō's daughter, by letter, July 1996. She wrote that the Christina Lake Resort Hotel was near Kamloops. However, there is a Christina Lake in southern BC near Grand Forks, where some Japanese families "self-evacuated" after Pearl Harbor.

8 Nakashima's wife was mentioned earlier under the pseudonym Nakashima Tami.

9 Interview with Zennosuke's nephew, George Inouye, Barriere, BC, September 1992.

10 Information from Beverley Inouye, August 1996.

11 Nakayama Jinshirō, *Kanada dōhō hatten taikan* [Encyclopedia of Japanese in Canada] (Tokyo, 1921), 316-17, gives some information on Saeki. He came from Kameyama village, quite near Imuro. Saeki was also mentioned in Chapter 3.

12 See Roy Ito, *We Went to War* (Stittsville: Canada's Wings, 1984), 18-76.

13 Ibid., 47, 287. David Iwaasa referred to "the 13th Cavalry Battalion which later became the famous Princess Patricia's." David Iwaasa, "Canadian Japanese in Southern Alberta, 1905-1945," in *Two Monographs on Japanese Canadians,* ed. Roger Daniels (New York: Arno Press, 1978), 27. Private communication from daughter Beverley Inouye, August 1996.

14 Information from a copy of a personal letter written by Inouye Zennosuke to Mackenzie King, 4 October 1944, in which Inouye protested the sale of his eighty acres. Received from daughter Beverley Inouye. See Peter Neary, "Zennosuke Inouye's Land: A Canadian Veterans Affairs Dilemma," *Canadian Historical Review* 85, 3 (September 2004): 423-50.

15 The Gentlemen's Agreement of 1908 had allowed the immigration of a special category of immigrants: "emigrants brought in under contract by Japanese resident agricultural holders of Canada and especially required for the promotion of such agriculture; such contract to be accompanied by the certificate of Japanese consular authority in the district where the labourers are to be employed." Howard H. Sugimoto, *Japanese Immigration: The Vancouver Riots and Canadian Diplomacy* (New York: Arno Press, 1978), 263. An example of the detailed documentation required is in William T. Hashizume, *Japanese Community in Mission: A Brief History, 1904-1942* (Toronto: Mission Copy Centre, 2002), 101-5.

16 Bill Hoshizaki, ed., *The Vision Fulfilled: Historical Sketches of Central Okanagan Japanese Canadian Families and Community Organizations, 1894-1994* (Kelowna: Kelowna and District Association of Japanese Canadians, 1995). See also Donna Yoshitake Wuest, *Coldstream: The Ranch Where It All Began* (Madeira Park: Harbour Publishing, 2005), 31.

17 Ed Ouchi, ed. *'Til We See the Light of Hope* (Vernon: Vernon Japanese Senior Citizens' Association, n.d.), 13.

18 Hoshizaki, *Vision*, 295, citing an article in *Kanada Nipponjin nōgyō hattengō* [Japanese Farming in Canada] (Vancouver: Canada Daily News, 1930).

19 Iwaasa, "Canadian Japanese in Southern Alberta," 3.

20 Ibid., 10, 14, 17.

21 Information received from interview with grandson, David Iwaasa, April 1993, in Tokyo, when David was on the staff of the Canadian embassy there.

22 Interview in Ottawa, October 1992.

23 Andreas Schroeder, *Carved from Wood: Mission, B.C., 1861-1992* (Altona, MB: D.W. Friesen, 1991), 109.

24 Hoshizaki, *Vision*, 304.

25 Ibid., 269.

26 Gordon G. Nakayama, *Issei* (Toronto: NC Press, 1984), 99; Hoshizaki, *Vision*, 72. A fairly complete biography of Maehara can be assembled since his story has appeared in these two books. I also interviewed Maehara's third daughter, Mitsuko (Mrs. Roy Ito), in Hamilton, November 1992.

27 Nakayama, *Issei*, 100.

28 Hoshizaki, *Vision*, 18-20.

29 Except for the 1941 *Tairiku* (BC Japanese telephone directory) in which he is listed as Kobayashi Takeyoshi, Box 773, Kelowna, BC, my documentary sources contain no references to him at this time.

30 Hoshizaki, *Vision*, 19.

31 Ibid.

32 Ibid., 13. The Okanagan Japanese Mission opened in 1920 and later became the Okanagan United Church. Cobyace and the *konwakai* tried to help the Japanese Canadians relocate to the Okanagan Valley during the Pacific War. They failed in this effort because, except in special cases, coastal Japanese Canadians were prevented from moving there. See Patricia E. Roy, "A Tale of Two Cities: The Reception of Japanese Evacuees in Kelowna and Kaslo, B.C.," *BC Studies* 87 (Autumn 1990): 23-47.

33 Iwaasa, "Canadian Japanese in Southern Alberta," 21. Although the information about Iwaasa Ito's two daughters was received from David in an interview in Tokyo in 1983, it was later disputed by two of her children.

34 In his conversations with southern Alberta pioneers, Iwaasa was told that the *yobiyose* paid their own fare to Canada and that they guaranteed three years' labour to their sponsors, who paid them $150 the first year; by the third year, however, they often received $300, as well as room and board. Ibid., 34. It appears that contracts varied from region to region.

35 Hino sold his farm to Iwaasa Jirō, a nephew of Kōjun, before returning to look after his adopted parents. When one of Kōjun's daughters visited him in Japan in 1972, she observed that Hino appeared to have done well. Married in 1936, he had fathered six children and was living in an impressive house. Hino Takao died in 1992 at the age of ninety-one.

36 Ken Adachi, *The Enemy That Never Was: A History of the Japanese Canadians* (Toronto: McClelland and Stewart, 1976), 138.

37 Kado Shizuo (1904-2000), a Surrey farmer, related how difficult it had been for his wife, Tokuyo (1908-), to immigrate in 1934. Shizuo had to show that he had assets valued at $2,000. The immigration authorities came to his farm to check whether he had suitable housing and other facilities. Interview, November 1992. John D. Meehan has noted that "legation staff and gaimusho [Ministry of Foreign Affairs] officials worked closely together to enforce the 1928 arrangement granting only 110 visas in 1930-31." John D. Meehan, *The Dominion and the Rising Sun: Canada Encounters Japan, 1929-41* (Vancouver: UBC Press, 2004), 47.

38 In the early 1960s, Kubota sold his farm, went to Japan, and remarried. Although in 1966 he had a colostomy after an operation for cancer of the bowel, he carried on, riding his exercise bike seven miles and running on his indoor power walker every day. Tamako proved to be a devoted partner who brought some well-earned sunshine to his long and difficult life. She teaches Japanese brush painting and calligraphy while basking in the love and companionship of Iwaasa Kōjun's children. Kubota was interviewed by David Iwaasa in 1972; the tape from the interview is available in the Lethbridge National Association of Japanese Canadians Archives. My interview of Kubota Tamako was conducted in Lethbridge in October 1993.

39 Yamaga, "My Footsteps in BC," 20.

40 John Cherrington, *Mission on the Fraser* (Vancouver: Mitchell Press, 1974), 120.

41 Yamaga Yasutarō, *Hene'e nōkaishi* [History of the Haney Agricultural Association] (Tokyo: Kasai shuppan insatsusha, 1963), 22.

42 Ibid., 24. Slightly edited translation.

43 David N. Laband and Deborah Hendry Heinbuch, *Blue Laws: The History, Economics, and Politics of Sunday Closing Laws* (Lexington: D.C. Heath, 1987), 215-19.

44 Information received from Ross Lambertson.

45 Quoted in Laband and Heinbuch, *Blue Laws,* 216.

46 Cherrington, *Mission,* 121.

47 Adachi, *The Enemy*, 147-51; Yamaga, *Hene'e,* 50.

48 Yamaga, *Hene'e,* 51.

49 Yuji Ichioka, *Issei: The World of the First Generation Japanese Immigrants, 1885-1924* (New York: Free Press, 1988), 211, 214.

50 Ibid., 211. According to the 1910 census, some 420 Japanese had been issued naturalization papers in the United States. However, following the Act of Congress of 1906, which standardized naturalization requirements and procedures,

the US attorney general ordered the federal courts to cease issuing naturalization papers to Japanese applicants.

51 Ibid., 224-25. This amendment "prohibited aliens ineligible to citizenship to purchase or lease agricultural land, to hold stocks in agricultural landholding companies, to transfer or sell agricultural land to each other, and disqualified them from being appointed as guardians of minors who had title to such land."

52 Yamaga, *Hene'e,* 50, 51.

53 Japanese, along with other Asians, were denied the franchise. See Andrea Geiger-Adams, "Writing Racial Barriers into Law: Upholding B.C.'s Denial of the Vote to Its Japanese Canadian Citizens, *Homma v. Cunningham,* 1902," in Fiset and Nomura, *Nikkei in the Pacific Northwest,* 20-43.

54 The Canadian Japanese Association claimed to represent the entire Japanese immigrant population. It was essentially oriented toward Japan and was the administrative organ of the Japanese consulate. Adachi, *The Enemy,* 123-24.

55 Yamaga, *Hene'e,* 52.

56 Adachi, *The Enemy,* 150.

57 Yamaga, *Hene'e,* 52.

58 Natural Products Marketing Act, S.B.C. 1934, C36, 121-123. Section 3(1) of the act states: "For the purpose of this Act the Lieutenant-governor in council may constitute a Board to be known as the British Columbia Marketing Board, which shall consist of not more than three members, who shall be appointed by the Lieutenant-Governor in Council" – that is, by the provincial cabinet.

59 Yamaga Yasutarō, "The History of Japanese Farming in British Columbia, 1904-1941," March 1948, UBC Special collections, Yamaga Yasutarō Papers, Boxes 6-15.

60 Ouchi, *'Til We See,* 29, 30.

61 I found this very interesting, because when I was a student between 1936 and 1942 at Strathcona School, the large public school in Vancouver in which the children from the Powell Street area were enrolled, few Japanese parents attended any of the school's activities. So I recall. My parents certainly did not.

62 Aso Makoto and Amano Ikuo, *Education and Japan's Modernization* (Tokyo: Japan Times, 1983), 34-35.

63 Mikiso Hane, *Peasants, Rebels, and Outcasts: The Underside of Modern Japan* (New York: Pantheon Books, 1982), 51-52.

64 The lives of these farm children were of course not unique. This can be seen from a study made of the childhood experiences of anglophone families living in the Bulkley Valley in B.C. in the interwar years. These children, too, were at times kept out of school when their labour was required. Neil Sutherland, "'I Can't Recall When I Didn't Help': The Working Lives of Pioneering Children in Twentieth Century British Columbia," *Social History/Histoire sociale* 24 (November 1991): 263-88.

65 In 1925 the Methodist, Congregational, and Presbyterian churches united to form the United Church of Canada. See Roland Kawano, ed., *A History of the Japanese Congregations of the United Church of Canada (1892-1959)* (Scarborough: Japanese Canadian Christian Churches Historical Project, 1998), xiv.

66 Misao Yoneyama, "The Pre-War Haney Community," in Randy Enomoto, ed., *Where the Heart Is* (Vancouver: NRC Publishing, 1993), 17. Dr. Yoneyama went on to become the first Japanese-Canadian female doctor.

67 Yamaga, *Hene'e,* 46.
68 Kawano, *A History,* xiv-xv.
69 The Gentlemen's Agreement of 1908 had provided for the *yobiyose*. See note 15.
70 Interview in Ottawa, October 1992.
71 Itō Gihachi was from Yoshitome village in Futami county in eastern Hiroshima prefecture. Kikuyo was from Fuchū village in Aki county. Okita was from Midori village in Asa county.
72 Hazel Takii Morikawa, *Footprints, One Man's Pilgrimage: A Biography of Jitsuo Morikawa* (Berkeley: Jennings Associates, 1990), 12, 22, 24. Hazel Morikawa (1915-2005) was the widow of Jitsuo Morikawa (1912-87), the son of Yasutarō and Tora. After Jitsuo died, Hazel wrote his biography.
73 When I met Essie in 1989, she was a vibrant woman who seemed much younger. She died in March 1996, survived by fourteen children, thirty-five grandchildren, thirty-one great-grandchildren, and three great-great-grandchildren.
74 Some families went into debt to educate their children. Nakashima Teizō and Tsutayo sent their son Kimiaki to the University of Washington in the 1930s.

Chapter 6: The Divided Urban Community

1 Charles H. Young and Helen R.Y. Reid, *The Japanese Canadians* (Toronto: University of Toronto Press, 1938), 68. They lived in Vancouver, Victoria, Toronto, Calgary, Winnipeg, and Montreal.
2 Ibid., 74.
3 I recall the regular visits of the "order taker" in the months preceding and following the birth of my younger brother. My mother relied on the Furuya (and another company, Union Store) for practically all family needs.
4 Sumida Rigenda, "The Japanese in British Columbia," MA thesis, University of British Columbia, 1935, 391. Presumably, the income quoted is per month.
5 He was on the interim board of trustees of the Hiroshima prefectural society in 1906, according to Nakayama Jinshiro, *Kanada no hōkō hatten taikan* [Encyclopedia of Japanese in Canada] (Tokyo, 1921), 1610. He was also one of the founding members of the Buddhist Church in Vancouver. Kanada Bukkyōkai kyōdan, *Kanada Bukkyōkai enkaku shi* [History of the Buddhist Church of Canada] (Kyoto: Nagata Bunshōdō, 1981), 21.
6 The adopted son's son, Paul, whom I interviewed in Toronto in October 1992, had been a young child at the time and remembered only that his father had been a teachers' training school graduate and was not accustomed to physical labour. So he had difficulty finding suitable employment. If Masashi immigrated when he was nineteen, he could not have put in the mandatory years of teaching, so there may be some misunderstanding here. See note 23 in Chapter 4.
7 "The 192nd Battalion of Blairmore, Alberta, enlisted 50 Japanese Canadians ... The Japanese Canadian volunteers were sent to France to join the 10th Battalion." Roy Ito, *We Went to War* (Stittsville: Canada's Wings, 1984), 61.
8 Shishido's service history was noted from a copy of a claim he later made to the Dominion H.Q. Service Bureau on 9 May 1931, appealing for a renewal of his pension since his injuries made it difficult for him to support himself and his family of five children. The copy was received from his granddaughter, Sharon Ault of Port Alberni, by mail, in January 1995. Shishido was "repatriated" to Japan in October 1946 with his wife, son, daughter-in-law, and two of

his daughters. They were unable to return to his home in Hiroshima city, which had been destroyed by the atomic bomb, and were forced to remain at Uraga, where they had disembarked. A nephew, back from fighting overseas, eventually took them to Tokyo. There, bedridden due to a stroke, Shishido was cared for by his daughter-in-law. Only after his death were his son and wife able to return to Canada to resume their lives. Information received from Sharon Ault, who received it from Katie Shishido, widow of Masajirō's son George.

9 Chiyeko returned to Canada in 1953 after her father died in 1950, and her mother in 1953. She had spent twenty-three years taking care of her parents. Determined to return to Canada someday, she married only after her return.

10 They are listed in the 1941 Japanese Business Directory as being located on the 300 block of Powell Street.

11 Interviews with Hayami Kaoru and her daughter Kathleen were conducted in Montreal, October 1992.

12 Sumida Rigenda, "The Japanese," 391-92.

13 There is very little written information about him. His daughter, Teruko, was a classmate of mine in 1937-38, but we have lost touch with each other. I recall that one of the drivers was another Hiroshima immigrant's son, a well-known singer, "Fatty" Kumano. He was one of the three sons of Kumano Kazuyoshi, who immigrated from Mukōjima-shi, Mitsugi county.

14 Amano's and Sakamoto's given names may have been pronounced differently, since the Chinese characters (*kanji*) that make up a given name can be read in different ways.

15 *Chūgoku shinbun, Imin* (Hiroshima: Chūgoku shinbunsha, 1992), 126.

16 The Vancouver and Area Japanese Telephone Directory, published in June 1941, gives the address as 2141 Dundas Street, Vancouver.

17 *Chūgoku shinbun, Imin,* 126-28. During the Pacific War, the two families "self-evacuated" to Revelstoke, where, after repeated requests by the Japanese Canadians for *miso* and soy sauce, they began manufacturing again. They have since returned to Burnaby. Amano's son-in-law and grandsons have continued the business, now under the trade name Amano.

18 A short biography of Hisaoka appears in Nakayama Jinshirō, *Kanada dōhō hatten taikan* [Encyclopedia of Japanese in Canada] (Tokyo, 1921), 314-16. My father at one time worked at his boatworks, in the mid-1930s.

19 Interview with Araki Buemon's second son, Takeru Araki, July 1993.

20 George Takeyasu to the author, 27 May 1996 and 23 October 1993.

21 Takeyasu, who had been a journeyman carpenter before he immigrated in 1906, thereafter worked as a boat carpenter in Vancouver from spring to fall. Letter from George, August 1996.

22 Sasaki Toshiji, *Yamamoto Kanji,* vol. 1 (Tokyo: Fuji shuppan, 1998), 68.

23 M. Miyasaki, *My Sixty Years in Canada* (Kamloops: author, 1973), 110. Dr. Miyasaki wrote in his memoirs that he had not been accepted by Queen's University Medical School because the hospital would not allow non-white students to serve an internship.

24 Information received from Dr. Shimokura's son, Howard Satoru Shimokura, April 2004.

25 Since the Japanese were barred from the franchise, professions such as law and pharmacy were restricted. Ken Adachi, *The Enemy That Never Was: A History of the Japanese Canadians* (Toronto: McClelland and Stewart, 1976), 52.

26 Toyo Takata, *Nikkei Legacy* (Toronto: NC Press, 1983), 76.

27 Interview with Takata Motoko, niece of Takata Hayato, in Hiroshima city, 22 April 1993. Toyo Takata, Motoko's Canadian-born cousin, son of Kensuke, was unaware of this. He had believed that the family had been soy sauce producers.

28 Miyajima is also called Itsukushima and is noted for its spectacular fall foliage, for the giant *torii* (Shinto shrine archway) surrounded by water, and especially for the beautiful Shinto shrines "dedicated to the three daughters of Susano-o: Tagori-hime, Takitsu-hime, and Itsukushima-hime, the last of whom has given her name to the island." E. Papinot, *Historical and Geographical Dictionary of Japan* (Rutland, VT: Charles E. Tuttle, 1996 [1910]), 219. Miyajima has been connected with the twelfth-century Taira clan, which was descended from one of the sons of Emperor Kwammu (Kammu), who ascended the throne in 782. See also *Kodansha Encyclopedia of Japan*, 1983, s.v. "Itsukushima," and "Itsukushima shrine."

29 Mrs. Takata's natal family was Miyake. She was from Yagi village in Asa county.

30 Interviews with their eldest son, Toyo Takata, carried out on a number of occasions, 1992 to 1995.

31 Kaminishi, from Nishihara village in Asa county, had immigrated in 1900 after teaching elementary school in Japan for two years. In Canada, within a few years he became a logging contractor. Shortly afterwards, with his wife Shigeno, he established himself with a rooming house on Powell Street, and began to participate in many social organizations in Little Tokyo. Shigeno, the well-educated daughter of a Buddhist priest, came in 1907 and was appalled at "the retrogression and decay" she found among the Japanese women; she took the initiative in volunteering to counsel them. Nakayama, *Kanada dōhō,* 557-58.

32 Interview with Kōichi "Kaye" Kaminishi, in Kamloops, September 1992.

33 Interview with his son, Fred Sasaki, in Toronto, October 1992.

34 *Vancouver Province,* 9 April 1943, 29.

35 Ross Lambertson, "After Union Colliery: Law, Race, and Class in the Coalmines of British Columbia," in *Essays in the History of Canadian Law,* vol. 6: *British Columbia and the Yukon,* ed. Hamar Foster and John McLaren (Toronto: Osgoode Society for Canadian Legal History, 1995), 390.

36 Adachi, *The Enemy,* 44, 45, 134.

37 For information concerning the deferment of military service, see Yuji Ichioka, *The Issei: The World of the First Generation Japanese Immigrants, 1885-1924* (New York: Free Press, 1988), 162. According to Ken Adachi, the CJA was "essentially oriented towards Japan, stressing the superiority of Japanese ethics and culture." Adachi, *The Enemy,* 124.

38 Adachi, *The Enemy,* 123.

39 Sasaki Toshiji and Shimomura Yuki, "Senzen no Bankūba nihonjingai no hatten katei" [The Development Process of the Prewar Vancouver Japanese Quarter], *Kobe International University Bulletin* 46 (15 June 1994): 36.

40 Interview in Vancouver, October 1995.

41 The day after his arrival in Vancouver, eager to further his education, Kazuta started working as a "school boy" for a white family. For performing a number of duties while he attended public school, he was paid five dollars per month including room and board. Later, he attended a business school. To pay for his tuition fees there, he shared a job as a night janitor with a friend and also set pins at a bowling alley. Gordon G. Nakayama, *Issei* (Toronto: NC Press, 1984),

171-72.) Such initiative was richly rewarded later when he worked as a bookkeeper for Kagetsu Eikichi. Kagetsu, the owner of Deep Bay Logging Company, was one of the wealthiest and most influential leaders in the Japanese-Canadian community (Takata, *Nikkei Legacy*, 84-85). Kazuta wrote agricultural reports in the *Kanada nichinichi* [Canada Daily] newspaper. The Japanese farmers told him that they read his daily articles on the current prices and trends of agricultural produce much more eagerly than the latest news of the events in Manchuria and China. In 1931, Japan had invaded and occupied Manchuria; by 1937, Japan was engaged in all-out war in China. News reports of these events were covered by Japanese-language newspapers such as the *Tairiku nippō* and *Kanada nichinichi.*

42 *Chūgoku shinbun, Imin,* 125. Unfortunately, very little remains of the records of the Hiroshima organization except for materials Kazuta had. He said that in the spring of 1942, at the last meeting of the Hiroshima Young Men's Association (a part of the Hiroshima Prefectural Association), the members decided that several of them would share the responsibility for safeguarding the prefectural association's records. Since the amount of baggage that was allowed per family was limited, it would have been impossible for any one person to be responsible for all of the organization's papers. Unfortunately, they were all lost except for the few that had been entrusted to Kazuta.

43 An explanation of a *tanomoshikō* is given by David J. O'Brien and Stephen S. Fugita: "The *tanomoshi* ... was an association of persons who made regular contributions to a common economic 'pot' whose goal was to provide the capital necessary to finance the startup or expansion of small businesses or other major purchases. Procedures varied from one *tanomoshi* to the other with respect to how individuals were chosen to get the money in the 'pot.' In some instances, lots were drawn; in others, a type of 'bidding' procedure was used.

"The underlying premise of the rotating credit association was that eventually every individual who contributed to the common pot would have a chance to use the money for a given time period. Obviously, some individuals experienced the benefits of the *tanomoshi* before others. Moreover there was no legal recourse to get money back should those who benefited early elect not to return money into the common treasury ... Ultimately, the success of the *tanomoshi* depended upon the trust which individuals had in one another." David J. O'Brien and Stephen S. Fugita, *The Japanese American Experience* (Bloomington: Indiana University Press, 1991), 27-28.

I participated in one in 1954 in Ottawa. A scientist from Tokyo who was a postdoctoral research fellow at the National Research Council needed financial assistance to have his wife and son join him, so a *tanomoshi* was organized. It was an interesting adventure in a Japanese tradition. When I told my parents about it, I was warned to "be careful" and that such ventures should be embarked upon only with trusted friends.

44 Ibid., 28.

45 Quoted in Rolf Knight and Maya Koizumi, *A Man of Our Times: The Life-History of a Japanese-Canadian Fisherman* (Vancouver: New Star Books, 1976), 34, 61, 38-39.

46 Edna Bonacich, "A Theory of Ethnic Antagonism: The Split Labour Market," *American Sociological Review* 37 (October 1972): 547-59; Gillian Creese, "Class, Ethnicity, and Conflict: The Case of Chinese and Japanese Immigrants, 1880-1923," in *Workers, Capital, and the State in British Columbia,* ed. Rennie Warburton and David Coburn (Vancouver: UBC Press, 1988), 55-85.

47 Audrey Kobayashi and Peter Jackson, "Japanese Canadians and the Racialization of Labour in the British Columbia Sawmill Industry," *BC Studies* 103 (Autumn 1994): 33-58.

48 Robin John Anderson, "Sharks and Red Herrings: Vancouver's Male Employment Agencies, 1898-1915," *BC Studies* 98 (Summer 1993): 75, 81.

49 Ibid., 73. Fee splitting was a process by which "an employment agent and an employer agree to divide the fee [paid by a job] applicant, who is kept on the payroll for a limited time. In order to maximize profits, a turnover of employees is accelerated through firing."

50 Ibid., 75-76.

51 Creese, "Class, Ethnicity, and Conflict," 72.

52 Anderson, "Sharks," 43.

53 Kudo Miyoko and Susan Phillips, *Bankūba no ai: Tamura Toshiko to Suzuki Etsu* [Vancouver Love: Tamura Toshiko and Suzuki Etsu] (Tokyo: Domesu shuppan, 1983).

54 Tamura Norio, *Suzuki Etsu: Nihon to Kanada o musunda jaanalisuto* [Suzuki Etsu: The Journalist Who Linked Japan and Canada] (Tokyo: Liburopōto Publishing, 1992), 141-49. Tamura noted that Ukita was unusually "liberal and wise" for a Japanese diplomat (145). Doubtless this was why Ukita's replacement in 1925 was an extremely nationalistic "hardliner," Kawai Tatsuo. A 1990 publication by the Consulate General of Japan, Vancouver, "Hands across the Pacific," refers to Ukita Gōji as Ukita Satotsugu (another reading of the Chinese characters) and notes that he was consul from 1916 to 1921, followed by Gōmyo Isago (1923-25) and Kawai Tatsuo. A paper by Sasaki Toshiji described Consul Kawai's highhanded activities. Sasaki Toshiji, "The Japanese Association of Canada: Its Democratic Reform and the Destruction of Its Democratic System by Vancouver Consul Kaai [*sic*]," *Kirisutokyōshakai mondai kenkyū* [Christian Social Problems Research] 41 (July 1992): 63-90.

55 Swanson Bay is 400 kilometres north of Vancouver Island on the mainland at Hartley Bay. See Map 4.

56 Tamura, *Suzuki,* 154.

57 A Hiroshima immigrant, Funamoto Shōichi (1889-1959), worked as an oiler on the Union steamships. He usually made day trips to Bowen Island, Squamish, and Woodfibre. But at times he went on the five-day trip to Prince Rupert, according to his son George, whom I interviewed in Hamilton in October 1992. Shōichi immigrated in 1908 from Hiura village in Asa county to marry Mitsuyo (1896-1972), the widow of his elder brother Zenichi (?-1918), who had been a victim of the 1918 influenza epidemic. I also interviewed Zenichi's son, Douglas, in Montreal, in October 1993.

58 Kudo and Phillips, *Bankūba no ai,* 113.

59 Tamura, *Suzuki,* 163.

60 Ibid., 166; Gillian Creese, "Exclusion or Solidarity? Vancouver Workers Confront the 'Oriental Problem,'" *BC Studies* 80 (Winter 1988-89): 42.

61 Tamura, *Suzuki,* 166-74.

62 Kobayashi and Jackson, "Japanese Canadians," 43, 44.

63 Tamura, *Suzuki,* 174.

64 Shimpo Mitsuru, Tamura Norio, and Shiramizu Shigehiko, *Kanada no nihongo shinbun* [Japanese-Language Newspapers in Canada], 2nd ed. (Tokyo: PMC shuppansha, 1992), 54.

65 In 1925 a new consul, Kawai Tatsuo, a strongly conservative nationalist, backed the business group. Suzuki and his cohorts resigned in frustration. The CJA later denied membership to labour union supporters. Tamura, *Suzuki*, 218. See also Sasaki, "The Japanese Association of Canada."
66 Tamura, *Suzuki*, 196.
67 Shimpo, Tamura, and Shiramizu, *Kanada*, 61.
68 Tamura, *Suzuki*, 249.
69 Knight and Koizumi, *A Man of Our Times*, 117-18. In a footnote, Knight elaborated on the activities of Winch and McInnis in the labour movement.
70 Creese, "Exclusion," 42-43.
71 Shimpo, Tamura, and Shiramizu, *Kanada*, 108-9.
72 Ibid., 228.
73 *Chūgoku shinbun, Imin*, 134-35.
74 Adachi, *The Enemy*, 146.
75 *Chūgoku shinbun, Imin*, 135.
76 Keibo Ōiwa, *Stone Voices: Wartime Writings of Japanese Canadian Issei* (Montreal: Vehicule Press, 1991), 157-205.
77 Knight and Koizumi, *A Man of Our Times*, 61.
78 Stephen S. Large, *Organized Workers and Socialist Politics in Interwar Japan* (New York: Cambridge University Press, 1981), 138.
79 Knight and Koizumi, *A Man of Our Times*, 119.
80 Ibid., 59.
81 National Association of Japanese Canadians, *Economic Losses of Japanese Canadians after 1941* (Winnipeg: Hignell, 1985), Schedule IV-5.

Chapter 7: Nisei, the Second Generation

1 British Columbia denied the franchise to citizens of Japanese, Chinese, Native, and East Indian ancestry. Homma Tomekichi, a naturalized British subject born in Japan, struggled to challenge this law. See Andrea Geiger-Adams, "Writing Racial Barriers into Law: Upholding B.C.'s Denial of the Vote to Its Japanese Canadian Citizens, *Homma v. Cunningham*, 1902," in *Nikkei in the Pacific Northwest: Japanese Americans and Japanese Canadians in the Twentieth Century*, ed. Louis Fiset and Gail M. Nomura (Seattle: University of Washington Press, 2005), 20-43.
2 Eileen H. Tamura, *Americanization, Acculturation, and Ethnic Identity: The Nisei Generation in Hawaii* (Urbana and Chicago: University of Illinois Press, 1994), 142.
3 "Enculturation" is the transmission of cultural values of the minority amidst the dominant culture of the larger society. Kyunghwa Kwak, "Adolescents and Their Parents: A Review of Intergenerational Family Relations of Immigrant and Non-immigrant Families," *Human Development* 46 (2003): 117.
4 Michiko Midge Ayukawa, "Japanese Pioneer Women: Fighting Racism and Rearing the Next Generation," in *Sisters or Strangers: Immigrant, Ethnic, and Racialized Women in Canadian History*, ed. Marlene Epp, Franca Iacovetta, and Frances Swyripa (Toronto: University of Toronto Press, 2004), 233-47.
5 Ken Adachi, *The Enemy That Never Was: A History of the Japanese Canadians* (Toronto: McClelland and Stewart, 1976), 111-18.
6 Terry Watada, *Bukkyō Tōzen: A History of Jōdō Shinshū Buddhism in Canada, 1905-1995* (Toronto: Toronto Buddhist Church, 1996), 30.

7 According to Kodama Masaaki, the former fief of Aki (see Map 1) had many followers of the Pure Land Sect of Buddhism. They treasured human life and thus did not believe in infanticide. Kodama Masaaki, *Nihon iminshi kenkyū josetsu* [Introduction to the Study of the History of Japanese Emigration] (Hiroshima: Keisuisho, 1992), 55. People from Shiga prefecture were also fervent Buddhists. See Audrey Kobayashi, "Emigration from Kaideima, Japan, 1885-1950: An Analysis of community and Landscape Change," PhD diss., University of California, Los Angeles, 1983.

8 Kanada Bukkyōkai kyōdan, *Kanada Bukkyōkai enkaku shi* [History of the Buddhist Church of Canada] (Kyoto: Nagata bunshōdō, 1981), 17-20.

9 Probably to conform with Canadian custom and to not appear to be "foreign," the term "church" was always used in Canada rather than "temple."

10 Watada, *Bukkyō,* 85.

11 *Chūgoku shinbun, Imin* (Hiroshima: Chūgoku shinbunsha, 1992), 129. After graduating from Britannia High School, she worked as a saleswoman at T. Maekawa Department Store. Her father, Satō Mohei, was one of the founders of the Buddhist Church.

12 Ibid., 129-31.

13 Okimura was from Asa county, Nagatsuka. He emigrated in 1908 followed by Shizuno in 1912. Interview with son, Fred Yutaka Okimura (1917-99), Montreal, October 1992.

14 Tom Sandō Kuwabara, with Hoyano Yumiko, *Toraware no mi* [Prisoner] (Edmonton: Print Shop, 1995), 193. English translation: Tom Sandō (with J.P. Desgagne), *Wild Daisies in the Sand: Life in a Canadian Internment Camp* (Edmonton: NeWest Press, 2002), 174.

15 Most of the Nisei who were interned had contravened government orders to go to road camps in the BC Interior or Northern Ontario, reluctant to leave their families. They had agitated for a "mass evacuation"; that is, they had demanded that families not be broken up. Adachi, *The Enemy,* 241-43.

16 Yamazaki Masakazu, *Individualism and the Japanese,* trans. Barbara Sugihara (Tokyo: Japan Echo, 1994), 12. Substitute "an alien land" for "the city" in the above quotation and the result is a description of the Japanese family in Canada.

17 Harry H.L. Kitano, *Japanese Americans: The Evolution of a Subculture,* 2nd ed. (Englewood Cliffs: Prentice Hall, 1976), 48.

18 Teachers at Strathcona School, where the Powell Street children went, constantly reminded Japanese students to speak English on school grounds.

19 In the 1920s and 1930s, there was of course no television; and few Japanese families, even if they owned radios, listened to English-language programs. Many preferred to listen to short-wave broadcasts from Japan, or to gramophone records of Japanese popular songs and old recitations. .

20 Roland Kudō, the son of Kudō Minoru and Hatsue (see Chapter 5), in a personal communication dated 24 January 1992, wrote: "Around 1922 when Kim Nakashima (son of Nakashima Teizō and Tsutayo) was sent home from his first grade because he did not understand English, the Barnetts took him in, to live with them, and tutored him." Later, Mrs. Barnett ran a kindergarten for Japanese children.

21 At the Japanese-language school on Alexander Street, a number of groups participated in the running of the school, including the Maintenance Association

(Ijikai) and the Women's Association (Bōshikai), which seem to have functioned like a Parent Teachers Association. Information provided by Noro Hiroko.

22 Noro Hiroko, "The Japanese Language Schools in Canada from 1902 to 1941: The Role of Ethnic Language Schools," working paper, University of Victoria, 1990. Also, Noro Hiroko, "Kanada ni okeru keishōgo to shite no nihongo kyōiku" [Japanese-Language Education as a Heritage Language in Canada] *Ijūkenkyū* [Migration Research] 30, 3 (1993): 87-94.

23 Information provided by Noro Hiroko.

24 Michiko Midge Ayukawa, "Yasutarō Yamaga: Fraser Valley Berry Farmer, Community Leader, and Strategist," in *Nikkei in the Pacific Northwest,* ed. Fiset and Nomura, 81.

25 Satō Tsutae and Satō Hanako, *Kodomo to tomoni gojūnen* [Together with the Children for Fifty Years] (Tokyo: Nichibo Publishing, 1969), 636.

26 Mrs. Yeiko Okita, née Ito, whom I interviewed in October 1993 in Lethbridge, said that she had lived in White Rock until she was seven years old and had lived across the road from the Honda family.

27 Honda Genichi of Furuichi village in Asa county married Tami when both were seventeen years old. Genichi came to Canada in 1917, followed a year later by Tami. In Japan she left their son Kiyoto, born in 1909. He was able to join them later. Interview with Roy Honda, October 1992, in Hamilton.

28 Satō and Satō, *Kodomo,* 636.

29 Adachi noted in *The Enemy* that "only one school in the Fraser Valley town of Haney adopted the California texts" (129). Gordon Nakayama wrote that "the Haney Japanese Language School used texts compiled by the Department of Education in the State of California, USA." Gordon G. Nakayama, *Issei* (Toronto: NC Press, 1984), 53.

30 For a short biography of Ariga, see Roy Ito, *We Went to War* (Stittsville: Canada's Wings, 1984), 247-48.

31 Personal communication from Tony Tateishi, Ottawa, July 1995. His father's criticism may be related to the fact that he had graduated from teachers' training school in Japan. For further discussion of Japanese-language school texts prepared for use in California and Washington state, see Teruko Kumei, "'The Twain Shall Meet' in the Nisei: Japanese Language Education and U.S.–Japan Relations, 1900-1940," in *New Worlds, New Lives: Globalization and People of Japanese Descent in the Americas and from Latin America in Japan,* ed. Lane Ryo Hirabayashi, Akemi Kikumura-Yano, and James A. Hirabayashi (Stanford: Stanford University Press, 2002), 108-25. See also Noriko Asato, "Americanization vs. Japanese Cultural Maintenance: Analyzing Seattle's *nihongo tokuhon,* 1920," in *Nikkei in the Pacific Northwest,* ed. Fiset and Nomura, 95-119.

32 Ayukawa, "Yasutarō Yamaga," 82.

33 Ito, *We Went to War,* 182.

34 Interviews with Harold Hirose of Winnipeg in Toronto, October 1993; with Hiroshi Okuda in Montreal, June 1991 and October 1992. For further information on Harold Hirose, how he became fluent in both Japanese and English, and his life and accomplishments, see Roy Ito, *We Went to War* and *Stories of My People.* Hirose's father, Tokugi, and Okuda's father, Kasaku, were mentioned in Chapter 2.

35 Satō and Satō, *Kodomo,* 186.

36 One of Mori Arinori's reforms as soon as he took office in 1885 was to promulgate the Normal School Ordinance by which the teacher training school curricula were rigidly "regimented," to mould those who were to "become teachers for children in the future." Candidates for these schools had to be recommended by chiefs of regional administrative units. In return for the scholarships they received, graduates were obligated to serve where they were sent after graduation. "The education these students, hailing from rural communities, received at normal schools was marked by a patriarchal order. Later they would return as teachers to schools rooted in rural communities, as it was by these teachers that a national sense of unity was formed." Aso Makoto and Amano Ikuo, *Education and Japan's Modernization* (Tokyo: Japan Times, 1983), 19.

37 Children in Japan were no more likely to be impressed by the attempts to teach "'traditional' moral education" in late Meiji, according to a study by E. Patricia Tsurumi of the "confusing array of ideals" in Japan's textbooks. E. Patricia Tsurumi, "Meiji Primary School Language and Ethics Textbooks: Old Values for a New Society?" *Modern Asian Studies* 8, 2 (1974): 260.

38 Certainly, extensive interviews and long observation do not suggest that years of Japanese schooling indoctrinated many Nisei with *yamatodamashii* (the Japanese spirit), let alone taught them much of the Japanese language. Some who did learn some Japanese, and many who did not, eagerly joined the Canadian army in 1945 to serve as interpreters in Southeast Asia. See Ito, *We Went to War.*

39 Adachi, *The Enemy,* 124.

40 Satō and Satō, *Kodomo,* 181-84. This is the same consul who was instrumental in ousting CMWU supporters from the CJA.

41 Satō Tsutae, *Kanada nihongo gakkō kyōikukai shi* [History of the Canada Japanese Language School Educational Society] (Tokyo: Miwa insatsukabushikigaisha, 1953), 223-24.

42 Adachi, *The Enemy,* 127.

43 Satō, *Kanada nihongo,* 228.

44 Satō, *Kodomo,* 82-83.

45 Hiroshi Okuda had similar Canadian academic qualifications, but he also had the advantage of a good knowledge of Japanese. Thus, he had obtained a position with Sasaki Shūichi's organization. Canadian authorities were well aware of Okuda's facility with Japanese. In 1943, when he was principal of the elementary school in Tashme, the relocation camp near Hope, he was brought to Vancouver and secretly asked to work for British Army Intelligence. He refused, was soon fired from his job as principal, and was ordered to leave for eastern Canada. He left for Montreal on 1 January 1944. He said he could not find any employment there until June; somehow, he managed to survive. Interview in Montreal, June 1991.

46 Adachi, *The Enemy,* 129, 166.

47 Ibid., 130.

48 Yamamoto Misako, "Cultural Conflicts and Accommodation of the First and Second Generation Japanese," *Social Process in Hawaii* 4 (1938): 47.

49 Hyang-Sae Kang, "Gender, Race/Ethnicity, Work and Family: The Experiences of Second Generation Japanese Canadian Women in Winnipeg, 1942 to Present," MA thesis, University of Manitoba, 1996.

50 Inouye Takuo was an Issei and thus was one of the first men to be sent to road camp in the spring of 1942. He was sent to the present-day Yellowhead Highway area, at Lempriere. For further information, see Yon Shimizu, *The Exiles: An Archival History of the World War II Japanese Road Camps in British Columbia and Ontario* (Wallaceburg: Shimizu Consulting and Publishing, 1993). The couple later settled in Salmon Arm and raised eight children. Suzue, who was widowed in 1969, has lived an active life surrounded by her grown children and her in-laws. Interview, September 1992.

51 Robert J. Smith and Ella Lury Wiswell, *The Women of Suye Mura* (Chicago: University of Chicago Press, 1982).

52 Mei Nakano, *Japanese American Women: Three Generations, 1890-1990* (Berkeley: Mina Press, 1990), 104.

53 Roy Kumano was the son of a Hiroshima immigrant from Mukōjima in Mitsugi county.

54 A rare exception was Masao "Massa" Kuwabara, the eldest son of Kuwabara Bunpei of Victoria. The 31 August 1940 *Victoria Daily Colonist* had a headline, "Tillicum Athletes Win City Baseball Honors," and in a sub-headline noted: "Double by [catcher] Massa Kuwabara Sends across Two Runs in Last Frame."

55 Pat Adachi, *Asahi: A Legend in Baseball* (Etobicoke: Coronex Printing and Publishing, 1992), 5. The National Film Board released a video documentary directed by Jari Osborne in 2003 on this team, *Sleeping Tigers: The Asahi Baseball Story.*

56 Adachi, *Asahi,* 10, 19, 2, 22, 64, 83.

57 Ibid., 45. When I interviewed Kaye in Kamloops in September 1992, he proudly showed me his Asahi uniform – his prized possession, which he has since donated to the Japanese Canadian National Museum, Burnaby, BC.

58 I recall with considerable nostalgia attending Asahi baseball games with my father. He was a rather stern but dedicated father who worked long hours as a carpenter to support our family. I suspect that he had little joy in his life, but in the bleachers at the Powell Street Grounds he was a completely different person from his usual sober self, cheering the team on, bantering with his contemporaries, and harassing the umpire. The Asahi brought out in him a side that I would otherwise have never known.

59 Adachi, *Asahi,* 5.

60 *The New Canadian,* 1 March 1939.

61 Nakano, *Japanese American Women,* 105.

62 Interview, Barriere, BC, September 1992.

63 Interview in Lethbridge, October 1993.

64 Michiko Midge Ayukawa, "The Memoirs of Imada Ito: A Japanese Pioneer Woman," BA essay, University of Victoria, 1988, 80-81.

65 Interviews carried out on a number of occasions.

66 *The New Canadian,* "The Voice of the Second Generation," published its first edition on 24 November 1938 and after 1 February 1939 was printed weekly. Stephanie Jean Marie Camelon, "Sandwiches or Sushi? Second-Generation Japanese Canadian Women and *The New Canadian*, 1938-1949," MA thesis, University of Victoria, 1996.

67 Marilyn Iwama, "If You Say So: Articulating Cultural Symbols of Tradition in the Japanese Canadian Community," *Canadian Literature* 140 (Spring 1994): 20.

68 Kang, "Gender, Race," 69.

69 Quoted in ibid., 70.
70 *The New Canadian*, 22 December 1939.
71 Adachi, *The Enemy*, 158.
72 In spite of this concern over the "low morality" of the Nisei, Judge Helen Gregory MacGill of the Vancouver Juvenile Court calculated that between 1928 and 1936 "the white delinquency rate was 15.6 times that of the Oriental." She attributed the good behaviour of Asian youth to "the strong family system of both China and Japan," which was supplemented "by control of the national group." Patricia E. Roy, *The Oriental Question: Consolidating a White Man's Province, 1914-41* (Vancouver: UBC Press, 2003), 153. See also Helen Gregory MacGill, "The Oriental Delinquent in the Vancouver Juvenile Court," *Sociology and Social Research* 22 (May-June 1938): 430, 434-35.
73 Tamura Norio, "Nikka Minshū shūka jijō nichibei kansen to Bankūba Local 31" [Last Issue Circumstances of the *Daily People:* The Japan-US War and Vancouver Local 31], *Communication kagaku* 3 (June 1995): 31.
74 Although Sada believed that Nisei behaviour was deplorable, other bystanders noted the opposite.
75 Charles H. Young and Helen R.Y. Reid, *The Japanese Canadians* (Toronto: University of Toronto Press, 1938), 49.
76 Peter Takaji Nunoda, "A Community in Transition and Conflict: The Japanese Canadians, 1935-1951," PhD diss., University of Manitoba, 1991, 398.
77 Roberto Perin, "Clio as an Ethnic: The Third Force in Canadian Historiography," *Canadian Historical Review* 64, 4 (1983): 466.
78 Roy Miki and Cassandra Kobayashi, *Justice in Our Time: The Japanese Canadian Redress Settlement* (Vancouver: Talonbooks, 1991), 112-15.
79 Adachi, *The Enemy*, 325-34.
80 Gary Okihiro, *Margins and Mainstreams: Asians in American History and Cultures* (Seattle: University of Washington Press, 1994), 140.
81 Gordon Hirabayashi, "The Japanese Canadian Identity: How We Perceive Ourselves," in *The Japanese Experience in North America: Papers and Proceedings*, ed. N. Brian Winchester, Laurel H. Fujimagari, and Akira Ichikawa (Department of Political Science, University of Lethbridge, 1977), 26-28.
82 Ross Mouer and Yoshio Sugimoto, *Images of Japanese Society* (London: Kegan Paul International, 1986), 405.
83 Yamazaki Masakazu, *Individualism and the Japanese*, translated by Barbara Sugihara (Tokyo: Japan Echo, 1994), 31.
84 Bill Hosokawa, *Nisei: The Quiet Americans* (1969; repr., Niwot: University Press of Colorado, 1992), 172.

Conclusion

1 James C. Scott, *Domination and the Arts of Resistance: Hidden Transcripts* (New Haven: Yale University Press, 1990), xii, 27.
2 Nicholas B. Dirks, Geoff Eley, and Sherry B. Ornter, eds., *Culture/Power/History* (Princeton: Princeton University Press, 1994), 6.
3 Charles H. Young and Helen R.Y. Reid, *The Japanese Canadians* (Toronto: University of Toronto Press, 1938), 129.
4 Quoted in David Cousens Hoy, "Power, Repression, Progress: Foucault, Louks and the Frankfurt School," in *Foucault: A Critical Reader*, ed. David Cousens Hoy, (Oxford: Basil Blackwell, 1986), 134.

5 There were attempts in 1900, 1903, 1905, 1906, and 1908 to enact a law that would require an immigrant to pass an English-language literacy test (similar to the Natal Act, a law passed in the South African colony of Natal in 1897). There were also attempts to establish a ten-year residency requirement, instead of the then three-year one, for "Orientals" before naturalization would be granted. Finally, there were efforts to introduce a head tax for the Japanese similar to the one for the Chinese. Ken Adachi, *The Enemy That Never Was: A History of the Japanese Canadians* (Toronto: McClelland and Stewart, 1976), 9, 42, 45, 71-72.

6 Canadian Japanese Association, "Report of the Survey of the Second-Generation Japanese in British Columbia," 1935, Rare Books and Special Collections, University of British Columbia.

Epilogue

1 Ken Adachi, *The Enemy That Never Was: A History of the Japanese Canadians* (Toronto: McClelland and Stewart, 1976), 191-93. These cards were coloured according to whether the person was Canadian born (white), a naturalized citizen (pink), or a Japanese national (yellow). On each card was the person's photograph, thumbprint, serial number, name, address, height, weight, marks of identification, and occupation.

2 Ibid., 199.

3 Roy Miki and Cassandra Kobayashi, *Justice in Our Time: The Japanese Canadian Redress Settlement* (Vancouver: Talonbooks, 1991), 17.

4 Adachi, *The Enemy,* 416.

5 For a detailed treatise on how the prejudices of certain BC politicians influenced the Canadian government, see Patricia E. Roy, "Lessons in Citizenship, 1945-1949: The Delayed Return of the Japanese to Canada's Pacific Coast," in *Nikkei in the Pacific Northwest: Japanese Americans and Japanese Canadians in the Twentieth Century,* ed. Louis Fiset and Gail M. Nomura (Seattle: University of Washington Press, 2005), 254-77.

6 Personal interviews conducted with Kaye Kaminishi in Kamloops in September 1992, and with Fred Sasaki in Toronto, October 1992.

7 Adachi, *The Enemy*, 351.

8 "Japanese Canadians," in *Encyclopedia of Japanese Descendants in the Americas,* ed. Akemi Kikumura-Yano (Walnut Creek: Altamira Press, 2002), 160.

9 Ibid., 161.

A Note about the Sources

1 W. Peter Ward, *White Canada Forever,* 2nd ed. (Montreal and Kingston: McGill-Queen's University Press, 1990), ix-x; Patricia E. Roy, *A White Man's Province: British Columbia Politics and Chinese and Japanese Immigrants, 1858-1914* (Vancouver: UBC Press, 1989), vii-x.

2 Adachi had been commissioned by the National Japanese Canadian Citizens Association to write the history of the Japanese in Canada. This assignment included the task "to reveal the demon of [racism] in all its scaly ugliness and perhaps to exorcise it." Adachi, *The Enemy That Never Was: A History of the Japanese Canadians* (Toronto: McClelland and Stewart, 1976), iv. See Roy Ito, *Stories of My People: A Japanese Canadian Journal* (Hamilton: Promark Printing, 1994), 432-41, for a picture of how Adachi struggled with this undertaking.

3 *Kanada iminshi shiryō* [Data on the History of Canadian Emigrants] (Tokyo: Fuji shuppan, 1995).

4 *Nikka jihōsha hōkō, Kanada zairyū sōran* [General Survey of Compatriots Resident in Canada] (Tokyo, 1920; repr., Tokyo: Nihon tōsho senta, 1993)

5 Much of the material in Yamaga's book was used in Michiko Midge Ayukawa, "Yasutarō Yamaga: Fraser Valley Berry Farmer, Community Leader, and Strategist," in *Nikkei in the Pacific Northwest: Japanese Americans and Japanese Canadians in the Twentieth Century,* ed. Louis Fiset and Gail M. Nomura (Seattle: University of Washington Press, 2005). Yamaga's book was translated in 2006 by W.T. Hashizume and is available through Nikkei Books, 74 Delaware Avenue, Toronto, M6H 2T1.

6 *Chūgoku shinbun, Imin* [Emigrants] (Hiroshima: Chūgoku shinbunsha, 1992), 397.

7 Tamura Norio, *Suzuki Etsu: Nihon to Kanada o musunda jaanalisuto* [Suzuki Etsu: The Journalist Who Linked Japan and Canada] (Tokyo: Liburipōto Publishing, 1992); "Nikkan Minshū shūka jijō nichibei kansen to Bankūba, Local 31" [Last Issue Circumstances of the *Daily People:* The Japan-US War and Vancouver Local 31], *Communication kagaku* 3 (June 1995): 27-41; Shimpo Mitsuru, Tamura Norio, and Shiramizu Shigehiko, *Kanada no nihongo shinbun* [Japanese-Language Newspapers in Canada], 2nd ed. (Tokyo: PMC shuppansha, 1992).

8 Rolf Knight and Maya Koizumi, *A Man of Our Times: The Life-History of a Japanese-Canadian Fisherman* (Vancouver: New Star Books, 1976).

9 Peter Rose, *Mainstream and Margins: Jews, Blacks, and Other Americans* (New Brunswick, NJ: Transactions, 1983), 205.

10 Robin W. Winks, ed., *The Historian as Detective* (New York: Harper and Row, 1969).

Bibliography

Japanese-Language Sources

Chūgoku shinbun. Imin. Hiroshima: Chūgoku shinbunsha, 1992.

Hiroshimaken. *Hiroshimaken ijūshi shiryōhen* [Hiroshima Prefecture Emigration History, Documents]. Hiroshima: Daiichihōkikabushikigaisha, 1991.

–. *Hiroshima kenshi, kindai I* [The History of Hiroshima Prefecture, Modern Period I]. Hiroshima: Toppan insatsukabushikigaisha, 1980.

–. *Hiroshima kenshi, kindai II* [The History of Hiroshima Prefecture, Modern Period, II]. Hiroshima: Hiroshimaken, 1981.

–. *Hiroshima kenshi, kindai gendai shiryōhen III* [The History of Hiroshima Prefecture, Modern Period, Present-Day Documents III]. Hiroshima: Hiroshimaken, 1976.

Ishikawa Tomonori. "Hiroshimawangan Jigozenson keiyakuimin no shakaichirigakuteki kōsatsu" [A Socio-Geographical Study of Contract Emigrants of Jigozen Village, Hiroshima Bay]. *Jinbun chiri* [Social Geography] 19, 1 (February 1967): 75-91.

–. "Setonai chiiki kara no (shutsu) imin" [Emigrants from the Inland Sea Area]. *Shigaku kenkyū* [History Research] 126 (1975): 54-71.

Kanada Bukkyōkai kyōdan. *Kanada Bukkyōkai enkaku shi* [History of the Buddhist Church of Canada]. Kyoto: Nagata bunshōdō, 1981.

Kodama Masaaki. *Nihon iminshi kenkyū josetsu* [Introduction to the Study of the History of Japanese Emigration]. Hiroshima: Keisuisho, 1992.

Kudo Miyoko and Susan Phillips. *Bankūba no ai: Tamura Toshiko to Suzuki Etsu* [Vancouver Love: Tamura Toshiko and Suzuki Etsu]. Tokyo: Domesu shuppan, 1983.

Kuwabara, Tom Sandō, with Hoyano Yumiko. *Toraware no mi* [Prisoner]. Edmonton: Print Stop, 1995.

Nakayama Jinshirō. *Kanada dōhō hatten taikan* [Encyclopedia of Japanese in Canada]. Tokyo, 1921.

–. *Kanada no hōkō* [Treasures of Canada]. Tokyo, 1921. Reprinted in *Kanada iminshi shiryō,* ed. Sasaki Toshiji. Tokyo: Fuji Shuppan, 1995.

Nikka jihōsha hōkō. Kanada zairyū dōhō sōran [General Survey of Compatriots Resident in Canada]. 1920. Reprint, Tokyo: Nihon tōsho senta, 1993.

Nishihama Hisakazu. "Kanadaimin no chichi, Kuno Gihei" [The Father of Canadian Emigrants, Kuno Gihei]. *Ijū kenkyū* [Migration Research] 30, 3 (1993): 170-84.

Nitta Jirō. *Mikkōsen, Suianmaru* [Stowaway Ship, *Suianmaru*]. Tokyo: Kōdansha, 1982.

Noro Hiroko. "Kanada ni okeru keishōgo to shite no nihongo kyōiku." [Japanese Language Education as a Heritage Language in Canada]. *Ijūkenkyū* [Migration Research] 30, 3 (1993): 87-94.

Sakamachi kaigai katsuyaku shi [History of the Overseas Activities of Sakamachi]. Hiroshima: Nakamoto sōgō insatsukabushikigaisha, 1985.

Sasaki Toshiji. "Kanada-Yunion tankō to Kobe imingaisha" [Canada-Union Colliery and the Kobe Emigration Company] *Han* [Pan] 6 (September 1987): 164-88.

–. "Meiji imingaisha ni yoru jiyūtokōsha no okuridashi." [Meiji Emigration Company and the Sending of Independent Voyagers] *Han* [Pan] 8 (April 1988): 156-81.

–. *Yamamoto Kanji*. Vol. 1. Tokyo: Fuji shuppan, 1998.

–. "Yunion tankō: dainiji keiyaku imin." [Union Colliery: Number Two Contract Emigrants] *Han* [Pan] 7 (December 1987): 170-98.

Sasaki Toshiji and Shimomura Yuki. "Senzen no Bankūba nihonjingai no hatten katei" [The Development Process of the Prewar Vancouver Japanese Quarter]. *Kobe International University Bulletin* 46 (15 June 1994).

Satō Tsutae. *Kanada nihongo gakkō kyōikukaishi* [History of the Canada Japanese Language School Educational Society]. Tokyo: Miwa insatsukabushikigaisha, 1953.

Satō Tsutae and Satō Hanako. *Kodomo to tomoni gojūnen* [Together with the Children for Fifty Years]. Tokyo: Nichibō Publishing, 1969.

Shimpo Mitsuru, Tamura Norio, and Shiramizu Shigehiko. *Kanada no nihongo shinbun* [Japanese-Language Newspapers in Canada]. 2nd ed. Tokyo: PMC shuppansha, 1992.

Tairiku nippōsha. *Kanada zairyū hōjin jinmei* [Japanese Residents in Canada]. Vancouver: Tairiku, 1941.

Taiyō insatsu. BC Japanese Telephone Directory, 1941. Vancouver: Taiyōinsatsu, 1941.

Tamura Norio. "Nikkan Minshū shūka jijō nichibei kansen to Bankūba, Local 31" [Last Issue Circumstances of the *Daily People:* The Japan-US War and Vancouver Local 31]. *Communication kagaku* 3 (June 1995): 27-41.

–. *Suzuki Etsu: Nihon to Kanada o musunda jaanalisuto* [Suzuki Etsu: The Journalist Who Linked Japan and Canada]. Tokyo: Liburipōto Publishing, 1992.

Tsurumi Kazuko. *Sutebusuton Monogatari* [Tales of Steveston]. Tokyo: Chūōkōronsha, 1962.

Yamaga Yasutarō. *Hene'e nōkaishi* [History of the Haney Agricultural Association]. Tokyo: Kasai shuppan insatsusha, 1963.

Yoshida Tadao. *Kanada no imin no kiseki* [The Situation of Immigrants in Canada]. Tokyo: Chūō shinsatsukabushikigaisha, 1993.

English-Language Sources

Adachi, Ken. *The Enemy That Never Was: A History of the Japanese Canadians*. Toronto: McClelland and Stewart, 1976.

Adachi, Pat. *Asahi: A Legend in Baseball*. Etobicoke: Coronex Printing and Publishing, 1992.

Anderson, Robin John. "Sharks and Red Herrings: Vancouver's Male Employment Agencies, 1898-1915." *BC Studies* 98 (Summer 1993): 43-84.

Asato Noriko. "Americanization vs. Japanese Cultural Maintenance: Analyzing Seattle's *nihongo tokuhon*, 1920." In Louis Fiset and Gail M. Nomura, eds., *Nikkei in the Pacific Northwest: Japanese Americans and Japanese Canadians in the Twentieth Century*, 95-119. Seattle: University of Washington Press, 2005.

Aso Makoto and Amano Ikuo. *Education and Japan's Modernization*. Tokyo: Japan Times, 1983.

Ayukawa, Michiko Midge. "Bearing the Unbearable: The Memoir of a Japanese Pioneer Woman." MA thesis, University of Victoria, 1990.

–. "Good Wives and Wise Mothers: Japanese Picture Brides in Early Twentieth Century British Columbia." *BC Studies* 105-6 (Spring-Summer 1995): 103-18.

–. "Japanese Pioneer Women: Fighting Racism and Rearing the Next Generation." In Marlene Epp, Franca Iacovetta, and Frances Swyripa, eds., *Sisters or Strangers: Immigrant, Ethnic, and Racialized Women in Canadian History*, 233-47. Toronto: University of Toronto Press, 2004.

–. "The Memoirs of Imada Ito: A Japanese Pioneer Woman." BA essay, University of Victoria, 1988.

–. "Yasutarō Yamaga: Fraser Valley Berry Farmer, Community Leader, and Strategist." In Louis Fiset and Gail M. Nomura, eds., *Nikkei in the Pacific Northwest: Japanese Americans and Japanese Canadians in the Twentieth Century*. Seattle: University of Washington Press, 2005.

Beardsley, Richard K., John W. Hall, and Robert E. Ward. *Village Japan*. Chicago: University of Chicago Press, 1969 [1959].

Beauchamp, Édward R. *An American Teacher in Early Meiji Japan*. Honolulu: University of Hawaii Press, 1976.

Bernstein, Gail Lee, ed. *Recreating Japanese Women, 1600-1945*. Berkeley and Los Angeles: University of California Press, 1991.

Bonacich, Edna. "A Theory of Ethnic Antagonism: The Split Labour Market." *American Sociological Review* 37 (October 1972): 547-59.

Bowen, Lynne. *Boss Whistle: The Coal Miners of Vancouver Island Remember*. Lantzville: Oolichan Books, 1982.

–. *Three Dollar Dreams*. Lantzville: Oolichan Books, 1987.

Camelon, Stephanie Jean Marie. "Sandwiches or Sushi? Second-Generation Japanese Canadian Women and *The New Canadian*, 1938-1949." MA thesis, University of Victoria, 1996.

Canada. Department of Labour. *Immigration Records*, 1908-20, "New Immigrants from Japan." Ottawa.

–. *Immigration Records*, 1908-20, "Returning Immigrants from Japan." Ottawa.

Canadian Japanese Association. "Report of the Survey of the Second-Generation Japanese in British Columbia," 1935. University of British Columbia Library, Rare Books and Special Collections.

Cherrington, John. *Mission on the Fraser*. Vancouver: Mitchell Press, 1974.

Creese, Gillian. "Class, Ethnicity, and Conflict: The Case of Chinese and Japanese Immigrants, 1880-1923." In Rennie Warburton and David Coburn, eds., *Workers, Capital, and the State in British Columbia*, 55-85. Vancouver: UBC Press, 1988.

–. "Exclusion or Solidarity? Vancouver Workers Confront the 'Oriental Problem.'" *BC Studies* 80 (Winter 1988-89): 24-49.

Dirks, Nicholas B., Geoff Eley, and Sherry B. Ortner, eds. *Culture/Power/History*. Princeton: Princeton University Press, 1994.

Dore, R.P. *Education in Tokugawa Japan.* Berkeley and Los Angeles: University of California Press, 1965.

Duus, Peter. *The Rise of Modern Japan.* Boston: Houghton Mifflin, 1976.

Embree, John F. *Suyemura: A Japanese Village.* Chicago: University of Chicago Press, 1969 [1939].

Enomoto, Randy, ed. *Where the Heart Is.* Vancouver: NRC Publishing, 1993.

Fukutake Tadashi. *Japanese Rural Society.* Translated by R.P. Dore. Ithaca: Cornell University Press, 1967.

Furuki Yoshiko. *The White Plum: A Biography of Ume Tsuda.* New York: Weatherhill, 1991.

Galloway, John D., Provincial Mineralogist. *Placer-Mining in British Columbia.* BC Geological Survey Bulletin. Victoria: British Columbia Department of Mines, King's Printer, 1933.

Geiger-Adams, Andrea. "Writing Racial Barriers into Law: Upholding B.C.'s Denial of the Vote to Its Japanese Canadian Citizens, *Homma v. Cunningham,* 1902." In Louis Fiset and Gail M. Nomura, eds., *Nikkei in the Pacific Northwest: Japanese Americans and Japanese Canadians in the Twentieth Century,* 20-42. Seattle: University of Washington Press, 2005.

Gosnell, R.E. *The Year Book of British Columbia and Manual of Provincial Information.* Victoria, 1897-1901, 1903, 1911, 1911-14.

Grove, Alan, and Ross Lambertson. "Pawns of the Powerful: The Politics of Litigation in the Union Colliery Case." *BC Studies* 103 (Autumn 1994): 3-31.

Hane, Mikiso. *Modern Japan: A Historical Survey.* Boulder: Westview Press, 1986.

–. *Peasants, Rebels, and Outcasts: The Underside of Modern Japan.* New York: Pantheon Books, 1982.

Hashizume, William T. *Japanese Community in Mission: A Brief History, 1904-1942.* Toronto: Mission Copy Centre, 2002.

Hirabayashi, Gordon. "The Japanese Canadian Identity: How We Perceive Ourselves." In N. Brian Winchester, Laurel H. Fujimagari, and Akira Ichikawa, eds., *The Japanese Experience in North America: Papers and Proceedings,* 26-42. Lethbridge: Department of Political Science, University of Lethbridge, 1977.

Hirabayashi, Lane Ryo, Akemi Kikumura-Yano, and James A. Hirabayashi, eds. *New Worlds, New Lives: Globalization and People of Japanese Descent in the Americas and from Latin America in Japan.* Stanford: Stanford University Press, 2002.

Hoshizaki, Bill, ed. *The Vision Fulfilled: Historical Sketches of Central Okanagan Japanese Canadian Families and Community Organizations, 1894-1994.* Kelowna: Kelowna and District Association of Japanese Canadians, 1995.

Hosokawa, Bill. *Nisei: The Quiet Americans.* New York: William Morrow, 1969. Reprint, Niwot: University Press of Colorado, 1992.

Hoy, David Cousens, ed. "Power, Repression, Progress: Foucault, Louks, and the Frankfurt School." In David Cousens, ed., *Foucault: A Critical Reader.* Oxford and New York: Basil Backwell, 1986.

Ichihashi Yamato. *Japanese in the United States.* Stanford: Stanford University Press, 1932.

Ichioka, Yuji. *The Issei: The World of the First Generation Japanese Immigrants, 1885-1924.* New York: Free Press, 1988.

Inouye Jūkichi. *Home Life in Tokyo.* London: KPI, 1985 [1910].

Irwin, Yukiko, and Hilary Conroy. "R.W. Irwin and Systematic Immigration to Hawaii." In Hilary Conroy and T. Scott Miyakawa, *East across the Pacific*, 40-55. Santa Barbara: Clio Press, 1972.

Isenor, D.E., E.G. Stephens, and D.E. Watson,. *One Hundred Spirited Years: A History of Cumberland, 1888-1988*. Campbell River: Ptarmigan Press, 1988.

Isenor, D.E., W.N. McInnis, E.G. Stephens, and D.E. Watson. *Land of Plenty: A History of the Comox District*. Campbell River: Ptarmigan Press, 1987.

Ishimoto, Baroness Shidzue. *Facing Two Ways: The Story of My Life*. Stanford: Stanford University Press, 1984 [1935].

Ito, Roy. *Stories of My People: A Japanese Canadian Journal*. Hamilton: Promark Printing, 1994.

–. *We Went to War*. Stittsville: Canada's Wings, 1984.

Iwaasa, David. "Canadian Japanese in Southern Alberta, 1905-1945." In Roger Daniels, ed., *Two Monographs on Japanese Canadians*. New York: Arno Press, 1978.

Iwama, Marilyn. "If You Say So: Articulating Cultural Symbols of Tradition in the Japanese Canadian Community," *Canadian Literature* 140 (Spring 1994): 8-33.

Jansen, Marius B., ed. *The Emergence of Meiji Japan*. Cambridge: Cambridge University Press, 1995.

–. *Sakamoto Ryōma and the Meiji Restoration*. Princeton: Princeton University Press, 1961.

Johnson, F. Henry. *A History of Public Education in British Columbia*. Vancouver: UBC Press, 1964.

Kang, Hyang-Sae. "Gender, Race/Ethnicity, Work and Family: The Experiences of Second Generation Japanese Canadian Women in Winnipeg, 1942 to Present." MA thesis, University of Manitoba, 1996.

Katoh, Amy Sylvester. *Blue and White Japan*. Boston: Tuttle Publishing, 2002.

Kawano, Roland M., ed. *A History of the Japanese Congregations of the United Church of Canada (1892-1959)*. Scarborough: Japanese Canadian Christian Churches Historical Project, 1998.

Kikuchi, Baron Dairoku. *Japanese Education*. London: John Murray, 1908.

Kitano, Harry H.L. *Japanese Americans: The Evolution of a Subculture*, 2nd ed. Englewood Cliffs: Prentice Hall, 1976.

Knight, Rolf, and Maya Koizumi. *A Man of Our Times: The Life-History of a Japanese-Canadian Fisherman*. Vancouver: New Star Books, 1976.

Kobayashi, Audrey. *A Demographic Profile of Japanese Canadians*. Department of the Secretary of State, Canada. September 1989.

–. "Emigration from Kaideima, Japan, 1885-1950: An Analysis of Community and Landscape Change," PhD diss., University of California, Los Angeles, 1983.

–. "For the Sake of the Children: Japanese/Canadian Workers/Mothers." In Audrey Kobayashi, ed., *Women, Work, and Place*, 45-72. Montreal and Kingston: McGill-Queen's University Press, 1994.

–. *Memories of Our Past: A Brief Walking Tour of Powell Street*. Vancouver: NRC Publishing, 1992.

Kobayashi, Audrey, and Midge Ayukawa. "Japanese Canadians." In Akemi Kikumura-Yano, ed., *Encyclopedia of Japanese Descendants in the Americas*, 149-76. Walnut Creek: Altamira Press, 2002.

Kobayashi, Audrey, and Peter Jackson. "Japanese Canadians and the Racialization of Labour in the British Columbia Sawmill Industry." *BC Studies* 103 (Autumn 1994): 33-58.

Koppel, Tom. *Kanaka: The Untold Story of Hawaiian Pioneers in British Columbia and the Pacific Northwest.* Vancouver: Whitecap Books, 1995.

Kwak, Kyunghwa. "Adolescents and Their Parents: A Review of Intergenerational Family Relations for Immigrant and Non-immigrant Families." *Human Development* 46 (2003): 115-36.

Laband, David N., and Deborah Hendry Heinbuch. *Blue Laws: The History, Economics, and Politics of Sunday Closing Laws*. Lexington: D.C. Heath, 1987.

Lai, Chuen-yan David. "A 'Prison' for Chinese Immigrants." *Asianadian: An Asian Canadian Magazine* 2, 4 (Spring 1980): 16-19.

Lambertson, Ross. "After Union Colliery: Law, Race, and Class in the Coalmines of British Columbia." In *Essays in the History of Canadian Law.* Vol. 6: *British Columbia and the Yukon,* ed. Hamar Foster and John McLaren. Toronto: Osgoode Society for Canadian Legal History, 1995.

Lang, Catherine. *O-bon in Chimunesu.* Vancouver: Arsenal Pulp Press, 1996.

Large, Stephen S. *Organized Workers and Socialist Politics in Interwar Japan*. New York: Cambridge University Press, 1981.

Lebra, Takie Sugiyama. *Japanese Women: Constraint and Fulfillment*. Honolulu: University of Hawaii Press, 1984.

MacGill, Helen Gregory. "The Oriental Delinquent in the Vancouver Juvenile Court." *Sociology and Social Research* 22 (May-June 1938).

MacKenzie, Norman, and Lionel H. Laing, eds. *Canada and the Law of Nations*. Toronto: Ryerson Press, 1938.

Makabe Tomoko. *Picture Brides: Japanese Women in Canada*. Translated by Kathleen Chisato Merken. Toronto: University of Toronto Press, 1995.

Marlatt, Daphne. *Steveston Recollected: A Japanese Canadian History.* Victoria: Aural History, Provincial Archives of British Columbia, 1975.

McDonald, Robert A.J. "Working Class Vancouver, 1886-1914: Urbanism and Class in British Columbia." *BC Studies* 69-70 (Spring-Summer 1986): 33-69.

Meehan, John D. *The Dominion and the Rising Sun: Canada Encounters Japan, 1929-41.* Vancouver: UBC Press, 2004.

Miki, Roy, and Cassandra Kobayashi. *Justice in Our Time: The Japanese Canadian Redress Settlement.* Vancouver: Talonbooks, 1991.

Miyasaki, M. *My Sixty Years in Canada.* Kamloops: author, 1973.

Modell, John. *The Economics and Politics of Racial Accommodation: The Japanese of Los Angeles, 1900-1942.* Chicago: University of Illinois Press, 1977.

Morikawa, Hazel Takii. *Footprints, One Man's Pilgrimage: A Biography of Jitsuo Morikawa*. Berkeley: Jennings Associates, 1990.

Moriyama, Alan Takeo. *Imingaisha: Japanese Emigration Companies and Hawaii, 1894-1908.* Honolulu: University of Hawaii Press, 1985.

Morley, Alan. *Vancouver: From Milltown to Metropolis*. Vancouver: Mitchell Press, 1961.

Mouer, Ross, and Yoshio Sugimoto. *Images of Japanese Society*. London: Kegan Paul International, 1986.

Nakane Chie and Oishi Shinzaburo. *Japanese Society*. Vermont and Tokyo: Charles E. Tuttle and Co., 1984 [1972].

Nakano, Mei. *Japanese American Women: Three Generations, 1890-1990.* Berkeley: Mina Press, 1990.

Nakayama, Gordon G. *Issei: Stories of Japanese Canadian Pioneers.* Toronto: NC Press, 1984.

National Association of Japanese Canadians. *Economic Losses of Japanese Canadians after 1941.* Winnipeg: Hignell Printing, 1985.

Neary, Peter. "Zennosuke Inouye's Land: A Canadian Veterans Affairs Dilemma." *Canadian Historical Review* 85, 3 (September 2004): 423-50.

Nolte, Sharon H. "Women's Rights and Society's Needs: Japan's 1931 Suffrage Bill." *Comparative Studies in Society and History* 28, 4 (1986): 690-714.

Nolte, Sharon, and Sally Ann Hastings. "The Meiji State's Policy toward Women, 1890-1910." In Gail Lee Bernstein, ed., *Recreating Japanese Women, 1600-1945.* Berkeley and Los Angeles: University of California Press, 1991.

Noro Hiroko. "The Japanese Language Schools in Canada from 1902 to 1941: The Role of Ethnic Language Schools." Working paper, University of Victoria, 1990.

Nunoda, Peter Takaji. "A Community in Transition and Conflict: The Japanese Canadians, 1935-1951." PhD diss., University of Manitoba, 1991.

O'Brien, David J., and Stephen S. Fugita. *The Japanese American Experience.* Bloomington: Indiana University Press, 1991.

Ōiwa Keibo, ed. *Stone Voices: Wartime Writings of Japanese Canadian Issei.* Montreal: Vehicule Press, 1991.

Okihiro, Gary. *Margins and Mainstreams: Asians in American History and Cultures.* Seattle: University of Washington Press, 1994.

Ouchi, Ed, ed. *'Til We See the Light of Hope.* Vernon: Vernon Japanese Senior Citizens' Association, n.d.

Papinot, E. *Historical and Geographical Dictionary of Japan.* Rutland, VT: Charles E. Tuttle, 1996 [1910].

Paulson, Joy. "Evolution of the Feminine Ideal." In Joyce Lebra, Joy Paulson, and Elizabeth Powers, *Women in Changing Japan.* (Stanford: University of Stanford Press, 1976.

Perin, Roberto. "Clio as an Ethnic: The Third Force in Canadian Historiography." *Canadian Historical Review* 64, 4 (1983): 441-67.

–. "Themes in Immigration History." In Paul Robert Magocsi, ed., *Encyclopedia of Canada's Peoples,* 1258-67. Toronto: University of Toronto Press, 1999.

Report of the Royal Commission on Chinese and Japanese Immigration. Session 1902. Ottawa: King's Printer, 1902. Reprint, New York: Arno Press, 1978.

Rose Peter. *Mainstream and Margins: Jews, Blacks, and Other Americans.* New Brunswick, NJ: Transactions, 1983.

Roy, Patricia E. "Lessons in Citizenship, 1945-1949: The Delayed Return of the Japanese to Canada's Pacific Coast." In Louis Fiset and Gail M. Nomura, eds., *Nikkei in the Pacific Northwest: Japanese Americans and Japanese Canadians in the Twentieth Century,* 254-77. Seattle: University of Washington Press, 2005.

–. *The Oriental Question: Consolidating a White Man's Province, 1914-41.* Vancouver: UBC Press, 2003.

–. "A Tale of Two Cities": The Reception of Japanese Evacuees in Kelowna and Kaslo, B.C." *BC Studies* 87 (Autumn 1990): 23-47.

–. *A White Man's Province: British Columbia Politics and Chinese and Japanese Immigrants, 1858-1914.* Vancouver: UBC Press, 1989.

Rubinger, Richard, ed. *An American Scientist in Early Meiji Japan*. Honolulu: University of Hawaii Press, 1989.

Saint-Gilles, Amaury. *Mingei: Japan's Enduring Folk Arts*. Union City: Heian International, 1983.

Sasaki Toshiji. "The Japanese Association of Canada: Its Democratic Reform and the Destruction of Its Democratic System by Vancouver Consul Kaai [sic]." *Kirisutokyōshakai mondai kenkyū* [Christian Social Problems Research] 41 (July 1992): 63-90.

Satō Tsuneo. "Tokugawa Villages and Agriculture," In *Tokugawa Japan: The Social and Economic Antecedents of Modern Japan,* eds. Nakane Chie and Ōishi Shinzaburō, trans. Conrad Totman. Tokyo: University of Tokyo Press, 1990.

Satzewich, Vic. "Racisms: The Reaction to Chinese Migrants in Canada at the Turn of the Century," *International Sociology* 4 (September 1989): 311-27.

Schroeder, Andreas. *Carved from Wood: Mission, B.C., 1986-1992.* Altona: D.W. Friesen, 1991.

Scott, James C. *Domination and the Arts of Resistance: Hidden Transcripts*. New Haven: Yale University Press, 1990.

Seager, Allen. "Introduction." In *Working Lives: Vancouver 1886-1986,* by Working Lives Collective. Vancouver: New Star Books, 1985.

Shimizu, Yon. *The Exiles: An Archival History of the World War II Japanese Road Camps in British Columbia and Ontario.* Wallaceburg: Shimizu Consulting and Publishing, 1993.

Smith, Robert J., and Ella Lury Wiswell. *The Women of Suye Mura*. Chicago: University of Chicago Press, 1982.

Smith, Thomas C. *The Agrarian Origins of Modern Japan*. Stanford: Stanford University Press, 1959.

Sugimoto, Howard H. *Japanese Immigration: The Vancouver Riots and Canadian Diplomacy*. New York: Arno Press, 1978.

Sulz, David. "Japanese 'Entrepreneur' on the Fraser River: Oikawa Jinsaburo and the Illegal Immigration of the *Suianmaru*." MA thesis, University of Victoria, Department of History, 2003.

Sumida Rigenda. "The Japanese in British Columbia." MA thesis, University of British Columbia, 1935.

Sutherland, Neil. "'I Can't Recall When I Didn't Help': The Working Lives of Pioneering Children in Twentieth Century British Columbia." *Social History/ Histoire sociale* 24 (November 1991): 263-88.

Takata, Toyo. *Nikkei Legacy*. Toronto: NC Press, 1983.

Tamura, Eileen H. *Americanization, Acculturation, and Ethnic Identity: The Nisei Generation in Hawaii*. Urbana and Chicago: University of Illinois Press, 1994

Tanaka, Tosh, ed. *Hands across the Pacific: Japan in British Columbia 1889-1989*. Vancouver: Consulate General of Japan, 1990.

Thomas, Cheryl Maeva. "The Japanese Communities of Cumberland, British Columbia, 1885-1942: Portrait of a Past." MA thesis, University of Victoria, 1992.

Totman, Conrad. *The Collapse of the Tokugawa Bakufu, 1862-1868*. Honolulu: University of Hawaii Press, 1980.

Tsurumi, E. Patricia. *Factory Girls: Women in the Thread Mills of Meiji Japan*. Princeton: Princeton University Press, 1990.

–. "Meiji Primary School Language and Ethics Textbooks: Old Values for a New Society?" *Modern Asian Studies* 8, 2 (1974): 247-61.

Tsurumi Kazuko. *Social Change and the Individual: Japan before and after Defeat in World War II*. Princeton: Princeton University Press, 1970.

Uyeunten, Sandra O. "Struggle and Survival: The History of Japanese Immigrant Families in California, 1907-1945." PhD diss., University of California, San Diego, 1988.

Vlastos, Stephen. *Peasant Protests and Uprisings in Tokugawa Japan*. Berkeley and Los Angeles: University of California Press, 1986.

Wakayama, Tamio. *Kikyō: Coming Home to Powell Street*. Madeira Park: Harbour Publishing, 1992.

Walthall, Anne. "Devoted Wives/Unruly Women: Invisible Presence in the History of Japanese Social Protest." *Signs* 20, 1 (Autumn 1994): 106-36.

Ward, W. Peter. *White Canada Forever*. 2nd ed. Montreal and Kingston: McGill-Queen's University Press, 1990.

Watada, Terry. *Bukkyō Tōzen: A History of Jōdō Shinshū Buddhism in Canada, 1905-1995*. Toronto: Toronto Buddhist Church, 1996.

Winks, Robin W., ed. *The Historian as Detective*. New York: Harper and Row, 1969.

Working Lives Collective. *Working Lives: Vancouver 1886-1986*. Vancouver: New Star Books, 1985.

Wuest, Donna Yoshitake. *Coldstream: The Ranch Where It All Began*. Madeira Park: Harbour Publishing, 2005.

Yamaga Yasutarō. *History of Haney Nokai*. Translation of *Hene'e nōkaishi* by W.T. Hashizume. Toronto: 4Print Div. of Musson Copy Centre, 2006.

–. "My Footsteps in BC." UBC Special Collections, Yamaga Yasutarō Papers, Boxes 1-15.

Yamazaki Masakazu. *Individualism and the Japanese*. Translated by Barbara Sugihara. Tokyo: Japan Echo, 1994.

Yamamoto Misako. "Cultural Conflicts and Accomodation of the First and Second Generation Japanese." *Social Process in Hawaii* 4 (1938): 40-48.

Yoshida, K., and T. Kaigō. *Japanese Education*. Tokyo: Japan Travel Bureau, 1937.

Yoneyama, Misao. "The Pre-war Haney Community." In Randy Enomoto, ed., *Where the Heart Is*. Vancouver: NRC Publishing, 1993.

Young, Charles H., and Helen R.Y. Reid. *The Japanese Canadians*. Toronto: University of Toronto Press, 1938.

Interviews

In Japanese

Hayami Kaoru (Montreal, October 1992)
Inouye Hatsuno (Burnaby, 1991, 1992)
Kado Shizuo (Burnaby, November 1992)
Kado Tokuyo (Burnaby, November 1992)
Kazuta Kiyosō (Vancouver, September 1995)
Kitagawa Kotoma (Vancouver, September 1992)
Kubota Tamako (Lethbridge, October 1993)
Kumamoto Toshiko (Vancouver, August 1992)
Miura Suguye (Onomichi, May 1993)
Nakamura, Mrs. (Victoria, 1990)
Niiya Yukio (Montreal, October 1992)
Okihiro Kōichiro (Toronto, October 1992)

Takata Motoko (Hiroshima, April 1993)

In English
Takeru Araki (Vancouver, July 1993)
Michi Ashikawa (Toronto, October 1992)
Sharon Kimoto Ault (Port Alberni, February 1995)
George Doi (Surrey, September 1992)
Manabu Doi (Toronto, October 1992)
Chieko Endo (Montreal, October 1992)
Suzue Enomoto Inouye (Salmon Arm, September 1992)
Frank Fudemoto (Ottawa, October 1992)
Toshi Sasaki Fudemoto (Ottawa, October 1992)
Douglas Funamoto (Montreal, October 1993)
George Funamoto (Hamilton, October 1993)
Kathleen Hayami (Montreal, October 1992)
Buck Higashi (Sooke, September 1993)
Sachi Hirahara (Hiroshima, April 1993)
Harold Hirose (Toronto, October 1993)
Roy Honda (Hamilton, November 1992)
Katsumi Imada (Kamloops, 1989)
Toshio Imada (Kamloops, 1989)
Ruth Ishihara Horibe (Montreal, October 1992)
Hatsumi Uyeno Hosoi (Kobe, April 1993)
Lily Shishido Inamoto (Toronto, October, 1992)
Beverley Inouye (Burnaby, 1990-96)
George Inouye (Barriere, BC, September 1992)
Mitsuko Maehara Ito (Hamilton, November 1992)
David Iwaasa (Tokyo, April 1993)
Hanae Iwaasa-Robbs (Lethbridge, October 1993; Cumberland, February 2006)
Ray Iwaasa (Cumberland, February 2006)
Yasuko Iwaasa Hironaka (Lethbridge, October 1993)
Sachiye Iwaasa Karaki (Lethbridge, October 1993)
Eileen Yaguchi Izumi (Hamilton, November 1992)
Tom Kaga (Lethbridge, October 1993)
Kōichiro Kaye Kaminishi (Kamloops, September 1992)
Masatoshi Kawakami (Hiroshima, April 1993)
Alice Kudo (Montreal, October 1992)
Jack Kudo (Vancouver, August 1992)
Roland Kudo (Owen Sound, Ontario, May 1992)
Kathleen Kudo Merken (Montreal, October 1992)
Rose Sato Kutsukake (Toronto, October 1993)
Masao Kuwabara (Hamilton, July 1991)
Miyori Miyake Mayeda (Montreal, October 1992)
Sherry Kitagawa Mototsune (Hamilton, November 1992)
Paul Nakagawa (Toronto, October 1993)
George Nakano (Toronto, September 1995)
Jim Nishiyama (Victoria, September 1993)
Frank Ohno (Lethbridge, October 1993)

Fred Okimura (Montreal, October 1992)
Yeiko Ito Okita (Lethbridge, October 1993)
Yoneso Okita (Lethbridge, October 1993)
Hiroshi Okuda (Montreal, October 1992)
Fred Sasaki (Toronto, October 1992)
George Shibata (Tokyo, April 1993)
Henry Shibata (Montreal, October 1992)
Bob Shigehiro (Lethbridge, October 1993)
Tom Shigehiro (Lethbridge, October 1993)
Raye Matoba Shin (Mississauga, correspondence 1992-96)
Howard Shimokura, (Vancouver, April 2004)
John Shintani (Vancouver, August 1992)
Masato Sunada (Lethbridge, October 1992)
Toyo Takata (Victoria, October 1992, and on many other occasions)
George Takeyasu (Lethbridge, October 1993, and correspondence 1992-96)
Eiji Tsukishima (Victoria, September 1993)
Mori Uyeno (Toronto, October 1992)

Index

Note: (m) after a page number indicates a map, (p) a photo, and (t) a table

Abe Masahiro, 6
agricultural associations: Consolidated Farmers' Association, 73; Hammond Japanese Agricultural Association, 69; Haney Agricultural Association, 69, 74, 128; Ichigo seisansha rengō kumiai (Union of Berry Producers Association), 72; Maple Ridge Berry Growers Cooperative Exchange, 73; Mission Agricultural Association, 62, 69; Vernon *nōkai* (Japanese farmers' association), 73; Whonnock Japanese Agricultural Association, 69
Aki county, xx, 2(m), 4-7, 7(m), 9, 20, 49, 51, 85, 88-89, 119, 133n4, 134n9, 135n29, 151n71, 157n7
Alberta, 21, 44-46, 58, 62-64, 67-68, 84, 149n34
Alberta Mill, 93, 122
Alexander, Richard H., 25, 121. *See also* Hastings Mill
Alexander Street Japanese Language School. *See* Japanese language schools
Alien Land Act (California), 71, 73, 149nn50-51
Alien Land Law, 72, 120
aliens, xiv, 35, 71-72, 150
Amano Teiichi, 82-83, 152n14, 152n17
"Amerika," xxii, 40, 42, 45, 68, 122
Amerika-mura, xix, 135n35
Angler internment camp, 101, 125
Anglo-Japanese Alliance, xxii, 72, 87, 121
Anglo-Japanese Treaty of Commerce and Navigation, 88
anti-Asian sentiment, xv, xxii, 120
anti-Japanese sentiment, xxii, 17, 19, 69-73, 87, 91, 108, 125. *See also* racism
Araki Buemon, 83
Ariga Chōkichi, 105-6
Arrandale Cannery, 81
Asa county, xx, 7(m), 26, 28, 32, 33, 52, 55, 62, 76, 86, 95, 119, 142n48, 144n21, 151n71, 153n29, 153n31, 155n57, 157n13, 158n27
Asahi baseball team. *See* Nisei
Asahi shinbun, (a major Japanese newspaper), 56, 92
Asiatic Exclusion League, xv, 37
Atlin Gold Mine, 31-32, 142n51

***b**aayan* (grannie), 53
Bakufu (the central administration of the Tokugawa regime), 5-6, 9
banto (clerks), 80
barbering, 80-81, 110
Barnett, Mr. and Mrs., 157n20
Barss, Dr., 73

BC Electric Company, 110
BC Legislature, 15, 87, 115, 121
BC Ministry of Education, 108
benefactor. *See* boss
berry farmers, 59, 65, 67, 71-75, 77. *See also* Fraser Valley
Bingo county, 2(m), 4-6, 8, 88, 133n4, 134n9
Bingo-gasuri, 8, 134n23
boarding house, 13, 20, 23, 26-29, 34, 46, 52, 56-57, 68, 79, 95, 101, 105, 120, 140n21, 140n23, 141n31, 153n31
boss (*bosu*), xxii, 13, 24-26, 29-32, 63, 78, 79, 86-88, 90-97, 113, 120-21
Bowen Island, 32, 155n57
British Columbia, xxii, 12-14, 58, 60(m), 64, 125, 156n1. *See also* University of British Columbia
British Columbia Magazine, 23
British Columbia Marketing Board, 150n58
British Columbia Security Commission, 12
Buddhism. *See* religion
bunke (branch family), 55
Bureau of Trade and Commerce, 16
Bussei (Young Buddhists' Associations; YBAs), 99
Bussei Baseball League, 99
Butchart Gardens, 85

Cameron Lake Logging Company, 87
Campbell River Sawmill, 76, 105
Canadian Department of Immigration, 42
Canadian Japanese Association (CJA), 26, 72, 88-89, 93-94, 107, 120-21, 140n15, 150n54, 153n37, 156n65, 159n40
Canadian Lumber Company, 86-87
Canadian Nippon Supply Company (Nikka yōtatsu kabushiki kaisha), 31, 63, 64, 93-94
Canadian Pacific Steamship Line, 15
Canadian-born Japanese/second-generation Japanese. *See* Nisei
Cariboo, 18, 21, 126, 139n52
cheap labour, 15, 25, 60, 91, 121
Chemainus, 28, 34, 142n56, 144n26
chigo parade, 99, 100(p)
child labour, 74-75, 77-78
"Chinamen," 16, 17, 71
Chinatown, xv, 21, 37
Chinese Exclusion Act (USA), 72
Chinese Head Tax, 15, 16
Chinese immigrants, xxi, 13-15, 16-18, 21, 25, 29-30, 71, 87, 92, 144n21, 156n1
chō, 6, 141n29
Christian/Christianity. *See* religion
Christina Lake Resort Hotel, 62, 147n7
Chūgoku shinbun (newspaper published in Hiroshima), xvii, 95, 129, 135n35, 143n58, 154n42
citizen/citizenship, 33, 62, 71-72, 115, 122, 126, 150n51, 150n53, 156n1, 162n1, 162n5
CMWU. *See* Japanese Camp and Mill Workers Union
Coldstream Ranch, 63, 65
Comox, 14, 21-22, 32, 54, 142n50
Confucianism, 3, 4
contract labourers (immigrants), xx, 13-15, 18-21, 24, 27, 29-32, 35, 38, 63-64, 76, 87, 90-92, 119, 129, 138n49, 148n15, 149n34
Coombs, 87, 127
Cooperative Committee of Japanese Canadians (CCJC), 116
Courtenay, 22, 54
CPR Railway, 31, 93
cross-border migration, 13, 21, 26, 28, 31, 32, 33, 35, 37, 51, 55, 61, 63, 64, 76; President Theodore Roosevelt, 35
Crystal Pool, 115
culture shock, 46
Cumberland, xx, 11, 14, 17-18, 21-22, 52, 54, 62, 64, 86-87, 106, 110, 111, 119, 129; Number Five Jap Town, 21, 106, 139n55; Number Five Mine, 21; Number One Jap Town, 21, 106, 139n55; Union Coal Company, 14; Union Colliery, 11, 14-15, 17-18, 20-21, 25, 32, 119, 137n19

daimyō (feudal lord), 3-4, 6, 45
Davidge, Frank Casper, 15, 17-18
dekasegi ("going out to work"), xxii, 9-11, 119, 134n9, 140n17
Department of Immigration, 42, 144n21
De Wolfe, Miss, 75
Doi Denjirō, 20
Doi Umatarō, 20, 138n44
dry cleaning business. *See* tradespeople and entrepreneurs
Dunsmuir family (Robert and James), 14-15, 17-18, 64, 85, 138n37
Dunsmuir-Kobe Emigration Company agreement, 15

Edo era (1600-1868), 4-5, 8, 134n9
education: of immigrants in Canada, 33, 76, 144n21, 153n41; in Japan, 6, 9, 32, 41, 43-49, 69, 89, 140n12, 143n16, 144n23, 145n36, 151n6, 159nn36-37; of Nisei, 65, 68, 69, 75, 98, 101-3, 114, 120, 145n43, 150n61, 157n11. *See also* Japanese-language schools
Emigrant Protection Law, 11, 16
Emigrant Protection Ordinance, 11, 16
Emperor Hirohito, 107
employment, 13, 15, 30, 32, 94-95, 108-9, 121, 151n6, 155n49, 159n45
employment sharks, 91
enculturation. *See* Nisei
Englewood, 105, 113
English Cannery, Steveston, 13
English language, 62, 75-78, 102-4, 111, 157n19, 162n5
Enomoto Suzue, 110
Enomoto Tsunetarō and Mume, 52
Era of the Warring States (1336-1590), 3
Esquimalt, 86, 113
Esquimalt and Nanaimo Railway, 14
"evacuation," 125-26, 157n15

farming, 4-5, 22, 44, 58-78, 111, 127, 133n15. *See also* agricultural associations; Alberta; berry farmers, Comox; Fraser Valley; Okanagan
female emigration (reasons for): adventure, 40, 42, 45, 46, 56; avoiding spinsterhood, 41-44, 122, 144n22; divorce, 43-45; escaping in-laws, 45, 86, 122; family pressure, 42, 44, 53-54; overeducation (age), 43-44; wavy hair, 40-41
first-generation Japanese. *See* Issei
First World War, 42, 55, 62, 69, 81, 120; Cruikshank, General E.A., 62; enfranchisement, 120; 143rd battalion, 142n54; 192nd Overseas Battalion, 81, 151n7; Princess Patricia's 52nd Battalion (Infantry), 63; Soldier Settlement Board, 33, 63; 10th Battalion, 151n7; Thirteenth Canadian Mounted Rifles, 62; 13th Cavalry Battalion, 147n13; Vimy Ridge, 63; Volunteer Corps of Japanese Canadians, 62
Fisgard Street, 86, 144n21
fishing, xix, xx, 13, 22, 24, 27-29, 33-34, 52, 83, 85, 133n15, 136n10
food, 46, 48, 77-78, 88; expense, 16, 28, 31, 63, 135n34; and lodging, 27; diet, 31; merchants, 80, 83, 86, 90, 94-96
Fraser Mills, 52, 97
Fraser Valley, 32, 43, 46-47, 58-59, 62-65, 67, 69, 72, 74, 77, 84, 158n29
fudai (loyal lords), 4, 6
Fudemoto Chiyoto Frank, 76, 109
Fudemoto, Toshi (née Sasaki), 65, 109
Fujiwara, Misao Yoneyama, 75
Fukayasu county, 8, 28
Fukui Yajū, 28
Fukuyama city, 4, 6, 7(m), 8, 28, 41, 82, 134n9, 141n29
Furuya Company, 80, 94, 151n3

Geibidōshikai (Association of Geibi Friends), 88. *See also* Hiroshima kenjinkai
girls' higher school (*kōtō jogakkō*), 45-45, 145n35
Gleichan, 64
Golden, 32, 142n50

Gorge Park, 85. *See also* Japanese Tea Garden
guriun Jappu ("Green Japs"), 19

hakujin ("white person"), xiii
Haney, 58-59, 65, 69, 74-75, 105, 109, 128, 158n29. *See also* agricultural associations
Haney Japanese Community Hall, 75, 105
Hastings Mill, 12-13, 22, 23, 25, 28-29, 93, 121, 140n23, 141n24; *otasuke gaisha* (saviour company), 12, 23
Hatley Park, 85
Hawaii, xv, xx, 9-11, 20, 26, 31, 32, 33, 35, 51, 55, 61, 66, 76, 77, 98, 119, 136n39, 141n24, 141n29
Hayami Kometarō (wife Kise, sons Gakuto and Masato), 81-82, 110, 111
Hiba county, 7(m), 83
hijiki (seaweed), 48
Hikone, 13
Hino Takao, 68, 149n35
hiragana (cursive script), xxi
Hirose, Harold, 106
Hirose Tokuji, 21
Hiroshima city, 4, 6, 9, 26, 34, 43, 50, 52, 56, 61, 95, 119, 129, 141n29, 146n49, 147n6, 153n27
Hiroshima City East (Higashi Hiroshima), 32, 81
Hiroshima kenjinkai (Hiroshima Prefectural Association), 27, 88-89, 89(p). *See also* Geibidōshikai (Association of Geibi Friends)
Hiroshima prefecture, xx, 2(m), 7(m)
Hiroshima University, 32
Hisaoka Bunji, 83
Hisayamada, xiii, 33, 123
Hoita Rikuzo, 33, 42
Honda family (Genichi, Tami, Roy) 105, 158nn26-27
Hong Kong, 15
honke (principal house), 55
Honshu, xix, 129, 133n4

Ichikawa Yasu, 41, 143n16
igusa (reed for *tatami*), 8, 135n25
Imada brothers, Toshio and Katsumi, 113
Imada Heiichi, 32
Imada Ito, xxi, 29-31, 46-48, 51, 65, 140n14, 145n43
Imada Kaichi, 29, 145n43
immigration, xv, xvi, 12, 14, 19(t), 22, 23, 25, 35, 36(t), 38, 119, 121, 127, 129, 148n15, 149n37. *See also* Department of Immigration, Immigration Building
Immigration Building, 46, 143n20
immigration restrictions. *See* Lemieux-Hayashi Gentlemen's Agreement
Imperial Hotel, 27, 140n23
Indian River, 30
Inoue Jirō, 59, 69
Inoue Kaoru, 9
Inouye, George, 113
Inouye Hatsuno, 76-77
Inouye Otoichi, 63
Inouye Takuichi, 110
Inouye Takuo, 110, 160n50
Inouye Zennosuke, 62, 63, 76-77, 147n14
Interior Vegetable Marketing Board, 73
Irwin, R.W., 9, 135n30
Ishihara Kikuno, 49
Ishii (family), xv, 123(p); Ishii Chōkichi, xiii, xv, xvi(p), 33; Ishii Kazuhiko, xiii-xiv; Ishii Kenji, xvi(p), 33, 38, 40(p); Ishii Misayo, xi, 40(p), 47 (*see also* Takata Misayo); Ishii Nobuko, xiv;
Ishii Seiichi, xiii
Ishikawa *ryokan* (hotel), 99
Ishiwara Meinosuke, 84-85
isolation, 24, 46-47, 64, 112
Issei, xvii, 75, 97, 98, 106, 109-10, 112-15, 120-3, 125-6, 130, 142n48, 160n50
Itō Gihachi, 76, 151n71
Itō Kikuyo, 76, 151n71
Ito Yeiko, 76, 109, 158n26
Iwaasa Ito, 44-45, 47, 67, 144n27, 148n33

Iwaasa Kōjun, 44-45, 64, 67-68, 144n27, 149n35, 149n38
Iwaasa Matsutarō, 20, 54, 64, 86

Japan Town/Japantown (Powell Street), xv, xxi, 24(m), 85
Japan Women's University, 145n36
Japanese Barbers' Association, 80
Japanese Camp and Mill Workers Union (CMWU), 94, 96-97, 115, 123, 159n40
Japanese Canadian Citizens Association, 116
Japanese Canadian Citizens League, 106, 116
Japanese Canadian soldiers, 62
Japanese Consul/Consulate, 12, 17-20, 22, 72, 75, 87-88, 92-94, 104, 107, 120-1, 148n15, 150n54; Kawai Tatsuo (Consul), 107, 121, 155n54, 156n65; Sugimura (Consul), 12; Ukita Gōji (Consul), 92, 155n54
Japanese Fishermen's Hospital, 84
Japanese Labour Union (*Kanada nihonjin rōdō kumiai*), 88, 92-95, 121. *See also* Japanese Camp and Mill Workers Union
Japanese-language schools, 101, 103-12, 115, 125; Alexander Street, 24(m), 106(p), 107, 157n21; Cumberland, 106, 159n45; *gakumuiinkai* (governing board), 103; Haney, 105-6, 158n29, 158n31; home education, 86; Mission, 62; new textbooks, 108
Japanese Ministry of Education (Monbusho), 104-5, 144n23
Japanese Ministry of Education Normal School Ordinance, 144n23
Japanese Students' Club, 112
Japanese Tea Garden, 85-86
Japanese Women's Association, 96(p)
Japtown 1/Town Number One. *See* Cumberland
Japtown 5/Town Number Five. *See* Cumberland
Jinseki county, 41
joshi kōtōgakkō (secondary school for women), 44

Kaga Sute, 52
Kagoshima prefecture, 15, 27, 66
Kagoshima-maru, 41
Kaideima, xix
kamaboko (boiled fish paste), 48
Kaminishi Kannosuke, xxi, 86, 101, 111
Kaminishi, Kōichi (Kaye), 101, 111, 126-7
Kaminishi Shigeno, 57, 153n31
Kamo county, 7(m), 12, 20, 22, 32, 53, 55, 68, 81
Kanada nichinichi (*Canada Daily*) newspaper, 153n41
Kanada Nipponjin nōgyō hattengō, 65
Kanagawa prefecture, 85
kanji (Chinese ideograms), xxi, 152n14
katakana (phonetic script), xxi
Katō Tōsaku, 30, 63
kazoku (peers), 7
Kazuta Kiyoso, 27, 89, 140n9, 153nn41-42
Kazuta Sentaro, 89
kika Nisei (lit., "returned to Canada Nisei"), 101
Kishida Isaborō, 85
Kishida Yoshijirō, 85
Kishimoto Yūkichi, 22
Kitagawa Kensuke, 55, 146n63. *See also* Yokota Kotoma
Knight Sugar Company, 64
Kōbai kumiai (cooperative store), 95
Kobayakawa Giichi, 22, 110
Kobayashi, Audrey, xix, 35, 129
Kobayashi Peter Takeyoshi (a.k.a. Peter Cobyace), 66-67, 148n32
Kobe, 15, 19, 20, 44, 81
Kobe Emigration Company. *See* Meiji Emigration Company
kōden (money gifts), 90
Kōi, 43
kōji (a type of yeast), 21
kokudaka, 4, 133n5
Kokumingakkō (Vancouver Japanese National School), 104
Kōmoto Kiyomi, xiv
Kōmoto Noriyoshi, xiv
konwakai (lit., "a gathering for familial talk"), 67, 148n32

Korea, xx, 3, 10, 54
Kōryō seinenkai (Hiroshima Young Men's Association). *See* Hiroshima kenjinkai
Koyama Eijirō, 63
Kubota Takayuki (wife Tamako), 68-69, 149n38
Kudō Minoru (wife Hatsue), 43, 62, 157n20
Kumamoto Jun, 55, 80-81
Kumamoto Kasaku, 81
Kumamoto prefecture, 10
Kumano, Roy, 111-12, 160n53
Kumatani Jiro, 72
kunimono (lit., "fellow country people"), 88
Kuno Gihei, xix-xx
Kure, 7(m), 59
Kurita Shōjirō (or Sōjirō), 27
Kuroda (later, Nakagawa) Masashi, 81, 151n6
Kusaka, Dr., 84
Kutsukake, Rose, 101, 141n29
Kuwabara family (Bunpei, Shigeno, Masano, and Masao), 42, 144n21, 160n54
Kyoto, 14, 84, 145n36

labour contractor. *See* boss
labour unions, 88, 91-97, 121, 129, 156n65; reds and radicals, 95-96; strikes, 18, 91-93. *See also* Japanese Camp and Mill Workers Union (CMWU)
Labour Weekly (*Rōdō shuhō*), 93-94
Lake Biwa, xix
land: buying, 59; clearing, 48, 59-63, 65, 70, 74; half-share contracts, 65; in Japan, 6; leasing, 22, 59, 65, 147n3; tax, 134n14
Lasqueti Island, 32
League of Nations, 96
legislation (BC), xxii; British Columbia Coal Mines Regulations Act, 15, 87; Crown Lands Act, 32, 142n47; Lord's Day Act, 69-71; Male Minimum Wage Law, 95, 115; Natural Products Marketing Act, 73, 150n58; School Act (BC Ministry of Education), 95, 108
Lemieux-Hayashi Gentlemen's Agreement, xvi, 37-38, 68, 76, 143n10, 148n15, 151n69
loss of property, 116, 125-7
Lumber Workers International Union, 93

Maehara Takuji, 31, 66
Maekawa Department Store, 92, 121, 157n11
Maekawa, T., 80
Mainichi shinbun (a Tokyo newspaper), 92
Manchurian Incident (1931), 96
Maple Creek, Saskatchewan, 31
Maple Ridge, 48
Marpole school, 107
marriage: arranged, xvi, 39, 53, 109-10, 114, 121; picture brides, 34, 39-46, 48, 62, 68, 122, 143n10
marumage (pompadour, or "round chignon"), 41
Maruten, 82
Masao Kobayakawa, 54, 110. *See also* Yokota Haruko
Matoba, Tom Niichi, 14, 111,
Matoba Toyokichi, 13-14, 137n13
Matsukata Masayoshi (Japanese finance minister), 7, 134n17
Matsumiya Kuye, 33
McGill University database, 129
medicine: doctors, 79, 84; medical licensing requirements, 84; pharmacist, 85
Meiji Emigration Company, 11, 14-19, 129
Meiji era (1868-1912), xviii, 5, 6, 9, 43, 47, 58, 85, 88, 100, 102, 109, 134n9, 145n30, 159n37
Meiji Restoration, 119
Meirō seinenkai (Meirō Youth Society), 67
Mihara, 4
Ministry of Foreign Affairs (Japan), 9, 11, 16-17, 19, 64, 83, 138n46, 141n38, 142n55

Minstrel Island, 32
Miomura, xix-xx
miso (fermented bean paste), 21, 28, 48, 54, 82-83, 152n17
Mission, 43, 62, 65, 69-70, 113
Mitsugi county, 7(m), 8, 33, 134n9, 152n13, 160n53
Miyagi prefecture, xix
Miyajima, 86, 153n28
Miyake Ryūkichi, 26, 32, 140n15
Miyamoto Sute, 52. *See also* Kaga Sute
mobility, occupational/geographic. *See* cross-border migration
Mongols, 107
Morikawa, Asano Essie, 77
Morikawa Yasutaro and Tora, 63, 76-77

Nagano Manzo, 144n21
Nagasaki, xvii
nagaya (longhouse), 49-50, 146n48
Nakagawa Gentarō, 81. *See also* Kuroda Masashi
Nakamura Tami, 40-41
Nakanishi Kanekichi, 21, 26, 32, 99, 139n52
Nakashima Giichi, 34, 142n57
Nakashima Kumakichi, 34
Nakashima Teizō, 61-62, 113, 147n7, 151n74, 157n20
Nakashima Tsutayo, 48, 151n74, 157n20
Nakata Ume, 52
Nakayama Jinshirō, 56-57, 128-30, 138n49, 141n38, 151n5
Nanaimo Free Press, 16-17
nappa (Chinese cabbage), 77
Nass River, 81
nationalists/nationalism, 105, 107, 155n54, 156n65
New Canadian, The (a Nisei newspaper), 109, 111-12, 114-15, 123
New Westminster Trades and Labour Council, 94
Nihōjima, 8-9
Nihongo gakkō kyōiku kai (Japanese Language Schools Educational Society), 107-8
Niiya Tsuruyo, 51
Nikka jihō (*Daily News*), 93
Nikka minshū (*Daily People*), 94-96, 115, 121, 129. *See also* Suzuki Etsu; Yoshida Ryūichi
Nikka publication, 130
Nisei, xxii, 21, 97-118, 120-23, 126, 157n15, 159n38, 161n72, 161n74; Asahi baseball team, 111-12, 133n17, 139n52, 160nn57-58; assimilation, 98, 101, 105-7, 112, 114; dual citizenship, 122; dual identity, 112-15; enculturation, 98, 101, 103, 106-8, 115-16, 120, 123, 156n3; franchise, 115, 150n53, 152n25, 156n1; Japanese Canadian Citizens Association, 116; parental control, 109-10, 112-15, 121; recreational activities, 111-12; second-class citizenship, 115, 120
Nishimoto Masami, xvii, 143n58
Nishimura Chiyoko, 13
nori (laver), 85
normal schools, 46, 145n36, 159n36
North America, xv, 35, 66, 117, 138n44
Numakuma county, 7(m), 82
Number Five Mine. *See* Cumberland

Ocean Falls, 56, 96(p), 97, 113
Oda Nobunaga, 3
Ohno, Frank, 113
Ohno Keizō, 13
Oikawa Jinsaburō, xix
Okanagan, 31-32, 46, 58, 63, 65-76, 73, 147n3, 148n32
Okanagan Japanese Mission, 148n32,
Okimura, Akira, 111,
Okimura family (Mataichi, Shizuno, and Shizuye), 101
Okita Yonesō, 109
Okuda, Hiroshi, 106, 111, 159n45
Okuda Kasaku, 21
onjin (benefactors). *See* boss
Onomichi city, xiii, 7(m), 13, 33, 40, 43, 45, 55, 123, 145, 172
Oriental, 23, 71, 73, 161n72, 162n5
Osaka, xiv, 9, 41

Osterhout, Dr. S.S., 75
Ōsuga, 43
otasuke gaisha (saviour company). *See* Hastings Mill
Ozawa Hotel, 86

Pacific War, 55, 58, 135n26, 148n32, 152n17
Parent Teachers Association (PTA), 74
patterns of immigration, 14, 23, 35-36
Pearl Harbor, xvii, xxii, 43, 108, 123, 125, 127, 147n7
Perin, Roberto, 116
Perry, Commodore Matthew, 5-6, 119
picture brides. *See* marriage
Pitt Meadows, 59
Powell Drugs, 84-85
Powell Street, 23-24, 27, 29, 32, 37, 58, 79-85, 87, 89, 99-103, 120, 152n10, 153n31, 157n18, 160n58
Powell Street Grounds (Oppenheimer Park), 24(m), 84
prefectural networks/associations, 26, 88-91, 111, 120, 154n42
public office (school trustee), 68

racism, xvii, xxii, 91-92, 108-9, 114-15, 120, 127, 131, 162n2. *See also* anti-Asian sentiment; anti-Japanese sentiment
Rainbow Ranch, 66
Raymond nihonjin kyōkai (Raymond Japanese Society), 67
real estate office, 21, 24, 26, 32, 62, 70
rebuilding lives, 127
redress, 116, 127
reds/radicals, 96
religion: Buddhism, xix, 3, 52, 57, 68, 70, 98-100(p), 103, 112, 151n5, 153n31, 157n7, 157n11; Christianity, 62, 66-67, 70-71, 75-76, 98-100, 103, 112, 148n32, 150n65
"repatriation," 126
ri, 59
Ritsumeikan University, 14
Rivers Inlet, 85
Rōdō shuhō (*Labour Weekly*), 93-94
Robinson School, 74
rōju (senior councillor), 6
rooming house. *See* boarding house
Royal Commission, 25, 30, 121. *See also* Hastings Mill
Royston, 84, 97
Royston Lumber Company, 18, 84, 86, 127

Sada Shōji, 93, 115, 161n74
Saeki county, xx-xxi, 7(m), 21, 22, 28, 32, 34, 52, 82, 84, 119
Saeki Tadaichi, 32, 62
Saga prefecture, 59
Sakamoto Noriyuki, 82-83, 152n14
Sakhalin, xx
San Francisco Examiner, 17
sankin-kōtai, 4
Sansei, 127
Sasaki Shūichi, xxi, 86-87, 127
Sasaki Tokubei (wife Shizu), 65
Sasaki Toshiji, 11, 14, 19-20, 129, 138n37, 138n49, 159n45
Satō Matsuyo, 57, 101, 111
Satō, Mickey Shigeru, 111
Satō Mohei, 28, 99, 101, 111, 141n29, 157n11
Satō Tsutae, 106-7
Second World War, xix, 12, 97, 101, 114
Sekigahara, Battle of, 3-4
self-employment. *See* tradespeople and entrepreneurs
senninbari (thousand-stitch belt), 107
senpai (senior), 12
Setonaikai (Inland Sea), 3
settlement (permanent), xvi, xxii, 32, 34, 35, 48, 58, 64-68, 92
Seymour Creek, 30,
Seymour School, 103
Shaughnessy Heights, 110
Shibata Hatsuzō, 50
Shibata, Dr. Henry Ryusuke, 50-51, 146n49
Shiga prefecture, xviii, xix, xx, 13, 26, 33, 63, 66, 80, 92-93, 141n24, 157n7
Shigehiro Otoichi, 77
Shimazu Shizuyo, 55-56, 83

Shimokura Sōtarō, 86
Shimokura, Dr. Harold Mitsugi, 84, 86, 152n24
Shin, Raye, 13, 137n15
Shishido, Lily and George, 111, 151n8
Shishido Masajirō, 81, 111, 151n8
shizoku (one-time higher-class samurai), 7-8, 15, 43-44, 135n26
Shokumin no tomo (The Settler's Friend), 13
Showa, xviii
Shoyama, Thomas K., 108, 111
Skagway, Alaska, 32
Skeena, 27, 52
Skeena Balmoral Cannery, 13
Southern Pacific Railroad, 14
soy sauce, 21, 54, 82, 152n17, 153n27. *See also* Amano Teiichi
split labour market, 90-91
St. Luke's International Medical Center, 84
Stave Falls, 26, 113, 140n14
Steveston, xx, 13, 22, 34, 83-84, 104
Steveston Fisherman's Association , 13
Strathcona School, 24(m), 103(p), 109, 150n61, 157n18
Suianmaru, xix
Sunada Naotarō, 32, 142n47
Surrey, 63, 76, 130, 149n37
Suye Mura, 110
Suzuki Etsu, 88, 92-96, 129. *See also* *Nikka minshū* (*Daily People*)
Swanson Bay, 92, 121, 155n55

Tairiku nippō (*Continental Daily News*), 43, 88, 92-94, 153n41
Tairiku, 1909, 13, 34, 81, 129-30, 136n12, 148n 29
Taisho, xviii, 92, 100
Taisho democracy, 92
Taiwan, xx
Takahashi Genshichi, 95
Takahashi Labor Agent, 29
Takata county, 7(m), 43
Takata (family), xiv, 38; Misayo, 38(p), 45; Tea Garden proprietors (Hayato, Kensuke, Motoko, Naoto, Toyo), 85-86, 113, 153n27, 153nn29-30 (*see also* Japanese Tea Garden); Tomoki, xiii
Takeyasu Nobuichi (wife Shimazu Shizuyo), 55-56, 83,
Tamaki family, 44
Tamura Toshiko, 92
tan, 6, 68
Taniguchi Kumatarō, 28-29
tanomoshi (credit association), 90, 154n43
tatami, xiii, 8, 135
taxi, 82. *See also* Yamashita Shintarō
terakoya (temple school), 26, 140n12
tofu (bean curd), 22, 48, 82. *See also* Amano Teiichi
Tōhoku region, xix, 10
Tokugawa regime/era, xviii, 3-6, 8, 10, 45, 56, 85
Tokyo, 17, 19, 53, 84, 116, 145n36, 148n21
Tokyo Women's School of Medicine (Tokyo joshi igaku semmon gakkō), 143n16
Tottori prefecture, 42
Toyota county, 7(m), 53, 55, 59, 81-82, 141n38
Toyotomi Hideyoshi, 3, 133n2
tōzama (feudal lords), 4, 6
tradespeople and entrepreneurs, xix, 4, 26, 59, 79-86; barbers, 80-81, 110; bathhouse managers, 22, 79, 81; boatbuilders, 83, 133n15, 133n17, 152n21; cleaners/pressers/dress-makers, 55, 79-80, 109; dry goods dealers/grocers, 28, 64, 79-80, 121; gardeners, 82, 126, 71, 133n17; taxi drivers, 82; tea garden operators, 85-86; tofu/soy/miso producers, 21-22, 48, 82-83, 152n17, 153n27
Treaty of Kanagawa, 5
Tsukiji, 84
Tsushima Strait, 3

Ueda Minoru, 12, 137n12
Ujina, 9, 85, 119, 135n26
Umegaya Restaurant, 13
unemployment, 8, 19, 21, 66

Union Coal Company. *See* Cumberland
Union Colliery. *See* Cumberland
Union Pacific Railroad, 14, 137n18
United Church Women's Association, 75
United States-Japan Gentleman's Agreement, 26
University of Alberta, 84
University of British Columbia, 33, 73, 84, 109, 111-12, 114, 127, 128
University of Toronto Medical School, 84
Upton Steamship Company, 15
U-turn, 129
Uyeki, Mr., 68
Uyeno, Kazuma, 116
Uyeno Ritsuichi, 26, 32, 99, 116, 140n18, 142n50

Vancouver City Council, 108
Vancouver City Hall, xv, 37, 108
Vancouver Coal Mining and Land Company, 14
Vancouver Daily Province, 71
Vancouver Trade and Labour Council, 93
Victoria, xv, xvii-xix, 15, 17, 19, 22, 28, 41, 42, 44, 46, 72, 79, 81, 85-87, 130, 142n54, 144n21, 151n1, 160n54; Gordon Head district, 72; Saanich Peninsula, 72, 144n21

wages, xxii, 14-16, 19, 35, 63-64, 73, 78, 88, 90-91, 93, 95, 98, 116, 121-22
Wakayama prefecture, xix-xx, 10, 27, 66
War Measures Act, 125
Washington Agreement on Naval Disarmament, 72
White Rock, 76, 105, 158n26
Winnipeg, 109, 114
women, Issei: childbirth, 47, 64, 67; community involvement, 74, 96; cooperative housing (*nagaya*), 49-50; early documentation, 56-57; family control (lack of independence), 54; farming, 48-49, 54, 64; isolation, 46-47, 64, 67, 102; raising children, 47, 51, 102; remarriage, 52; return to Japan, xxi, 20, 51, 55-56, 66, 81, 86; romantic love, 55-56, 110; strenuous labour/work, 46-49, 57, 64-65, 74; widowhood, 51-52

***y**agō,* 55, 145n30
Yama Taxi, 82
Yamada Suteya, 25
Yamaga Yasutarō, 58-61, 64-65, 69, 71-75, 122, 128
Yamaguchi prefecture, 15, 59, 133n4
Yamasaki Yasushi, 94
Yamashita Shintarō, 82
yasuri (files or rasps), 8
yobiyose (lit., "called over"), 63, 68, 76, 148n15, 149n34, 151n69
Yokohama, 9, 15-17, 135n30
Yokota family, 53-54
Yokota Haruko, 53-54, 110, 146n62. *See also* Kobayakawa Masao
Yokota Kotoma, 53-55, 146n62. *See also* Kitagawa Kensuke
yome (bride), 45
yōshi (adopted husband), xiv, 51, 76, 146n52, 146n64
Yoshida Ryūichi, 29, 90, 94, 97. *See also Nikka minshū* (*Daily People*)
Yoshida Tomekichi (and Hina), 43-44
Yoshiye Saburō, 93

Printed and bound in Canada by Friesens
Set in Stone Artegraphica Design Co. Ltd.
Copy editor: Matthew Kudelka
Proofreader: Deborah Kerr
Cartographer: Tim de Lange Boom
Indexer: Louanne Mah